NOTES

on Bible Readings

1982

INTERNATIONAL BIBLE READING ASSOCIATION
Robert Denholm House, Nutfield
Redhill, Surrey, RH1 4HW, England

ISSN 0140–8275
ISBN 0 7197 0301 8

Cover picture: The Church of All Nations at the foot of the
Mount of Olives
Photograph by Maurice Thompson, Bible Scene Slides

*Typeset, printed and bound in Great Britain by
Hazell Watson & Viney Ltd, Aylesbury, Bucks*

CONTENTS

International Bible Reading Association

Dear Friends,

During the early months of 1981 I paid my first visit to Ghana and Nigeria. The purpose was to visit the IBRA staff and to meet some of our members. It was a thrilling experience to see for myself the tremendous contribution which the IBRA makes to the life of Christians there and to be welcomed with such warmth and enthusiasm. Everywhere I went I was told of the importance of the IBRA books. But, more important, I was able to see and appreciate some of the problems faced by our colleagues and to look for further ways in which we can help.

In both Ghana and Nigeria I pledged continued support for the work, and we also make this pledge to our friends in other countries where help is needed in promoting the work of the IBRA. If the IBRA can enable Christians to read and understand God's word for them in the 1980's this will be a fitting celebration of the first hundred years of the IBRA's existence.

During this Centenary Year there are new developments taking place to widen the scope of our Association. In Liberia there are opportunities for initiating IBRA branches; in India there are hopes of an expansion of the Telugu work; in Ghana there is a request for the translation of IBRA notes into a fifth language; there is news of IBRA notes being translated into Portuguese; and everywhere there is a demand for more copies of the IBRA notes in English.

We can rejoice that God is blessing the work of the IBRA and giving us new opportunities for further service. Our membership of the IBRA links us with hundreds of thousands of Christians around the world in a fellowship of Bible reading.

Let us pray for one another, asking that we may discern God's word to his people and that we may all have courage to act upon it.

With every blessing,
Yours sincerely,

G. R. Chapman

IBRA Staff: Revd G. Roy Chapman (General Secretary)
              Joy R. Standen (Editor)

INTRODUCTORY NOTES

We recommend that readers of this book use the *New English Bible* or another modern version of the Bible. All biblical quotations are from the *New English Bible* unless otherwise stated. Abbreviations used in this book are given below. Sometimes it is suggested that you read the Bible passage **after** reading some of the notes and this is indicated by the symbol ▶. On most days there is a short prayer or an idea for meditation and these are marked by the symbol □. Sunday readings from the Joint Liturgical Group Lectionary are indicated by a ★.

After each Saturday's notes a question is given for personal thought or for discussion in a group. Help and information on these questions is given in *Bible Study Handbook*, and more details about this are to be found on page 34.

Acknowledgments

We are grateful for permission to quote the following:

From *Everyday Prayers* (IBRA) on January 6;

A verse from hymn 532 in *Congregational Praise* on January 22;

From the prayer for Lent 4 from *The Methodist Service Book* (Methodist Publishing House) on March 21;

The prayer for Ascension Day from *The Methodist Service Book* (Methodist Publishing House) on May 20;

A verse from *The Key Next Door* (Hodder & Stoughton Limited) by Leslie D. Weatherhead on July 22;

A quotation from *Praying the Psalms* (SPCK) by Leslie E. Stradling on July 26.

Abbreviations

The following abbreviations are used in this book:

AV	*Authorised Version*
GNB	*Good News Bible*
LB	*The Living Bible*
NEB	*New English Bible*
RSV	*Revised Standard Version*

1, 2, 3 JOHN

Notes by Revd Frank Hanson, BA, BD

Frank Hanson, a Methodist minister, is Director of the Education Division of the Methodist Church of New Zealand, and Chairman of the Wellington District Synod.

The Centenary Year of the IBRA, which we now begin, reflects an unbroken tradition of a hundred years of worldwide service in biblical insight and knowledge. The aim of the IBRA is not dissimilar from that of the letters of John with which we begin this year's readings: to encourage the people of God to maintain and grow in the faith of our Lord and Saviour Jesus Christ and to show that faith in day-to-day living.

When the letters of John were written, probably about the end of the first century AD, the young faith was faced with fierce competition for the hearts and minds of people. There was also much antagonism. There was a temptation to water down the gospel to make it more palatable and acceptable to a wider circle of people. There were current ideas, too, which, though strange to us, threatened to take the gospel along dangerous by-ways.

John struggles to help his readers maintain the purity of the faith, at the same time reminding them that faith is useless unless it leads to action.

Suggestions for further reading

The Letters of John and Jude by William Barclay, Daily Study Bible (Saint Andrew Press);

One Volume Bible Commentary by William Neil (Hodder and Stoughton).

Friday January 1   1 John 1.1–4

There is an old saying, 'Seeing is believing.' Although the tricks of magic caution us that that is not always so, yet most of us are more persuaded by what we see than by what we hear. John represents a group of people fortunate enough to have seen Jesus. Notice how the words, 'we have seen', 'we have heard', keep coming through like a refrain. They give added weight because they are personal.

Ideas and beliefs can be argued about and disagreed with. It is much more difficult to argue with what people have experienced for themselves. Christian faith is not only about doctrines; it is about how we experience God for ourselves.

When God wanted to translate his message and purposes in ways people could understand he placed them in a series of personalities and events. When he wanted to transmit his major news he did not write a letter or send a signal – he embodied it in a person.

Sometimes our human words can lead to death or violence or conflict. By contrast, God's words are full of life and love and hope. In some of our traditions, New Year's Day is a time for words – for resolutions. Are they, like God's words, wholesome and life-affirming?

☐ *O God, fill my life with words and deeds that matter.*

Saturday January 2   1 John 1.5 to 2.2

When we think about the world today, it is easy to list all its wrongs and woes, but it is much more difficult to do something about putting those wrongs right. We can easily dwell on human error – and then give up in despair.

John makes it perfectly clear that his aim is positive rather than negative: 'In writing thus to you my purpose is that you should not commit sin.' (2 verse 1) That seems to imply a background of error and wrongdoing in the Christian community receiving the letter. Many Christians today would admit to a feeling of being inadequate and prone to falling below Christ's standards. But that is not where things rest. In Jesus, God has taken decisive action to provide a cure for human shortcoming and wrong.

How would you describe yourself today? When we contrast ourselves with God's light and purity of purpose our sense of worth may sink all the further. The reality of our own sin and failure is obvious, especially to ourselves. But it is only part of the picture. God has provided a way by which what is wrong can be put right. He is working for our true fulfilment.

☐ *O God, enable me to feel my stature in Christ, rather than be swamped with personal misgivings.*

For group discussion and personal thought

Read again John's personal testimony in 1 John 1.1–4. How does this compare with your own experience of Jesus as a friend and Saviour?

Sunday January 3   Luke 2.41–52*
THE VISIT TO JERUSALEM

Adults are sometimes shocked by the indifference shown by young people towards values and customs they have always regarded as important. On the other hand, older people are sometimes put to shame when a young person takes with profound seriousness truths which have become dulled for his seniors by familiarity, cynicism or carelessness. There are times when older people have become so concerned with the externals of religion, that they lose sight of the heart of the matter, while the young impatiently dismiss the 'wrappings' and point to the reality.

The parents of Jesus had brought him to Jerusalem to experience their greatest religious festival. When Jesus was missing, they looked everywhere except the one place which to him was the obvious place to go after such an occasion. There is puzzled impatience in the boy's response to his mother's anxious rebuke. For him, the heart of Passover was not in family meals, celebrations and meeting old friends, but in the wonder of the love of God. It was in the temple that he could meditate on that. Throughout his life, in his approach to all matters, he cut through the inessential to the truth.

☐   *Lord, that I may learn of thee,*
     Give me true simplicity.   *Charles Wesley*

Monday January 4   1 John 2.3–11

When an electrician has repaired an appliance he must test it out before he allows it to be used again. This checking-out is important for safety reasons.

How do we check-out our lives as Christians? John has two practical ways. In one, we measure our actions against the commands which find their origins in God (verse 3). In the other, we test out our words and actions against those of Jesus (verses 5b–6). In a sense, these are two ways of saying one and the same thing, for the motivating force in the life of Jesus is the law of love.

This is why the command is both **old** and **new**. It is as **old** as God himself, for God is love. He always has been – in creation, in the history of the people of Israel, in his actions in people and nations. Yet it is as **new** as Jesus, for in him it is brought to light in a new way. Love takes on new depths in the attitudes, words and life of Jesus.

Verses 9–11 give an example of this kind of testing being worked out. Do we love or hate our 'brother'? The presence of love shows we are on God's wavelength, while its absence shows that we are still floundering around in the darkness.

☐ *Belovèd, let us love :*
     In love is light,
And he who loveth not,
     Dwelleth in night.   *Horatius Bonar*

Tuesday January 5   1 John 2.12–17

Every Christian group includes a diversity of people – young and old, male and female, introvert and extrovert. In verses 12–14 John is making this point. It is not so important to match the age-group with a specific message, but rather to see the diversity of age-groups and the range of faith which is found among them. Knowing God, experiencing forgiveness, defeating evil impulses and powers – all these represent areas of spiritual maturity. They are signposts of growth in the inner tumults and battles which are part of every one of us.

Verses 15–17 do not mean that John is anti-world. He uses the term 'world' in a technical sense. It stands for all life which is alienated from God and opposed to his will. In this sense the 'world' is the focus of opposition to God's purposes. When we say that 'God loved the world so much that he gave his only Son' (John 3.16), we mean that Jesus came right into the centre of the opposition camp – the 'world' – and that is the object of God's love and concern. The world in this sense is alluring and can readily draw us away from God's purposes. It can snare and trap us so that we become caught in short-lived and dangerous escapades.

☐ *Lord God, help me not to be satisfied with short-term answers as substitutes for long-term qualities.*

Wednesday January 6 (Epiphany) 1 John 2.18–27

How do you feel when you see the results of your effort and hard work being swept away by people who do not seem to care? In today's reading the writer is caught up in emotions which have been aroused by error and defection. He is fighting for the hearts and souls of his people – and he does it with conviction and passion. So stirred is he, that he applies the words, liars, misleaders and antichrists, to those who were attempting to draw or force away the Christians from what they believed.

There are times when those who do not believe in Christ must be treated sensitively and gently. Can you identify people like that? But there are other times when such people must be strenuously opposed, and shown up for what they represent. John regards it as such a time for this congregation.

Having been soundly knit into the network of believers, they must now decide whom they can and whom they cannot trust, who will lead them into a confirmation of their faith and who will lure them away. There are times when we are all faced with such decisions. Let us pray that Christ may dwell in us, leading us to the truth.

☐ *An Epiphany prayer*

Father, we celebrate the coming of Jesus as the light of the world: let his light be in our minds that it may scatter the shadows of our unreason, our confusion, our resistance to the truth; let the light shine in our hearts and Christ's love reach every part of our lives. (Everyday Prayers)

Thursday January 7 1 John 2.28 to 3.6

What do you think you are worth? What is your value? What is your image of yourself? This reading gives two starting-points. One is to see ourselves as sinners who need to be thoroughly reformed (verses 4–6). The other is to see ourselves as God's children who need continually to be confronted by what we can become (verses 1–3).

As Christians, we live with this tension. On the one hand we have a personal value which is worth well beyond anything we possess, because God puts it on us. He believes in us, he encourages us in the direction of personal integrity and growth. He builds up our confidence and sense of worth.

But, on the other hand, we demean ourselves and let ourselves down. And we let him down in the process. We are not sinners by birth. We are born with God's price on our head. We only become sinners when we think and decide and act in ways that are anti-God, anti-humanity and anti-self. Sin then is a trespasser, a transient fellow-traveller, albeit a stubborn one, not a permanent part of our constitution. Admittedly it can become so much a part of us that we never want to let it go. But basically we are persons who are the recipients of God's grace and worth and acceptance.

☐ *O Jesus Christ, grow thou in me,*
 And all things else recede :
 My heart be daily nearer thee
 From sin be daily freed.   *Johann C. Lavater*

Friday January 8   1 John 3.7–12

Jesus told a story about two sons (Matthew 21.28–32). One of them said he would help and didn't; the other said he wouldn't help and did. Which of the two was more helpful?

We could base a similar story on today's reading. There were two people: one said he believed in Jesus but did not live it out in action; the other said he did not believe but lived out a life based on love and right relationships. Which of the two is the Christian?

We can think that it is most important in the Christian faith to believe the right things. But what is the point of **believing** the right things if that is as far as it goes. The yardstick for John is the ability to **do right** and to **love** one another. That is a mixture of right thought and right action.

Wrong thoughts and wrong actions abound, but they do not have their origins in God. They are part of that pervasive force which tries to organise God out of existence. Even worse for us, they are part of a disease which can take control of us personally and bind us up in selfishness and greed.

☐ *Think and pray about these words : 'Faith, if it does not lead to action, is in itself a lifeless thing.' (James 2.17)*

Saturday January 9   1 John 3.13–24

People can give us a bad time. The phrase 'the world hates you' (verse 13) can come very close to how we are feeling about life. But remember, it can work both ways! We can make it hard for others, too.

Like a haunting refrain John keeps on bringing us back to genuine love. This is for him the pearl of great price. Even when people are antagonistic toward us this is still the answer.

The good news of the gospel commences in the way God thinks about us and feels towards us. His attitude is clearly seen in the words and actions of Jesus. God does not suddenly change his mind because you or I happen to be the people involved. His love is persistent and his love is consistent; and being his people means allowing this same attitude to permeate and control more and more of what we think, and say, and do.

☐ *O give us hearts to love like thee,*
 Like thee, O Lord, to grieve
Far more for others' sins, than all
 The wrongs that we receive.

 One with thyself, may every eye
 In us, thy brethren, see
The gentleness and grace that spring
 From union, Lord, with thee.

Edward Denny

For group discussion and personal thought

Read again 1 John 3.16–18. John underlines that Christian love must be practical love. In what practical ways are you showing God's love to people in your area? What other ways might be considered?

Sunday January 10   John 1.29–34*

THE BAPTISM OF CHRIST

As we read these verses, we may assume that the baptism of Jesus had already taken place. Of the various points John made about Jesus, one is of outstanding importance: 'There is the **Lamb of God; it is he who takes away the sin of the world**' (verse 29). Here, in a few words, we find the central message of the gospel – this great truth was expounded at length by Paul in his letters.

The whole of mankind is in a state of alienation from God. 'The sin of the world' is a phrase which does not refer to specific sins, but to the all-pervasive state of being cut off from God. To try to grapple with this situation – to bridge the gap between men in their guilty isolation and God in his holy perfection – the Jews had organised a system of sacrificial ritual. The sacrificing of a lamb at Passover was one means by which they hoped to get back to God. But it was **their** lamb they offered. No, said John in effect. God in his love takes the initiative; he provides a sacrifice. It is the Lamb of God – God's lamb, not man's – that overcomes the alienation. It is not our efforts, but God's love, revealed in Christ, that bridges the gulf.

☐   *'God was in Christ reconciling the world to himself.'*

(2 Corinthians 5.19)

Monday January 11   1 John 4.1–6

Whom can we trust? That is a real issue. It applies to politicians, advisors, officials, newspaper reporters, even friends. Further, with so much contradictory advice being offered in the religious field, it is an important question there also. It is possible to take the statements and comments of religious 'experts' at face value – and to accept them without query. But, unless we have implicit faith in the person we are listening to, that is naïve. How can we distinguish 'the spirit of truth' from 'the spirit of error' (verse 6)?

● **By asking whether the statements square up with the life of Jesus.** If Jesus is the clearest and most perfect picture of the character of God that we possess, then anything that clashes with him or does not measure up with him is suspect. On that basis a number of ideas which pass from some people's lips as religious truth are questionable. They may well be part of that concentration of evil, error and malice which is summed up in John's concept of 'Antichrist'. While some find it helpful to personalise that phrase, others find it makes better sense to allow the phrase to summarise all the forces that are hell-bent on destruction.

● **By checking out our own ideas with other Christians.** Individualistic ideas can be superbly right or drastically wrong. They need talking through with others.

● **By playing our own hunches.** Any statement that rouses in us the query, 'But God can't be like that', needs looking at again.

☐   *Lord God, build in me such a sure image of yourself that I may be able to discern what is true and reject the false.*

13

Tuesday January 12 1 John 4.7–21

Every letter has its heart – the paragraph or sentence which sums up better than any other the central theme on which it is based. Today's reading is the heart of *1 John*. In any discussions on the Christian understanding of God these verses are crucial. They provide us with the basic clues. At the heart of the universe, interwoven into its purpose and creation, is the feeling and caring, the respect and the self-giving which are caught up in the activity of love.

God's aim is to arouse confidence not fear; to instil a sense of value not of degradation; to build hope rather than to dash us on the rocks of despair.

One of our temptations is to transfer our human limitations and resentments on to God – and make him like us. The biblical message encourages us to be like him! That is not easy. But neither was it easy for God to attempt to live out his life on earth. It left him forlorn, alone, and (hopefully for some) dead – a stark symbol of what we humans do with the goodness we cannot cope with.

Love gives itself away. It uses itself up for others. It puts aside self-centred desires for the sake of a wider sensitivity and caring.

Love is a lived-out quality – not an idea or a word. That is as true for God as it is in human relationships. He does not just say it. He does it.

☐ *Encourage me, Lord, to grow more like you – in love.*

Wednesday January 13 1 John 5.1–12

There are times when we all feel that life is getting the better of us – or that other people are. For some that is a constant feeling that never leaves them. The Christian faith is concerned with reversing that trend. It helps us to cope, and to play a positive role in life, instead of being pushed around like flotsam. Paul senses this when he writes, 'If God is on our side, who can be against us?' (Romans 8.31) Part of that reversal comes through an increased awareness of ourselves and the way we respond – and the changes we can make which will enable us to react to life more positively. But an important ingredient is the inner strength we draw from a heightened awareness of God's presence and concern. If God values us as deeply as the Scriptures declare, then the realisation of this makes us stronger.

Personal and visible declarations of this are important if we are to believe it: hence the significance of the Sacraments and the inward presence of Jesus. John writes about the water, the blood and the Spirit:

● In the **water of baptism** there is a declaration of God's undeserved and unmerited love – even for those who cannot yet respond.

● In the **blood of the Passion** and its symbolism in Holy Communion there is a declaration of the suffering and self-giving which God considers we are worth.

● In the **indwelling presence of Jesus through the Spirit** we have the declaration of God's constant involvement with us.

☐ *May 'the means of grace' help to build and integrate me as a person, so that I may live victoriously.*

Thursday January 14   1 John 5.13–21

As people we want to be assured and re-assured – about love within our family relationships, about our value as workers, about the worth others see in us. To feel positive about our-selves enables us to do things; to feel negative inhibits us.

John reinforces human value by stressing that we may ex-perience eternal life – that is, life in God. And so our approach to God can be person to person. It needs to be shot through with genuine openness and mature honesty. That is what true prayer is. It is not necessarily the right sounding phrases or the high-sounding thoughts; it is the sincere and honest outpouring of our hopes and despairs, our concerns and our achievements. God listens to things like that!

John's statement about 'deadly sin' brings to mind our Lord's concern about 'eternal sin' (Mark 3.29). We can bring to God an attitude to sin which is willing to see things as they are, to express sorrow, and is ready to be renewed. Or, we can bring an attitude which is stubborn, blind, unbending, haughty, dog-matic, and self-opinionated. Such an attitude bears the seeds of self-destruction as it inevitably leads to the closing of more and more of our lives from God. And one thing we cannot have is eternal life without God.

John's parting words are not a threat but a warning. Be careful not to let go of God; rather, claim your heritage as part of his family!

☐ *Lord, keep me from becoming so insensitive that I tear myself from your grace.*

As you read this letter, try to put yourself in the place of the person receiving it. What would impress you? It may be:

● **A reminder**. Verse 5 reiterates a message spelt out at greater length in *1 John*. The Christian gospel is not about new ideas or philosophies; it is a restating of things we have heard before – sometimes time and time again. Admittedly we need refreshing and up-to-date examples which will reinforce the truth – but the basic, underlying law of love is eternal.

● **A warning**. Not everyone who mouths God's name speaks Christian truth. John is clearly committed to the vital and intimate link between God and Jesus. From a Christian viewpoint you cannot understand the Father without Jesus, nor Jesus without the Father. Religious faith offers wide scope for irrational ideas and emotional blind alleys. Do not believe everyone you listen to!

● **A hope**. Written communication is inadequate compared with face to face discussion. New dimensions of love, physical communication and dialogue open up when people can be together. A misunderstanding which would take many letters might be cleared up through being together for a few minutes.

☐ *Lord, keep on writing your letters to me through the words and actions of genuine Christian people.*

John found it difficult to get a message through to the congregation. It still happens! Too much paperwork, lack of time, personal disagreement with what it contains, can result in a message being halted by a minister or official. On some occasions that can be healthy; for it can save a congregation from being bombarded with too much information. But at other times it can be distressing, preventing people from giving their support to something they feel to be worthwhile.

John seeks out an ally, and with tact and diplomacy encourages Gaius to get the message through. The fact that he succeeded is proved by the existence of the letter itself. For it was as easy then as it is now to assign unwanted correspondence to a waste-paper basket.

The bond of Christian fellowship encourages us to share hospitality with people whom we do not know. So it is here. A testimonial from John brings together Demetrius and Gaius.

Although presumably they have not met before, they will greet each other and help each other because of their common friend – and their common Lord. Today this is a world-wide phenomenon as Christians from differing countries and cultures share experiences, faith and resources.

Perhaps Diotrephes had an horizon which was no larger than the local congregation. Perhaps ideas and leadership from outside appeared as a threat rather than full of possibilities. The local church is God's possession rather than our own, and God can enrich it from without as well as within.

☐ *Lord, help me to be tolerant and open-minded; and give my church openness to new ideas both from within and without.*

For group discussion and personal thought
Read again 1 John 4.7–11,19a. How can we love people we don't agree with, or whom we find difficult, or who are hostile to us?

Sunday January 17   John 1.35–51*
THE FIRST DISCIPLES
What is it that brings people together to form a group or a club or some other fellowship? Usually it is a common interest or quest. Andrew, Simon, Philip and Nathanael were all serious-minded men cherishing the Jewish hope of a Messiah. This is what, by various means, brought them to Jesus.

In what ways were they brought to Jesus? In each case, except that of Philip, it was through the recommendation of another. Very occasionally, the call to Christian discipleship may be a 'direct' one, but for most of us our first knowledge of Christ came via others – parents, teachers, friends. This is the way the Church grows – through the witness of those who have come to love Christ and who want to share their joyous experience.

Why do some churches grow and thrive, while others are weak and dying? Has it something to do with the assurance, enthusiasm and faith – or lack of these things – in the church members? Men and women today long to find some meaning in their lives, some ideal to follow. Some find their answer to these longings in pop stars or football teams. But they need more – something deeper, something personal. **Do they find it in us?**

☐ *'Lord make me an instrument of thy peace.'*   (*Francis of Assisi*)

HOW THE IBRA BEGAN ...

The International Bible Reading Association grew out of the movement for Christian education in the nineteenth century. The Sunday School Union of England and Wales (now the National Christian Education Council) was active in developing lesson notes and other teaching materials. When those involved in church work in the USA proposed that the lesson courses available in Britain and America should be based on the same scheme, the idea was adopted, and in 1874 the 'International' lesson scheme came into use on both sides of the Atlantic. At the same time, 'Home Bible Readings', based on the scheme, were published.

A few years later, the Sunday School Union set up a committee to explore ways of strengthening 'the spiritual work of Sunday school teaching'. One member of that committee suggested the formation of an organisation to promote the regular use of the 'Home Readings'. His name – **Charles Waters** – was destined to achieve a unique place in the hearts of a great multitude.

The proposal was eventually adopted late in 1881. A membership card was printed and a circular despatched to Sunday Schools inviting them to form branches. Charles Waters was appointed Honorary Secretary and the first circular letter was sent to members in the following June. By the end of 1882, more than 10,000 people had joined. In this way the International Bible Reading Association was launched with Charles Waters at the helm. Until his death in 1910 he remained the inspiration behind the growth of the organisation.

The Association, named *'International'* through its link with the lesson course, soon began to be truly international, for its members were to be found in New Zealand, Canada, South Africa, the West Indies as well as the United States and Britain – thus foreshadowing modern IBRA developments across the world.

In this way the IBRA began – its aim, then as now, being to promote the daily, intelligent and prayerful reading of the Bible.

FIRST HUNDRED YEARS

IBRA

1882-1982

This is the **CENTENARY YEAR OF THE IBRA** and celebrations will be taking place around the world. You can join these celebrations:

● By **giving thanks to God** for all that has been accomplished during the first 100 years and by asking for his blessing upon the work today.

● By **sharing in a celebration service** in your own church. A special festival service is available from the IBRA; also a prayer leaflet for personal and corporate use.

● By **inviting others to become members of the IBRA** and share in the fellowship of daily Bible reading. Complimentary copies of two weeks' readings are available from the IBRA or from your group secretary.

● By **sending a special thank-offering to the Missionary Fund** which will enable the international work to continue and grow (see page 176 for details).

● By **making known the work of the IBRA** through your church magazine or local newspaper – articles are available from the IBRA.

One hundred years of work can best be celebrated by going forward boldly and with confident faith into the next hundred years. The aim of the IBRA – to encourage daily Bible reading and to help in the understanding of the Bible – remains constant. Please help us to promote this work in every way you can as **your** contribution to the Centenary celebrations.

☐ *Almighty God, we give you thanks for the written word of the Bible, and for the fellowship of the IBRA whereby we are encouraged to read the Bible and find your word for us today. Let your blessing be upon us as you open to us the truths of your word; may we have the strength of purpose and the confidence of hope to follow your leading.*

(Please send a large stamped addressed envelope for festival service and other leaflets.)

THE LORD'S PRAYER

Notes by Revd David M. Owen, BA, BD, ThD

David Owen is a minister of the United Reformed Church, now at Reigate in Surrey. He has also held pastorates in Monmouthshire and Bournemouth. He is the author of 'Sounds of the Passion' (Denholm House Press) and 'Sharers in Worship' (NCEC).

Robert Louis Stevenson used to conduct family prayers every morning in his South Seas home. One morning, in the middle of the Lord's Prayer, he rose from his knees and left the room. His wife, accustomed to his ill health, thought he had become unwell again, and went after him and asked what was wrong. He replied that a feeling of terrible unworthiness had come over him as he prayed the Lord's Prayer. 'I am not fit,' he said, 'to pray that prayer today.'

Who, indeed, is fit to pray it? Yet pray it we must, for this prayer that Jesus entrusted to his first disciples, and to us, has become one of the most priceless possessions and tools of our faith, for here is something to be used, something to help us grow in the Spirit.

January 18–25 is the **Week of Prayer for Christian Unity.** As we think about and pray the Lord's Prayer during this week, let us remember that it is the most universal and ecumenical prayer of the Christian Church.

Monday January 18   John 17.1–8, 20–26

**'Our Father in heaven,
hallowed be your name.'**

There were great celebrations in ancient Rome as one of the emperors returned home victorious from a battle. At one point in the procession a small boy broke through the soldiers' cordon and ran towards the emperor. When restrained by a soldier, the boy cried out, 'I know he's the emperor, but he's also my father, and I want to be with him.'

Apocryphal or not, this story helps to take us to the heart of the Christian faith and to illustrate the relationship we have with God our Father. Whilst we know him to be the almighty God, creator and provider, whose name is holy, we have a longing to be near him because we have been brought into a personal relationship with him. This we owe entirely to Christ.

The 'High Priestly Prayer' of John 17 from which today's reading comes, tells first of that most personal and perfect relationship between Jesus and God his Father. He hallowed and glorified God's name in everything, never abusing the relationship, yet enjoying the intimacy it afforded.

The wonder is this – we, too, who are Christ's disciples may enter that relationship and know God as Father. Paul said: 'The Spirit you have received is a Spirit that makes us sons, enabling us to cry "Abba! Father!" We are God's heirs and Christ's fellow-heirs.' (part of Romans 8.15, 17)

☐ *Father, let your name be hallowed in my life today.*

Tuesday January 19

'Your kingdom come,
your will be done, on earth as in heaven.'

We normally think of a kingdom as a territory or land governed by a king, but in the Bible 'kingdom' means God's universal sovereignty and lordship. Whilst the Old Testament looks forward to God's rule in his Messiah, the New Testament declares that the Messiah Jesus has arrived; therefore God's kingdom has come. It is true that his rule is opposed by enemy forces, but it can never be destroyed. We must pray that the few Christlike things which are done at the present time will eventually be done by people everywhere.

The kingdom was Jesus' ideal, and constituted the heart of his teaching, and it was expressed in simple, everyday stories.
▶ Read **Matthew 13.31–33, 44–50.**

In these simple stories lies our Lord's supreme purpose. He calls us to be citizens of his kingdom, and to work and pray for its fulfilment.

☐ *A little girl in Perth, Scotland, prayed mistakenly, 'Thy kingdom come, thy will be done, in Perth as it is in heaven.' Pray that the same may happen where you live and work.*

Wednesday January 20   John 6.1–13, 25–27

'Give us today our daily bread.'

In his Gospel John deliberately set Jesus' long discourse on spiritual food after the miraculous feeding of the multitudes.

Clearly they are complementary. In the miracle Jesus was obviously concerned about bodily hunger, and he knew it was fruitless offering them spiritual food unless he first gave them bodily food.

This petition in the Lord's Prayer is a prayer for food for the body. We are to pray that our basic physical needs will be met each day. It is a prayer for necessities, not luxuries, and underlying it is a deep thanksgiving to God for his provision, and a recognition of the debt we owe to our fellow-workers who labour for our needs.

But Jesus insisted that people need spiritual as well as physical food. To those who followed him after their hunger had been satisfied, he spoke of that eternal and imperishable food which he was able to give. He went on to say that the manna eaten by the Israelites in the wilderness was a mere shadow of what he was offering, and that he was the bread of life (verse 35).

☐ *Ever may my soul be fed*
   With this true and living bread.   *Josiah Conder*

Thursday January 21   **Matthew 18.21–35**

'Forgive us our sins
as we forgive those who sin against us.'

The parable of the two debtors is a deliberately exaggerated story to stress the connection between being forgiven and forgiving others. Sin is a violation of God's character and makes us debtors, but the debt is so colossal as to be unpayable, so that the only plea left to us is that we may be forgiven the debt. Jesus says that God does not expect to be recompensed. He is so loving-hearted that he forgives . . .

   However great our trespass,
   Whatever we have been.   *Oswald Allen*

God's kingdom is based on a love-relationship. We neither purchase nor merit his love – we take it. How great then is our obligation to exercise that same love toward others who wrong us! Jesus' word to Peter to forgive seventy times seven was not cold, calculated arithmetic, but a way of saying, 'Go on forgiving!' It is the merciful who obtain mercy (Matthew 5.7). Forgiveness of others is not an optional extra but an obligation of Christian discipleship.

☐ *Accept Christ's forgiving love today, and let that love flow*
   through you to others.

Friday January 22

'Do not bring us to the time of trial but deliver us from evil.'

The traditional rendering, 'Lead us not into temptation,' poses a big problem. To 'tempt' means to 'entice to evil' – something God can never do. What we do find in the Bible is the idea that the afflictions of individuals and nations may be the means by which God **tests** their integrity.

But again, should we really ask that we might avoid being tested? Are not tests necessary and beneficial? The point is that the first part of this petition has meaning only when the second part is added. What we are praying for, in effect, is that we may be kept away from situations of moral danger which might break us, but that if we are so tested we may be given strength to overcome. (See 1 Corinthians 10.13.)

▶ Now read **Ephesians 6.10–18.**

Paul gives spiritual significance to each item of the Roman soldier's armour. Only as we stand in the strength of Christ can we be sure to resist our tribulations.

☐　*Give me, O Christ, the strength that is in thee,*
That I may stand in every evil hour;
Faints my poor heart except to thee I flee,
Resting my weakness in thy perfect power.　　Henry C. Carter

Saturday January 23　　　　　　Revelation 5.9–14; 7.9–12

'For the kingdom, the power, and the glory are yours now and for ever.'

On the day that Handel's *Messiah* was first performed in London, King George II was in the royal box. When the oratorio reached its climax in the 'Hallelujah Chorus' with its 'King of Kings and Lord of Lords,' the crowd, following the king's example, surged to its feet and remained standing until the end. It was a truly regal gesture for a monarch to make.

Great religious compositions seem to require a doxology – a concluding crescendo of praise to God. As if by design, the book of *Revelation* consummates the New Testament, especially in the praise of the angels and martyrs in heaven, and the whole creation to the victorious Lamb of God.

The doxology to the Lord's Prayer which we think about today is not found in the most ancient manuscripts. It was probably a later addition when the prayer was first used in the corporate worship of the Church. It has been described as the Church's 'Hallelujah and Grand Affirmation', following upon the words her Lord has taught her children to say from the heart.

☐ *Say to God with confidence:*

Your kingdom will never fall;
your power will never fail;
your glory will never fade.
You are God for ever. Amen.

For group discussion and personal thought

Why do you think that the Lord's Prayer is the Christian's greatest prayer? How helpful do you find modern versions of the prayer (a) in private devotions, (b) in church worship?

Sunday January 24   John 2.13–22*

THE NEW TEMPLE

Unlike the other Gospel writers, John placed the cleansing of the temple at the beginning of Christ's ministry. To John this incident seemed to be a very suitable introduction to the controversy between Jesus and the religious authorities which dominates his Gospel.

Jesus was angered by the desecration of his 'Father's house'. He saw that trading practices were turning people's minds away from a real sense of God's presence. Also he wanted people to know that the presence of God was not limited to certain places. He knew that the dwelling-place of God was to be found in himself and in the fellowship of those who followed him. The 'body of Christ' would be the true temple.

The meaning of his reply to those who challenged his action in the temple is probably this: With your practices, you are destroying all that the temple stands for; soon the temple will be no more but, in me and my followers, all that it stood for will find fulfilment. Within a short time the temple was indeed no more. But the truth went marching on, in the hearts and lives of those who loved Christ.

☐ *For thou, within no walls confined,*
Inhabitest the humble mind;
Such ever bring thee where they come,
And going take thee to their home.   *William Cowper*

24

GENESIS 1–11

Notes by Revd H. Daniel Beeby, BA, ThD

Dan Beeby, President of the NCEC for 1981–82, is a minister of the United Reformed Church and lecturer in Old Testament at Selly Oak Colleges, Birmingham. Previously he has served in China and taught theology at Tainan Theological College in Taiwan.

From *Genesis 12* through to *Revelation*, first Israel and then the Church are the centre of attention. To them God reveals himself; through them he proclaims his love and salvation. But love for whom? And what is salvation from? Why salvation at all?

The answers are mainly to be found in **Genesis 1–11**, which forms an essential preface to all that comes after. In these chapters the stage is set. First, God creates the heavens and the earth, the plants, animals and fishes; then he makes man 'in his own image'. But man disobeys and all is threatened.

The material in these chapters has been drawn from various sources, some very old and obscure. Scholars can tell us much about where the stories came from and what they meant originally, but this is of secondary importance. Our concern will be with what they mean as a whole – with the quilt, not the patches – and we shall see how their meaning helps us to understand the rest of the Bible.

Suggestions for further reading

Genesis 1–11 by Alan Richardson, Torch Bible Commentaries (SCM Press);
Creation by Claus Westermann (SPCK);
Genesis by G. Von Rad, Old Testament Library (SCM Press).

Monday January 25

In *Genesis* there is much which appears to deny God's Lordship. Man, God's viceroy, mutinies; brother kills brother; and a flood brings utter destruction. Nevertheless, the author insists, this is our Father's world – he made it, he is its beginning as he will determine its end. All the world is his stage and he built a perfect theatre.

▶ Read **Genesis 1.1–19.**

What most troubled ancient man was: How do we keep disorder at bay? The act of creation, therefore, is seen as God turning disorder ('without form and void') into a serene, orderly habitation. So light overcomes darkness, land wins the battle with unruly water and the sun and moon bring order to time and seasons.

The movement from chaos to order is symbolised by the biblical view of a day – evening and then morning. The rhythm of life is not from light to darkness but from dark to dawn. We move towards the light; we live in hope. This is not because suffering is illusion or that darkness, disorder and evil are unreal, nor because of an inevitable movement of progress, but because under all things and in all things is God whose love is new every morning.

To those who meet the future with faith in Christ, the best is yet to be.

☐ *Chase the dark night of sin away;*
   Shed o'er the world thy holy light.   *Bernard of Clairvaux*

Tuesday January 26

What is man? Is he a 'naked ape', or a tool-bearing animal, or the creature of economic forces? Or is he divine, a spark from the eternal flame? The quality of human society depends on how we answer these questions.

▶ Read **Genesis 1.20 to 2.4a.**

Man is made on the sixth day, along with the animals. He has his affinity with the animals; he must eat and sleep; he is born and he dies. This cannot be denied but it is not the whole story. He is not only an animal – he is created as the 'image of God'. This means that just as other 'gods' had idols to represent them, God's representative is man and to this representative great tasks are committed. They are kingly tasks; man is God's viceroy. He is steward of much of his environment, with tremendous power and authority, but all to be exercised as the great king commands and not only for his own delight and pleasure.

So man comes between animals and God, and this is where he must be kept. If we forget God we become like animals and treat other races or our enemies as animals. If we forget our humble 'cousins' we make ourselves 'gods' and this is even more disastrous.

26

◻ *We, the stewards, have betrayed your trust, O King;*
forgive us, and this day make us your faithful servants.

Wednesday January 27 Genesis 2.4b–17

As in the New Testament, the message of the Old Testament is
'all of grace'. Man's life and personality come to him directly
from God (verse 7). For man the desert is made to blossom and
provide beauty and nourishment. It also produces one tree which
hints at eternity and another – the tree of the knowledge of good
and evil – which offers wide experience, but also threatens death.
Increase in knowledge is a dubious blessing – an ambiguous gift.

If man is to love God, he must be free **not** to love him. He is
given this freedom – even the freedom to choose death (verse 17)
– but he is protected from the dire consequences resulting from
any abuse of his freedom by the prohibition not to eat. God
gives man a law not that he might earn grace, but so that he can
continue to enjoy all that God has freely given him. The law is
an extension of the grace; it makes it possible to continue within
the grace because it keeps us in fellowship with God.

How does man know this law? Only because God speaks it. It
is not carved on the tree; it is not natural to man. It comes as
part of the word of God – in the Bible and in Jesus Christ.

◻ *In love you make us free;*
in mercy you restrain us.
Thanks be to you, O God.

Thursday January 28

How are we to explain human sexuality? Why are men and
women drawn together as by magnets? Genesis 1.27 gives as the
reason that the image of God belongs to man and woman jointly.
It cannot be complete in either gender on its own, only in some
combination of the two. When male and female are united har-
moniously, the image of God is set forth fully.

▶ Read **Genesis 2.18–25**.

These verses also seek to answer questions about sexual
attraction. Why is it so powerful – almost irresistable? And the
answer in some ways is the same as in chapter 1. Male and
female belong together. Separate, they are incomplete; the male
seeks his lost rib, the female longs to return to the body of which
she is a part.

Both accounts deal with human sexuality as a matter of supreme importance. Both see it as a gift from God essential to his purposes and existing before sin has made its entry. Both distinguish it from animal sexuality and both are concerned with male and female complementing each other rather than being equal. The sexes are presented as equally important, rather than as equal. They are made for each other, and together they reveal something of God's nature – something which they cannot reveal as separate individuals.

☐ *Pray for all married couples – that they may*
  so love each other that their loving reflects what God is.

Friday January 29

In Genesis 1–2 we have been introduced to the five great themes that occupy the pages of Scripture:
- God's relationship with 'nature';
- God's relationship with mankind;
- mankind's relationship with nature;
- man's relationship with his fellows;
- and man's relationship with himself – his self-consciousness.
▶ Now read **Genesis 3.1–13.**

In these verses we see how the relationships listed above begin to go wrong. An 'infection' enters into God's world which speaks to every part and flaws the whole. And the trouble starts with the second of the relationships listed – God's relationship with mankind. This seems to be the key to the whole. Here is the Achilles' heel – the vulnerable part – of creation: man's obedience or otherwise to the word of God. All depends on whether man listens to God's word of prohibition or whether he is led into disobedience by evil promptings (verses 1–5), the desire for experience (verse 5), the tug of the senses or the invitation of others (verse 6).

Man falls and, quite literally, all hell is let loose. In quick succession the five relationships are distorted – even God's relationship with nature because, as we shall read tomorrow, he curses the serpent and the ground. Nothing remains as God intended except his purpose of love for his creation which one day will lead to salvation and re-creation through Christ.

☐ *Let our life be new created,*
  Ever-living Lord, in thee.   *Hugh Falconer*

These wonderful stories in *Genesis* defy all categorisation. They are not just myth or folklore. They transcend history and are more profound than science. Today's reading shows the dilemmas and sadness of female and male existence.

Woman's punishment strikes at her greatest contribution – child-bearing. Instead of continuing the joy of conception, birth will now involve pain and suffering. The 'rib' will always seek to return home but it will be to domination and agony as well as to the joys of motherhood (verse 16).

In the same way, the breadwinner finds life hardest at the point most distinctive of his role – his relationship with the land. He is bound to the land in countless ways. He is made of its dust, his name 'Adam' comes from the word for soil *adamah*, and the generations born to woman can only survive if man tills the ground. But the ground is now his enemy as well as his friend. It will resist his efforts to win food from it by producing thorns, thistles and weeds and finally, at death, he will sink back into the dust.

☐ *Lord, for our heavy yoke give us your light one, and of our dust make us your sons and daughters in Christ.*

For group discussion and personal thought

The opening chapters of *Genesis* leave us in no doubt that this is God's world, and that men and women must use it responsibly. In what ways are we discovering this to be true in our own generation?

LIFE FOR THE WORLD

In the heat of the day, Jesus wanted a drink of water. He asked for one from a very startled woman, for she was a **Samaritan**. Further, rabbis did not usually converse with **women**. But it was typical of Jesus to override prejudice. He was always ready to establish relations with anyone. Some years later Paul wrote that in Christ there is neither male nor female, Jew nor Gentile, slave nor free (see Galatians 3.28). Jesus saw every individual as able to give him service and worthy to receive his own great gift.

Jesus knew the woman had a more urgent thirst than a

physical thirst – a thirst of the spirit. So he spoke to her about 'living water' – water that gives eternal life. Not surprisingly, she thought Jesus was referring to 'running water' as distinct from well water; so she asked in effect: 'Who do you think you are? Greater than Jacob who gave this well to us?'

Yes, greater indeed than Jacob! That 'living water' included:
● Jesus' vision of God which could give people hope and a sense of worth;
● Jesus' friendship which could always renew people's flagging spirits with a knowledge of the divine companionship;
● Jesus' teaching about love which could bring an end to people's enmities and fears of one another.

☐ *Think about that 'living water' and pray for it.*

Monday February 1   Genesis 4.1–16

In chapters 1–3 a creation which God saw was very good has been corrupted by sin in the first generation. In the second generation, we are shown how sin becomes more pernicious, and also what are some of the danger points of human existence.

Worship and the desire to make offerings to God are shown to be integral to human existence but, at the same time, we are made aware that these can lead to jealousy, hatred and murder. We talk easily of 'brotherly love'. This story warns us that just as deep – perhaps deeper – is brotherly hate. Are not civil wars the worst ones? The story of Cain and Abel suggests that there is a fundamental conflict – between equals, even brothers.

Is there then any hope? Without Jesus Christ, no, there is not; but even in this grim and sombre account there are pointers to Jesus – hints of silver linings. Bitter punishment falls on Cain the murderer but that is not the whole story. Wherever he wanders on the earth, God's mercy will follow him. This marked man is shadowed with 'grace', for his mark protects him.

☐ *Lord, keep us from turning good into evil, and help us to see mercy in your chastisement.*

Tuesday February 2   Genesis 6.1–22

Genesis 1 describes how God made an orderly creation out of disorderly water and chaos; chapter 6 tells how man's disobedience led to the reversal of the process with a return to water and chaos. But that is not quite all – there is to be a second Adam, Noah, who will provide a new start with a new covenant.

And it is not really chaos because it is planned, beginning just when God decides with the waters rising to the precise point intended, and the end coming when God appoints.

The pattern already present in chapters 3–4 is being repeated. Man responds to grace with sin; God has to respond with judgement and punishment, but this is not the last word. Even before the disaster of the flood takes place God is preparing for a hopeful future. Is it possible to see here, even before the call of Abraham and the chosen people, the vague foreshadowing of the cross and resurrection? Is there in the nature of all things an inbuilt tendency that links despair with hope, punishment with love, abasement with exaltation, a cross with a crown? The Christians who can somehow associate their own suffering with God – 'make up that which is lacking (the lack is ours) of the sufferings of Christ' (see Colossians 1.24) – are the ones most likely to experience the fullness of God's mercy and joy.

☐ *Jesus' prayer on the cross, 'Father, into thy hands I commit my spirit' (Luke 23.46), was preceded by his cry 'My God, my God, why hast thou forsaken me?' (Mark 15.34). Think about this in relation to today's notes.*

Wednesday February 3   Genesis 7.1–23

The story of the flood did not originate in Israel; it was borrowed from surrounding cultures; but, transplanted into the soil of *Genesis*, it is made to say things undreamt of elsewhere. We saw yesterday how it fits into 'the cross and resurrection' pattern of Scripture. Today let us discover another link with the gospel of Christ.

The author of *Genesis* was writing for people whose greatest fear was the nightmare of a watery chaos, when all order and meaning would disappear, when seedtime and harvest, summer and winter, heat and cold would vanish in inundating seas. The story of the flood proclaims that the thing feared has occurred. 'Fear not,' he says, 'the flood is history, behind, not before.'

In New Testament times mankind's greatest fear was of death. One way Paul combated this fear was to tell people that they had died with Christ and were already risen with him. In other words, the thing they feared would happen in the future had already happened. Death for the Christian is not an impending threat, an approaching horror, it is over and done with, buried in the past. We have died to sin and risen to life eternal.

☐ *We rejoice this day that we have died and risen with Christ.*

Some people are still troubled by an imagined conflict between science and religion. Many are inclined to deny God's 'intervention' in his world and the possibility of miracles happening, on the ground that such occurrences are contrary to the laws of nature.

Today's reading, especially verses 21–22, presents a somewhat different point of view. Whereas we see natural law as something independent of God, indeed almost opposed to him, the first readers of these words were desperately afraid that their environment was not dependable. They longed for a God who could provide stability – in other words, a nature that was law-abiding and not capricious and unruly. We are told that this is precisely what we have. Our surroundings are trustworthy because God has made them so. The times and seasons essential to human existence are fixed by God. Natural law is God's constant intervention, his hourly miracle. It is the bedrock of certainty, the grace of reliability that life cannot do without.

This is not in conflict with science. It is this that makes science possible inasmuch as science exists to comprehend the laws and study the patterns of nature. We live, not in a 'clockwork' universe from which God is locked out, but in a home where the Father is wonderfully present in every cell.

☐ *For the laws and patterns of nature,*
   the Lord's holy name be praised.

Punishment has followed sin, but now comes grace on grace. A new blessing restores the gift of fertility; the right to rule has not been withdrawn; the diet is no longer vegetarian (Genesis 1.29) but includes meat. The God who gave detailed instructions on building an ark now sees that no detail of human life is left uncared for. The danger is over, man and creation have a new start. But can't things go wrong again? Is the new start really 'for keeps'?

Two things give assurance: a **covenant** and a **sign**, the rainbow. The covenant is sure and utterly steadfast because it is God who promises, not Noah. If it had been conditional on an oath by Noah then it would have been a dubious affair; but it rests on the unshakable mercies of God, and not on frail man.

Covenants and signs abound in Scripture, but all of them are summed up in and contribute to the new covenant in Christ's blood and the sign of broken bread and poured-out wine. Noah's covenant and sign spoke of a safe and sure world for man to live in; Christ's new covenant and the sacrament speak of a safe and sure salvation in this world and the next.

☐ *Take from our souls the strain and stress,*
And let our ordered lives confess
The beauty of thy peace.　　　*John Greenleaf Whittier*

Saturday February 6　　　　　　　　　　Genesis 11.1–9

Chapter 10 lists the nations of mankind as the result of God's blessing. Today's reading shows us the other side of the coin. The distinct nations with their different habitations and languages are the result not of blessing but of curse. And it is 'curse' which has the last word in this narrative; these early chapters of *Genesis* end with this dismal picture of the human condition.

Fearful of losing unity, men seek it for the wrong reason (verse 4) and in the wrong way. The tower of tremendous height, built to attract people and draw them together, is not a symbol of unity but of pride. Their advanced technology (verse 3) brings them not security and harmony but disaster, and in vain we look for the grace we have found in the previous narratives.

Is all lost then? By no means. All that is recorded in Genesis 12.1 to Revelation 22.21 can be seen in some sense to be God's response to the plight of mankind as demonstrated by the tower of Babel story. Abraham is called in order that he and his descendants may be a channel of blessing to man under the curse. This is the promise whose looked-for fulfilment holds our attention through the whole of the Old Testament. The suspense is great. Will the nations ever be blessed?

☐ *Thanks be to God that he sent his Son to be 'a light for revel-ation to the Gentiles, and for glory to thy people Israel.' (Luke 2.32, RSV)*

For group discussion and personal thought

As we struggle today with differences of race, colour, language and nationality, what could make us all one? Consider Acts 2.1–11 alongside the story of the tower of Babel (Genesis 11.1–9) in answering this question.

Sunday February 7 (Education Sunday)   Luke 8.4–15*
CHRIST THE TEACHER

In the parable of the sower, Jesus reminded his friends that there are those who, for one reason or another, do not accept or retain God's word. But always there are some who do respond. Throughout his ministry Jesus continued his work with quiet patience and he called his disciples – and that includes us – to do the same, without any anxiety about the results.

Verses 9–10 are rather puzzling. They seem to give the impression that Jesus taught by parables in order to hide the truth from some listeners. Ideas behind modern education and counselling may help us here. Nowadays it is recognised that facts which are forced upon people's minds are not necessarily taken in; they may even be vigorously rejected. Only as insight dawns, can the facts become one's own, and this takes time. We cannot learn the secrets of God's kingdom by rote. They only come alive for us when we are spiritually ready to grasp them. The parables put these secrets within our grasp, but do not thrust them upon us. Only as we absorb and reflect upon Jesus' parables can we fully understand the truth he is offering to us.

☐ *On this Education Sunday, pray for Christian teachers, that they may be enabled to communicate to their pupils a knowledge of the loving presence of God in all aspects of life.*

MARK'S GOSPEL

Notes by Revd Michael Walker, BD, MTh

Michael Walker is a Baptist minister at Beckenham, Kent. He has also served in parts of London and in Edinburgh. He is the author of several books, including 'From Glory to Glory' (Collins Publishers).

Mark's Gospel was written at a time when the Church faced danger both from within and without. Inside the Church, there were those who were so emphasising the divinity of Jesus that they were losing sight of his humanity. From outside the Church there was the threat of persecution and the possibility that Christians would be called upon to die for their faith.

Mark's portrait of Jesus bears both these in mind. The humanity of Jesus is stressed. His power is limited to the faith of those who come to him for help. He is rejected by his contemporaries. In human terms, his ministry is a failure; his life ends in darkness and a feeling of utter abandonment. This emphasis on the humanity of Jesus is an exhortation to Christians who may have to suffer. In their suffering they are like Jesus and, like him, they are to be sustained by faith and hope alone.

Suggestions for further reading

The Gospel of Mark by William Barclay, Daily Study Bible (Saint Andrew Press);

Mark: Evangelist and Theologian by Ralph P. Martin (Paternoster Press).

Monday February 8   **Mark 1.1–8**

This Gospel (good news) 'begins' with an event – the announcement of one who is about to come. Mark's Gospel does not begin as an idea in a human head, it is not a religious speculation, a philosophical notion or an inspired guess at how the world might be made a better place. It begins with the announcement of an event. Something is about to **happen**.

The Christian gospel is made out of the stuff of history. It relates events that took place in specific places at a particular time. It records the words and deeds of one who lived in the same flesh, blood and bone that all other human beings inhabit, and tells of the way that people, as frail and sinful as ourselves, reacted to him. The good news of our salvation begins with the man Christ Jesus.

The temptation to detach the gospel from the world of time and space, and by the same token, to remove Jesus to another plane of existence, was already facing the Christians of Mark's time. It faces us still. Too often we attempt to disentangle the gospel from the ambiguities and weaknesses of our human life. If we have any good news, however, it must be rooted in the world as it is.

☐ *Lord, may I find you in my humanity, not by trying to escape from my humanity.*

Tuesday February 9   Mark 1.9–20

One of the themes of Mark's Gospel is **the cost of discipleship.** It is a phrase familiar to us as contemporary Christians. The German pastor Dietrich Bonhoeffer used it as the title of a book he wrote before World War II, when he and other Christians were coming increasingly to realise that to follow Jesus means to suffer with him. As Bonhoeffer said, there is no such thing as 'cheap grace'.

When Jesus comes he comes to call us. After his baptism, as Mark records, Jesus began to proclaim the gospel and to call the first disciples – Simon, Andrew, James and John. He called them from their place of work and he uttered his call in the language of their daily work (verse 17). Their lives had been a preparation for this moment – the fishermen of Galilee were now to become the fishermen of the kingdom.

Jesus calls us still, coming to us wherever we are, summoning us to risk everything in the supreme vocation of being his disciples. Too often we miss that call because we are too busy creating what we feel is the appropriate environment for God to say something to us or to do something special in our lives. If only we would listen we might hear him more often in the commonplace circumstances of our daily lives.

☐ *Lord, may today's ordinary happenings provide a place for you and me to meet each other.*

The words of Jesus to the first disciples had evoked a wonderful response: they had left everything and followed him. In today's reading his words evoke a different reaction. The disciples' re-action was like the beginning of a journey, a pilgrimage in which all are moving together in the same direction. The reaction in today's verses is like a collision, the clash of two contrasting forces moving in opposite directions. The disciples heard the words of Jesus as a loving and joyous invitation; the man pos-sessed by the unclean spirit heard his words as a threat and he reacted violently.

There are still people for whom meeting Christ is more of a collision than an encounter. Set on their own paths, pursuing their own ambitions, determined to achieve their own ends, his words – a call to unselfish love – are like a barrier placed across their way. These strange, disturbing words of his seem to run counter to the madness in our human souls and, faced with them, people ask to be left alone. Yet these are the only words that can set us free from those spiritual enemies that try to dominate us.

☐   *Pray for those who hear the words of Christ:*
> *those who find in them their life;*
> *those who are afraid of them;*
> *those who try to oppose them.*

In Mark's Gospel some of the earliest recorded actions of Jesus are in the realm of healing. Inevitably, the reputation of a man capable of driving out disease will quickly spread. The experi-ence of suffering and pain is almost universally shared and feared and if someone is able to bring healing and an end to pain then he will be sought after.

The Christian faith has always been committed to the healing of the sick. It has seen victory over disease as one of the signs of God's kingdom and has thrown itself into the work of medical care. Today many things, that in previous generations would have been regarded as miracle, are now standard practice in medicine and surgery. Knowledge and skills now exist that would have been undreamed of only a short while ago.

The Church, however, still has a role to play alongside the medical services. The interaction of body, mind and spirit in the experience of those who suffer is still a profound mystery. In prayer and in our caring we work by the side of Christ as he continues to heal the sick and make people whole.

☐ *From thee all skill and science flow,*
All pity, care, and love,
All calm and courage, faith and hope;
O pour them from above.

Charles Kingsley

Friday February 12   Mark 2.1–12

This marvellous story tells us two things: the first concerns ourselves; and the second what Jesus is able to do for us.

● First, **we should come to Jesus in faith and expectancy.** There was nothing negative about this paralysed man or his friends. They believed that Jesus was able to heal him and, whatever the obstacles, they were not prepared to leave until the work of healing had been done. Sometimes our faith is limited because we fear disappointment or we see situations in the light of our own slender resources. Faith is the willing commitment of a situation into the hands of Christ, believing that his love will not let our prayers go unheard or unanswered. We are not dealing with a reluctant Christ who has to be persuaded to love us.

● Secondly, **Jesus was willing to give more than was asked for.** What was asked for was the healing of a man's body; what Jesus was prepared to give was the even deeper healing of a man's heart and mind (verse 5). Sometimes we see only the outward symptoms of disease and fail to detect the deeper signs of a broken heart and a distressed mind. The ministry of Jesus reached deep into the paralytic's need. His ministry to us remains the same. He wants our healing to be complete, not partial.

☐ *Let us remember those we know to be ill and offer to God our faith and love in our prayers for their healing.*

Saturday February 13   Mark 2.13–22

One of the themes of Mark's Gospel is to trace how one who began his ministry to such tumultuous applause (Mark 1.28) could end his life in the loneliness and agony of the cross. In today's reading we see the beginning of the shadows that were to grow deeper in the course of Jesus' ministry.

If Jesus had wanted to be accepted by the establishment of his time then he would have joined a monastic community, or earned himself a reputation as a devout rabbi, or associated with one of the strong religious parties such as the Pharisees or Sadducees, or worked in collaboration with the priestly group in Jerusalem. Instead, he mingled with those who had no standing in the community and committed the unpardonable social sin of eating with them at the same table (verses 15–16).

The Church cannot choose the company it keeps and, at the same time, keep its eye on what is socially acceptable. Jesus sat with 'bad characters' because they were prepared to receive him and to listen to him. We, too, have good news to share with whoever will receive it and, like Jesus, we should share it, regardless of people's race or social standing.

☐ *Pray for the witness of the Church to those whom society rejects.*

For group discussion and personal thought
Consider Mark 1.30–34 and 2.1–12 as an indication of the Gospel writer's emphasis on the healing power of Jesus. How important is faith in the healing of the sick? Is failure to be healed a sign of deficiency in faith?

Sunday February 14   **Mark 1.35–45***
CHRIST THE HEALER
It had been the Sabbath. Straight from a session in the synagogue Jesus went to heal Simon's mother-in-law. That same evening the whole town clamoured at the door and he healed many (Mark 1.21–34). After that there was no 'lie-in' for Jesus on the following morning, but an early, solitary prayer session. The local crowds were still clamouring for him, but at once he began an extensive tour of preaching and healing.

We are struck by the immense energy and urgency of Jesus, and also by his refusal to let the success of one aspect of his work (healing) hinder the other (preaching), and by his determination to fit into his crowded programme time for quiet communion with his Father. Healing, preaching, prayer; action, proclamation, worship – his was a balanced life of commitment to God's will.

We do well to reflect on this and ask, in respect of our own lives, as individual Christians and as members of our local church: Are all three aspects properly catered for? Are we too busy to allow time for prayer, or for study of our faith? Are we too academic to see and deal with the immediate needs of our neighbours?

☐ *Lord, may our prayer and our proclamation of your gospel enable us to be instruments of your healing mercies.*

Monday February 15   Mark 2.23–28

Mark here relates a story that illustrates a second reason for what was to be the mounting hostility to Jesus – his attitude to the law. For Jesus' fellow-countrymen the law covered every detail of their lives and mapped out the path of religious duty that they believed would lead them to God. Jesus did not challenge the law itself but rather their attitude to it; what had been designed as a means of serving God had become an end in itself.

The law of the Sabbath was particularly rigorous in its application to every part of life. Many times in his ministry Jesus was to challenge any interpretation of this law that was inhuman or that put principle before people. The needs of his hungry disciples had to be met as much on the Sabbath as on any other day.

There is always a danger of laws and customs coming adrift from the reasons for which they were designed. No law should be allowed to diminish our concern for people or to displace our compassion. The law of the Sabbath was meant to lead people nearer to God, not to drive them further away. For Christians, that should still be the aim of all rules and principles.

☐ *Lord, help me to live truly in the spirit of your laws that I may grow nearer to you.*

Tuesday February 16   Mark 3.1–6

Matthew and Luke left out from this story the reference to Jesus' anger in verse 5. Perhaps later Christians felt that anger was an emotion unworthy of the Jesus whom they worshipped. Mark, however, was concerned to convince his readers of the real humanity of Jesus and being angry is part of being human. Jesus was angry because he saw the law being erected as a barrier to what was humane and compassionate.

Too often we make the mistake of imagining that Christian love precludes all passion and especially passionate anger. Yet there is a place for anger. We cannot remain unmoved and indifferent when we are the witnesses of other people's sufferings. We cannot remain sweetly calm when we see injustice, brutality, hunger and countless other ills bearing down upon and threatening to break the backs of so many of our fellow-men and women.

Jesus, however, went beyond anger. He channelled it into loving action on behalf of the man with the withered arm. Anger, in itself and untempered by love, can be a destructive emotion. We should use our anger to motivate our love, and our love to motivate our actions.

☐ *Let us remember those whose need particularly baffles and hurts us and ask God how our love might be more effective in helping them.*

Wednesday February 17   Mark 3.7–19

Mark tells us that Jesus had three aims in his mind when he called the Twelve to be his disciples (verses 14–15). They were to be his companions, to proclaim the gospel and to cast out devils. Let us try to put that in terms of our own discipleship:

● Christ calls us **to be his companions.** The Christian enterprise is one in which we co-operate with our Lord in striving to see God's will done on earth. Jesus does not keep us in the dark, nor does he do his work apart from us. Rather, he calls us to share in the tasks of the kingdom.

● Secondly, he calls us **to proclaim the gospel.** This is something that we would prefer to delegate to others. We are aware of the difficulties in witnessing to our faith – difficulties of language, of understanding, of openness to the deeper spiritual questions of our human life. Yet all of us, with the help of Christ, must seek to find the words and the deeds that will effectively communicate the truth of the gospel to other people.

● Lastly, the disciples were called **to cast out devils.** In our own terms, that means facing whatever is evil, all the darkness in humanity that tries to overpower the light.

☐ *Lord, show me the task I must carry out to do your will;*
    help me to witness;
    give me courage in the face of evil.

41

The hostility to Jesus now began to infect even the attitudes of his closest family. They had heard rumours that he had become insane (verse 21) and they came to find him in order to talk to him. His reply in verse 33 must have seemed a snub. However, a new family had come into being around Jesus, bound not by ties of flesh and blood but by a commitment to do the will of God.

Even the deepest and most loving relationships are subjected to stress, perhaps because of a clash of loyalties or the need to follow different objectives or, sometimes, through sheer mis-understanding. That stress is easier to bear if those involved recognise that they are held together not only by the immediate ties of human love, but also those ties that are formed by de-votion to Christ and his Church.

There are times when our Christian duty will clash with our human inclinations, or when love for God and the desire to do his will may seem to run counter to what those closest to us expect of us. God's love embraces us all. The family of Jesus wanted to claim Jesus and thus exclude others. He, on the other hand, wanted to enlarge the family of God.

☐ *Pray that you may be true to God and to your loved ones.*

Out of this group of parables let us look particularly at the parable of the seed growing silently and secretly in the night (verses 26–29).

Jesus always encouraged every effort towards virtue and every resolve to persevere in the path of discipleship. He also reminded us that God is on our side, working with us and through us.

We have to throw all our efforts into the work that God gives us to do. At the same time, we have to recognise our own limitations. A locomotive driver has the skills to drive the train, but he does not have the strength to push it. We have the gifts that God has given us but, as we use them, we must not imagine that God becomes a sleeping partner and leaves everything to us. We do our part and then leave it to him to breathe the spirit of life into our work and to bring about the harvest for which we long.

It needs faith to trust God to do his part. The farmer in the parable had that faith when he planted the seed – otherwise he would have had some sleepless nights!

☐ *From thee, the overflowing spring,*
Our souls shall drink a fresh supply;
While such as trust their native strength
Shall faint away, and droop, and die. *Isaac Watts*

Saturday February 20 Mark 5.1–20

Animal lovers, businessmen and conservationists find great problems with this story: the animal lovers, because the slaughter of the pigs seems callous; the businessmen, because what Jesus did was bad for profits; the conservationists, because of what they see as a waste of resources and the polluting of the lake.

At the heart of the story is a solitary man, insane, frightened and frightening, grievously ill and desperately unhappy. And it is that man of whom we must never lose sight as we try to understand this story. Perhaps a man who believed he was inhabited by an army of devils needed to **see** them destroyed. The squealing pigs running down the hillside into the waters and drowning there would have persuaded him of his own healing.

There are many good causes to be defended and fine principles to be upheld. We owe a responsibility to the animal kingdom to protect it. Prosperity is created by profits and none of us today would disagree with the arguments of the conservationists. But what matters most is the salvation and wholeness of people.

☐ *Pray for those who are desperately in need, that they may meet with great compassion.*

For group discussion and personal thought

Read Mark 2.23–28. In what ways do churches today put laws and principles before the needs of people (for example, in the matter of divorce or the openness of the Lord's table)?

Sunday February 21 Mark 4.35–41*

CHRIST, WORKER OF MIRACLES

The disciples were swamped with **terror**. Jesus invited them to share his **tranquillity**. He, who was so open to God that he could be an instrument of the conquest of sickness, was equally confident of God's ability to control the powers of nature. Do we share with Christ his confidence in God? This confidence was stated compellingly in different words by Paul: 'I am convinced that there is nothing in death or life, in the realm of spirits or superhuman powers, in the world as it is or the world as it shall be, in the forces of the universe, in heights or depths – nothing in all creation that can separate us from the love of God in Christ Jesus our Lord.' (Romans 8.38–39)

The miracles of Jesus were not conjuring tricks to persuade people of his divinity; they were expressions of his trust in the love of God which held all things within its embrace and control. The real miracle of our lives is not that God intervenes in this or that crisis to save us from trouble, but that he is in all events to save us from despair.

☐ *Lord, help me to know your loving presence in all aspects of my life.*

Monday February 22   Mark 5.21–34

All of us like our privacy. We resent intrusions into what we believe to be our own business. There are areas of our experience and our feelings that we want to keep hidden from other people. The woman who came to Jesus to be healed wanted to cling to her privacy. We can sympathise with her – we, too, react against having our personal frailties blazoned in front of others.

Encounters with Jesus, however, cannot be completely solitary or private. We cannot meet him, receive his grace and then withdraw from him to be lost in the crowd. We cannot go on our way deceiving the rest of the world into believing that nothing has changed. If Christ has given us something then he wants us to share it openly with others.

The woman's passion for privacy may have been part of a timid attitude to life, a desire to shut herself away from others. By compelling her to confess her faith publicly Jesus made it possible for her to come out of her private citadel and share her life with others. That too, was part of her healing.

☐ *Jesus, may all confess thy name,*
  Thy wondrous love adore;
  And, seeking thee, themselves inflame
    To seek thee more and more.   *Bernard of Clairvaux*

Both the story of the woman with the haemorrhage (see yesterday) and that of the raising of Jairus' daughter emphasise the role of faith. Here Jesus exhorts Jairus to go on having faith even in the face of what is seemingly impossible (verse 36). If the girl was dead, what point was there in hoping for anything to be done? There is nothing more final than death. The end of the story, however, is the raising of the little girl.

This story is a sign of hope, a pledge of Christ's unfailing love towards those who put their trust in him. The first readers of Mark's Gospel were being faced with persecution, the loss of things they loved dearly, even death itself. This story reminded them that, no matter how impossible a situation might appear, nothing could alter the firm resolve of Christ's love.

We have to go on trusting even when life is painful and it seems that nothing can turn the tide of affliction that bears down upon us. Jairus was asked to go on believing even though he had no idea of what Jesus could do in the situation. We, too, have sometimes to trust without evidence, trust without knowing what Christ may do for us. In the end, we shall see his love at work in ways we never imagined.

☐ *Lord, keep my faith strong, no matter what happens.*

Ash Wednesday, February 24   Mark 6.1–6a

If faith created the conditions in which Christ's power could be seen at work, lack of faith stifled that same power. The people of Nazareth did not deny the wisdom of what Jesus was saying, nor did they deny the reports they had heard of the miracles he was performing, but what they could not do was to bring themselves to accept him as others had done. They thought they knew him better than others; in fact, they understood him less.

Sometimes we act as spectators of what Christ does in the life of other people, yet lack the faith to believe that he can work just as effectively in our own lives. We stifle the power of his Spirit, setting limits to our faith and to what we think is possible. As Lent begins today, let us ask God for the gift of greater faith that will release the power of Christ in our lives.

☐ *A prayer for Ash Wednesday*
  Lord, help me to use this time of Lent for the deepening of my faith. So much has still to be done in the service of your king-

dom: I want to help your work, not hinder it. May no lack of faith on my part become an obstacle to the spreading of your truth or the work of your love in the lives of those around me. So help me to pray and to believe.

Thursday February 25 Mark 6.6b–16

Anyone who has done any backpacking and hill-walking will know that one of the impediments to progress is a heavy pack. Experience gradually teaches us just how much we need and how much is surplus, so that we do not make the mistake of carrying spare clothes that are unnecessary. The lighter the pack, the quicker and easier the journey.

When Jesus sent out his disciples on a mission he told them that they were to carry nothing extra. His restrictions may seem too austere to us – no bread, no pack and no money – but there was a sense of urgency in the mission and nothing could be taken that would impede the disciples' progress.

In the pilgrimage of our lives we have to learn what is important and what is trivial, what we need and what we can dispense with. We all make the mistake of carrying too much unnecessary baggage in our lives and find it hard to understand why we do not make the spiritual progress we expect of ourselves. Maturity is, in part, learning to distinguish the simple necessities of the Christian life from the worldly concerns with which it is sometimes cluttered.

☐ *Pray for grace to live simply and to move swiftly in the service of Christ.*

Friday February 26 Mark 6.17–29

The violence and the cruelty that underlie this story are, unfortunately, familiar to anyone today who reads a newspaper or watches a television newsreel. The plot hatched by Herodias was wicked. Yet her youthful daughter did not question it, Herod lacked the courage to oppose it, and the guests were swept along by it. The monstrous deed was done and John's head was cut off.

It is said that the success of evil men is made possible by the silence of good men. In Herod's court, no one even tried to be good. They had become trapped in their own vice, the victims of their own indulgence and apostasy. Evil deeds are done because people lack either the courage or the moral authority to oppose them. Yet that frailty finally offers us no basis for excuses. The severed, bleeding head of John, was a grim condemnation of the evil of which all who saw it were a part.

We should never become so familiar with cruelty and violence that they cease to shock and offend us. It is not a sign of sophistication when we are no longer shocked, but of insensitivity. For every cruel deed, somewhere a voice should be raised in anger, a protest made, a loud shout uttered in the name of justice and humanity.

☐ *Lord, save us from silence in the face of evil.*

Saturday February 27 Mark 6.30–44

When the disciples came to make the tally of their resources and found it amounted to nothing more than five loaves and two fishes they must have felt desperate, faced with the crowd's obvious need of sustenance. Contrasting with the few resources available was the unlimited compassion of Jesus that somehow embraced the whole multitude (verse 34). Here then, was a union of contrasts, the unconditioned love of Jesus and the limited resources of the disciples.

If we were to make an honest count of our resources as Christians we might well grow desperate as we realise the size of the task in front of us. We have so little to offer in the face of a needy world. We are often few in numbers, we cannot lay claim to endless material resources, and we feel overwhelmed by the challenge with which the world faces us.

What transforms our resources is our willingness to offer them to Christ and to allow him to use them as a vehicle of his compassion. What is inadequate in our hands is more than sufficient in the hands of Christ. Given his compassion, even our slender resources are enough to match the needs of the people around us.

☐ *Let us pray that we may share Christ's compassion and that Christ will use our gifts.*

For group discussion and personal thought

Do we, like the people of Nazareth in Mark 6.1–6a, lack the faith that Christ can work mightily in our lives? What do we find are the greatest barriers to faith in our lives? How can we use Lent to increase our faith?

THE TEMPTATIONS

When the leader of a nation loses his integrity, the nation disintegrates. Some modern world leaders have begun by leading their people out of slavery or inferior status because they have had a shining ideal and a burning enthusiasm, but later they have succumbed to the allure of personal power and wealth and in the end toppled their nation into a worse chaos than before!

Jesus had his brilliant vision of the kingdom of God. His whole ministry was devoted to inviting men and women to enter this kingdon. But first he had to face the test that comes to all leaders – the test of his integrity. The Spirit led him into a forty days' desert experience to face this test. He was tempted to exploit his status as Son of God. He was tempted to use unworthy means of winning people's allegiance – pandering to their materialistic desires, using satanic methods (eg force), and overcoming unbelief by doing marvels. He was 'tempted by the devil', but his integrity could not be shaken.

Jesus chose the one way God required him to take – the appeal of love – even though that way would render him seemingly helpless, powerless and eventually lead him to crucifixion. But that was to be the way of his victory. It is still the only way to win people into the kingdom. How does the Church today stand up to this test?

◻   *O Jesus, King most wonderful !*
    Thou conqueror renowned.

                                              Bernard of Clairvaux

Monday March 1   Mark 6.45–56

The beginning of this reading, like the beginning of the reading for last Saturday, suggests that, in the ministry of Jesus, there was a clash between his desire to withdraw in order to pray and the demands that were made on him by the crowds who seemed to dog his footsteps wherever he went. In today's verses Jesus turns from prayer to the desperate need of his disciples.

The same clash between action and prayer is familiar in all our lives. Sometimes we find it impossible to disentangle ourselves from our responsibilities toward others in order to pray. The danger is that we shall see some virtue in this and be content permanently to substitute action for prayer. The attractions of being busy can seduce us from the more private and disciplined pursuit of contemplative prayer.

Jesus, however, was not prepared to resolve the tension between action and prayer by abandoning prayer. He **made** time to pray. Perhaps that is the only way we are going to fit prayer into our lives.

☐ *O thou by whom we come to God,*
   The life, the truth, the way,
The path of prayer thyself hast trod:
   Lord, teach us how to pray !   *James Montgomery*

Tuesday March 2   Mark 7.1–13

Jesus claimed that some laws are more important than others and that the inward attitude of the heart is most important of all.

If a man placed any of his possessions under pledge to God, then it was deemed to be *Corban* (verse 11), which meant that under no circumstances could the vow be revoked and the possessions retrieved. Jesus argued that there could be an occasion when the more basic demands, such as filial duty to one's parents, should take precedence over *Corban*. If a man's parents were in desperate need it was wrong that any interpretation of the law should forbid him to help them.

Here again we come up against Jesus' insistence that law must be governed by compassion and used to enrich human relationships, not to cripple them. The most devoted application to legal systems could serve no devout purpose if it hardened men's hearts and pushed them further away from God and his compassion. It is a heart that is attuned to God that perceives, with simple clarity, the priority of compassion in all things. All laws are subject to the command that we should love God and our neighbour.

☐ *Lord, grant to me a simplicity of heart that I may see you more clearly, and be quick to respond to the needs of others.*

Wednesday March 3   Mark 7.14–23

Jesus was still dealing with the question of ritual washings that was raised in verse 5 of this chapter. He stated a principle in verses 14–15, which he then went on to explain.

Although admirable from the point of view of hygiene, the Jewish laws governing the washing of hands and dishes were totally inadequate as an expression of religious virtue. As the psalmist had said, it is he 'who has clean hands and a pure heart'

(Psalm 24.4) who can ascend the hill of the Lord. A man is in greater spiritual peril from the inhabitants of his own heart than he is from any 'foreign bodies' that enter his body through his mouth.

We may go to great lengths to ensure that we are not contaminated by the more unsavoury aspects of our life in the modern world. But this in no way sets us free from the vigil we have to keep over our own heart and mind, for it is there, in the bubbling cauldron of our own sin, that we mix a 'witches' brew' of envy, greed and arrogance.

☐   *Breathe on me, Breath of God,*
     Until my heart is pure,
  Until with thee I will one will,
     To do or to endure.

                                                  Edwin Hatch

Thursday March 4   Mark 7.24–37

By the time the story of the Phoenician woman came to be written in Mark's Gospel the mission of the Church had already extended to the Gentiles. This story illustrates that mission.

Jesus came first to the people of Israel. It was they who were to be the first to receive the word of God. Yet that word would inevitably spill over into the Gentile world, just as scraps of food fall from a table. That time had not yet come; but the woman, acting almost prophetically, claimed the grace that would one day be available to the whole human race. Her daring and faith were rewarded and her daughter was immediately healed.

Jesus' reference to a meal reflected his people's hope that, when Messiah came, he would gather his people to a great banquet where they would together celebrate the victory of his kingdom. Jesus' countrymen believed it was they alone who would sit at that banquet. Like them we, too, limit the banquet to a chosen few. But, as Martin Luther King saw in his dream, **all** nations will sit down to the messianic banquet, whatever their race or their colour.

☐ *Lord, we thank you for sharing the feast with us; may we share it with others.*

Friday March 5   Mark 8.1–13

More than once we have put our daily reading in the setting of the early Church and the Christians who first read Mark's

Gospel. We know that in their corporate life they met on the first day of the week, which they came to call the Lord's Day, and celebrated the Lord's Supper or Eucharist. In that celebration they remembered how the Lord had taken bread and broken it, on the eve of his death, making it a symbol of his life offered for them and to them.

The language of our story today is similar to that used in the Lord's Supper (see verse 6). Would the early Christians have made the connection in their minds between the miraculous feeding of four thousand people and the weekly 'feeding' of the Church, the gift of bread to all who needed it and the love offered in the Eucharist to all who would receive it?

We still share in the miracle of that gift. Still Christ's love is shared among us in broken bread, and still the gift is available to the countless people who come, in faith, to receive it.

☐ *Prayer for the (Women's) World Day of Prayer*

> *O Lord, may our prayers encircle the world today.*
> *Grant us the peace for which we long;*
> > *build us up in the unity for which we strive;*
> > *use us in the service to which we are called.*

Saturday March 6   Mark 8.14–26

The healing of the blind man dramatically illustrates features of Jesus' healing ministry that are stressed in Mark's Gospel. There is the growing privacy with which Jesus sought to surround his healing work. The blind man was taken away from his village to be healed and was ordered to tell no one what had taken place. The miracle itself also took place by stages, illustrating the human factors, as well as the divine power, that were at work.

Jesus never used miracles to enhance his own reputation. They were signs of the kingdom, acts of compassion towards the sick and disabled. Jesus did not use the miracles to impress people or to win them to himself.

As Christians we may be tempted to gauge the effect that compassionate action might have on other people and their attitudes to us or to the Church. Perhaps we hope that by being compassionate to needy people we may win them to our way of thinking. But compassion is never a means to an end. It is offered for its own sake. The love of Christ is unconditional love; it has no strings attached; it is not motivated by a desire to impress people.

☐ *O God, help me to love like Jesus, with no thought of personal gain or reward.*

For group discussion and personal thought

Read and think about Mark 7.24–30. Why did Jesus hesitate to help this woman? What should the Church's response be to requests for help from non-Christian individuals and organisations? (Try to consider some specific examples.)

2nd Sunday in Lent, March 7   Matthew 12.22–32*
CONFLICT

There are people who try to depreciate a good action by questioning the motive of the one who did it. For example, they say: 'He only gave the money to a charity in order to get his name in the papers.' This unpleasant habit is a way of trying to belittle someone we do not like, or whose kindness shows up our own selfishness, by attempting to make his virtues appear as vices. The Pharisees tried to belittle Jesus' healing miracle by ascribing it to the power of the 'prince of the devils'. He replied, first, with an amused comment which came to this: 'Well, if this is Satan's work, he is not making much of a showing of it, is he? He is destroying himself!'

An attitude of refusing to acknowledge good when it is plainly there can turn into a permanent moral blindness which is never able to recognise goodness. It becomes a way of life – life which is a lie, cut off from reality, cut off from God. People who live in this way are sinning against the Holy Spirit and are in peril of spiritual death. In the end, Jesus' amused first comment turned into a terrible condemnation (verses 31–32).

☐ *Lord, save us from self-deception. Give us minds open to perceive and appreciate goodness. Save us from cynicism. Help us humbly to seek your forgiveness.*

Monday March 8   Mark 9.14–29

Time and again, Mark emphasised the role of faith in the healing of the sick. Where faith is present then healing is possible, where it is absent then miracles are impossible. Faith, however, is an elusive attribute, it does not come naturally, especially to twentieth century people who have been taught to question everything and trust nothing that cannot be proved.

There are many people for whom the father's agonised cry in verse 24 will find an echo in their own hearts. They want to have faith but faith is hard to come by.

We should distinguish between wanting to believe and refusing to believe, between a faith that wrestles with doubt and unbelief and a faith that does not exist at all. The father longed to have more faith and that longing itself was enough for his son to be healed.

We should not boast of a faith we do not have. On the other hand, we should not despair of the frailty of our faith. Faith comes to those who long for it, fight for it, pray for it and open their hearts to receive it.

☐ *His call we obey, like Abram of old,*
Not knowing our way, but faith makes us bold;
For, though we are strangers, we have a good guide,
And trust, in all dangers, the Lord will provide.   *John Newton*

Tuesday March 9   Mark 9.30–37

Jesus, aware of the mounting hostility to his ministry, prophesied his own death (verse 31). The failure of the disciples to understand him was forcefully illustrated by the discussion they had soon afterwards. They argued about who was the greatest, as if Jesus had said nothing about death and sacrifice.

The crassness of the disciples' failure to grasp what Jesus was saying should not delude us into thinking that we avoid the errors into which they had fallen. In our faith we are surrounded on every side, in word and symbol, by the evidence that the way of Christ is the way of unconditional love. Yet pride, ambition and selfishness still intrude themselves into our Christian lives. We find the way of the servant (verse 35) no easier than did the Twelve. We are more concerned with our rights than with our duties to others.

The disciples argued about their status under the shadow of the cross. If we are to live beneath its shadow then we must allow ourselves to be influenced by the self-renunciation and sacrificial love that it represents.

☐ *Pray that you may have the willingness to be a servant for Christ's sake.*

53

We all tend to be suspicious of people who are 'not one of us' (verse 38). All human groups are defensive and eager to protect themselves against outsiders. The regular patrons of a youth club may look askance at any new group of people who wander in. Members of golf clubs fret about newcomers or outsiders who may not wear their ties in the appropriate places. Some nations barricade their borders to keep their own people in and foreigners out. It is small wonder that the Church, being made up of human beings, sometimes shares in this mistrust of others and becomes edgy and suspicious of newcomers or Christians of another persuasion.

Our attitude becomes even more intractable when we inflate it into religious principle or loyalty to our traditions. Simple hostility is concealed beneath doctrinal argument; plain human defensiveness is dressed up as religious conviction.

The suspicion that leads us to build fences between people is a worldly flaw in our Christian witness. Jesus did not feel threatened by a man healing in his name, in fact he accepted him. We too, must covet our Lord's openness to people, learning to understand them, not to fear them.

☐ *Lord, may I strive to walk with all who confess your name.*

The way we interpret these words of Jesus is a cause of great division among Christians. There are those who take his words in verses 11–12 as the statement of a law in the same category, and just as binding, as all other divinely inspired laws. For them, divorce simply cannot take place.

There are other Christians who would argue that Jesus is here presenting the ideal of marriage – that is, a lifelong union between a man and a woman. They would not put that ideal in the realm of law, any more than they would the injunction to give away a shirt, or turn the other cheek, or pluck out a right eye if it is a cause of offence.

All Christians would agree, however, that Jesus presented us with a view of marriage that in no way allows us to trivialise it or allows it to be spoilt by selfish lust or disloyalty. The promises made in marriage are not to be put on one side as a matter of convenience. Neither is marriage to be treated as a casual and temporary relationship. It is nothing less than the making of

one flesh (verses 8–9), a union as mysterious as that which binds
Christ in love to his Church (see Ephesians 5.32–33).

☐ *Pray for the marriages of your friends, that they may be true
and full of love.*

Friday March 12   Mark 10.13–16

Those who have close contact with children, such as parents and
teachers, may feel that the view of childhood presented here is a
highly idealised one. Martin Luther is said to have observed the
antics of his own children and sighed, 'Dear God, are we really
meant to be such fools!' Children can be antisocial and down-
right exasperating.

Yet sometimes our exasperation is prompted by a furtive envy.
We see in children qualities that we have lost. We realise how
the years have hardened us, blunting the edge of our perception,
colouring our vision of the world with the greys of compromise
and cynicism. It is these lost qualities that we would describe as
childlike as opposed to childish.

To follow Jesus in childlike faith is to be flexible and open to
what he has to reveal to us. It is the refusal to allow ourselves to
be made hard, bitter and sarcastic by the set-backs of life. It is
trusting in the goodness of God and looking with confidence,
born of hope, to tomorrow and all the days that are yet to come.
It is being ready, as C. S. Lewis put it, to be 'surprised by joy'.

☐ *Lord, may I never lose my joy, wonder or hope.*

Saturday March 13   Mark 10.17–31

Why is wealth a stumbling-block to faith (verses 21,23–24)?
We should try to find an answer because most of us, at least in
the western world, are likely to be more acquainted with prosperity than we are with poverty. Is that why, in many of those
same countries, faith has been in decline?

One of the dangers of wealth is that we invest too much of
our happiness in it. The more happiness we feel we can buy, the
less happiness we find within ourselves or create out of our own
resources. When our happiness lies in our possessions, any
threat to them is a threat to our own peace of mind.

Wealth also faces us with divided loyalties. The time and
energy devoted to the amassing of wealth can drain away resources that could otherwise be used in the deepening of human

relationships and the building of love. Families that grow rich sometimes fall apart because, in the struggle to make money, their members have forgotten the cultivation of love.

Finally, wealth makes more difficult that attitude of unselfishness, that willingness to sit light to material things, which characterises the way of Christ.

□ *Let us pray that we may value no earthly possession too much.*

For group discussion and personal thought

Study Mark 10.17–27. In what ways does prosperity affect our lives? As Christians what criteria should we apply in the way we handle our money and material possessions?

3rd Sunday in Lent, March 14   Luke 9.18–27*
SUFFERING

A suffering Messiah! Whoever would believe such a thing? His followers called not to victory parades, but to self-renunciation! Who would be likely to respond to a call like that? Yet, clearly and unequivocally, Jesus set suffering as a central element in the Christian way of life. It is something we cannot evade if we take our faith seriously, for we are engaged in a war. At all times the forces of self-interest, ignorance, greed and fear are seeking to destroy Jesus' vision of love. So we have to fight, inside ourselves as well as in the world. Every new day the fight is renewed. There is no let-up. And our weapons in this war are the weapons of love – they can be no other. There is a cross at the heart of the Christian way.

At the same time, there is the resurrection. We may have to suffer, but we also gain a victory. We find our true selves (verse 25) and our status as children of God; we experience the joy of knowing we are in touch with the creator of the universe and in touch with reality. So, suffering for Christ's sake is not to be seen as a wretched and fearful thing, but as an experience of the energy of love in which we are safe (verse 24).

□   *The fire our graces shall refine,*
     Till, moulded from above,
  We bear the character divine,
     The stamp of perfect love.

                                         Charles Wesley

Mark tells us that Jesus was leaving Jericho when Bartimaeus, hearing the crowd go by, began shouting for help. His determination to be heard equalled his determination to be healed. Perhaps he believed this was the one opportunity in his lifetime to get back the one thing he longed for – his sight.

Bartimaeus contrasts with the father who found faith so difficult (see Mark 9.24). He knew what he wanted, he believed Christ was able to give it to him and he refused to hold his peace until his sight was restored.

The robustness of Bartimaeus' faith is characteristic of ages other than our own. But in every age, even this one, there have been people for whom faith has been a fearless affirmation, people who have believed passionately in the loving power of Christ, people who have trusted without a moment's hesitation. Such people are like the birds on a poster which bears the caption: 'They fly because they think they can.' They are an encouragement to us all.

☐ *Lord, may we be encouraged by the faith of others.*

The rightness of Jesus' action in cleansing the temple should not lessen for us the shock of it. It was an act liable to lead to a disturbance of the peace, to loss of revenue, to the enflaming of passions and to physical confrontation. The success of Jesus' action can only be accounted for by the enormous authority of his presence. No one had the confidence to resist him.

In some areas of the world today, where there is political oppression allied to social injustice, there are Christians who believe that they must take the law into their own hands in order to make possible the justice and freedom that are hallmarks of the kingdom of heaven. Some of them are prepared to go to extremes that many of us, remote from their situation and living in happier circumstances, find impossible to accept.

If we reject extreme violence, however, we must on no account reject the cause of those who claim rights that we take for granted every day of our lives. Let us not join the ranks of the smugly indifferent who refuse to lift a finger to make the world a happier place for those who suffer at the hands of tyranny.

☐ *Let us pray for those of our fellow-Christians who claim for their fellow-men the liberation that Jesus has given to us.*

Yesterday we used the word 'authority' to describe Jesus' action in cleansing the temple. That authority was evident not only to those who believed in Jesus but also to those who opposed him. What they questioned was its source. Jesus used the example of John to put the issue starkly before them, for the question of John's authority was the same as his own – it came either 'from God, or from men' (verse 30). They refused to answer Jesus' question.

To believe in Jesus is to believe that his authority derives from God. Here is not someone simply presenting the example of a good man, or a man who had gone beyond all of us in his ascent of the way that leads to God. The authority of Jesus came from God himself. If we believe this, his actions must set the style of our lives and his words will be God's word to us.

If we accept the source of Jesus' authority then our lives cannot remain unchanged once we have met him and believed in him.

☐　*Thou art the everlasting Word,*
　　　The Father's only Son;
　　God manifestly seen and heard,
　　　And heaven's belovèd One.
　　　　Worthy, O Lamb of God, art thou
　　　　That every knee to thee should bow.

　　　　　　　　　　　　　　　　　　　　　　　Josiah Conder

This is one parable that those for whom it was intended seemed to understand. Under the guise of a story, Jesus spoke of the long history of rejection of prophets who had spoken the word of God and, so often, only been listened to after they were dead. He himself was the latest in that long succession, closer to God than any of his predecessors (verse 6), yet already his enemies were plotting to murder him (verse 7).

The parable prodded their conscience in three places: the record of resistance by Israel's rulers to the prophets in the past; their own refusal to accept Jesus; and the plans that were already afoot to have him put to death. Stung by his words, they only became more determined to arrest him.

Conscience plays the same trick with all of us. We all have sensitive areas where the memory of past failures or the pursuance of present sins makes us feel uneasy and guilty. We can take the same path as Jesus' enemies, stifling the voice of our conscience, burying our memories, strengthening our resolve to continue in the wrongdoing to which we have already put our hand.

Alternatively, we can let our conscience bring us to repentance, and repentance to forgiveness and peace. We choose. The cross is either the sign of our rebellion or of our salvation.

☐ *Lord, may I hear your voice when it speaks in my conscience.*

Friday March 19   Mark 12.13–17

The flattery was cynical and the question barbed (see verse 14). If Jesus had answered by denying the need to pay taxes to Caesar then they could have accused him of treason. On the other hand, to have given an unqualified support to the payment of Roman taxes would have offended the patriotism of the people and damaged his standing among them. Jesus' answer in verse 17 was memorable. We owe a duty to those who govern us and we owe a duty to God; we can escape neither the secular or the sacred; we can isolate ourselves neither from our life in the world nor from our answerability to God.

Jesus was describing just one of the knife-edges on which his followers live. The State has a right to expect that we play our part as citizens, but cannot expect from us the worship that belongs to God alone. To make a god out of the State is to fall to one side of the knife-edge and drop into blasphemy. On the other hand, our first loyalty is to God, but this does not cancel out the responsibilities that are ours as members of the State. Keeping a sense of balance is sometimes difficult, but it is inescapable.

☐ *Let us pray for our nation, for our fellow-countrymen and our duties to one another, for strength to live our lives in loyalty to God, and for the coming of God's kingdom.*

Saturday March 20   Mark 12.18–27

The Pharisees and the Herodians had already tried to trap Jesus (verse 13). It was now the turn of the Sadducees who came to argue against the resurrection, in which they did not believe. They recounted to Jesus a plausible story that seemed to them to make a nonsense of any theory of resurrection. The story, however, rested upon the assumption that life in the resurrection is simply a continuation of life here on earth, like an endlessly extended ball of string. Jesus rejoined by telling them that resurrection is more than resuscitation, the re-animation of a corpse, the simple continuance of things as they were. It is a new dimension of life (verse 25) in which physical relationships are superseded.

Clearly, Jesus moved towards his death trusting in the power of God to raise the dead to everlasting life. Because he has now passed through death and been raised, we can live our lives in hope and trust, knowing that we also move towards that eternal life which God will give to us. That life is not to be thought of as endless time, but of life in God, a life lived in a dimension we can only attempt to describe because it is so different from the setting of our life here in time and space.

☐ *Pray for those who mourn that they may be comforted, and for those who fear death that they may be set free from fear.*

For group discussion and personal thought

What should be our attitude to Christians who, living under oppressive régimes, believe that active resistance possibly with violence is the only way to gain freedom? Does Jesus' action in clearing the temple court (see Mark 11.15–17) help us to answer this? If so, how?

4th Sunday in Lent, March 21   Luke 9.28–36*
THE TRANSFIGURATION

It is not uncommon for a person who has been enduring a long and wearisome illness for many weeks, to wake up one morning feeling considerably better. Temperature is down and the pain is less nagging. Although he knows it may still be many weeks before he is really fit, this moment encourages him, gives him a foretaste of what things will be like and an inner strength to continue enduring the illness. Such moments of encouragement come to us in all kinds of difficult experiences – they stimulate flagging spirits and help us to continue the struggle.

Perhaps the disciples were feeling bewildered by the opposition their Master was receiving from some quarters and by what he had told them about the necessity of his death and their suffering. Now, both for him and for them, came a foretaste of the outcome of the struggle, if only they would remain faithful. Two great leaders of the past stood with him. Like him, Moses and Elijah had had to face opposition; yet that had been the road to their great achievements. Moses, representing the law, and Elijah, representing the prophets, stood there with their Master. And in this highly significant scene there came an assurance to the disciples that Jesus was the fulfilment of all that was best in their tradition and their religion. Encouraged, they could continue.

☐ *'Almighty Father, give us faith to perceive Christ's glory, that we may be strengthened to suffer with him, and be changed into his likeness.' (Methodist Service Book)*

Monday March 22   Mark 12.28–34a

There were those, even in the religious establishment of Jesus' time, who listened sympathetically to him and agreed with what he said (see verse 32). The common ground upon which Jesus and the lawyer stood was their commitment to the two great commandments as the foundation of all faith and religious practice.

We often meet people who are 'not far from the kingdom of God'. They have made no open commitment to Christ, they might not even claim the name of Christian; yet there is a genuine search for God, endeavour to glorify him and an unselfish commitment to their neighbours. It should not astonish us that outside the bounds of any religious faith there are people who are kind, generous, compassionate and practical in their concern for others.

Jesus did not see this man, on his way to the kingdom, as a problem. We sometimes speak as if we do. We puzzle about good and uncommitted people as if they were a theological conundrum and nothing more. Like Jesus, we should accept them and encourage them in their seeking.

☐ *O brother man, fold to thy heart thy brother:*
   Where pity dwells, the peace of God is there;
To worship rightly is to love each other,
   Each smile a hymn, each kindly deed a prayer.
                          John Greenleaf Whittier

Up to this point Jesus had been defending himself against the
questions of the religious leaders. Their questions exhausted he
turned the tables and went on the attack. In particular, he
attacked those who did the right thing for the wrong reason:
the religious who prayed in order to attract attention (verse 40)
and the wealthy who were generous in order to be noticed (verse
41).

Both piety and generosity are twisted and dishonoured when
they are used to feed our own pride. Our prayers are not a sign
of our spiritual superiority, but of our dependence upon God,
our love towards him and our desire to co-operate with him in
his work. Generosity should be practised gratefully, in thankfulness that God has given us resources to share with other people.
It was in that spirit of generosity that the poor widow gave all
that she had (verse 44).

Whatever we do that is good, we should not be looking all
the time over our shoulders to see what effect it is having on
other people. It is enough that God hears our prayers and sees
our giving – they should be intended for the ears and eyes of no
one else.

☐   *Let us ask God to deepen our life of prayer;*
            to make us more generous;
            to help us pray and give with humility.

Wednesday March 24   **Mark 13.1–13**

We have already noted that the first readers of Mark's Gospel
were facing a time of persecution. For them, the recollection of
Christ's words had a grim significance, for they were already
being punished and hauled before judges. They knew well the
cost involved in holding out to the end.

The prayer that we might 'hold out to the end' should be the
prayer of all of us. In the course of a lifetime our discipleship
has to suffer many stresses and temptations. There have always
been those for whom these proved too much, the people who
fall away from the faith and from the Church. Falling away
from the faith is grievous for the person concerned and for the
rest of the Church.

It does not take a savage persecution to make people abandon
their faith; in fact, affluence and ease breed more apostates than
the fires of martyrdom ever did. All of us, in the place and cir-

cumstances where God has set us, have to resolve not to let go, not to quit before we reach the end. For how can one compensate for the loss of faith? What treasures can the world offer to compare with that pearl of great price that is the kingdom of heaven?

☐ *Lord, keep me faithful, never letting go,*
to the end, to the very end.

Thursday March 25   Mark 13.14–23

It is possible that the events spoken of in verses 14–20 describe or portend the turbulent years which led to the collapse of Jerusalem in AD 70 after a terrible siege. Be that as it may, our Lord's words conjure up images of crises that have faced men and women in every generation – the crises of war, of famine, of natural disaster. Ordinary life is dislocated, sometimes nature itself makes the events more terrible – disease can easily accompany floods, hunger is inevitably aggravated by drought.

Disasters of this sort always raise questions for faith – why do such things happen in a world watched over by a loving God? The words of Jesus do not deny the reality of such events, or give us any reason to suppose that they will not occur. What these verses are saying is that disaster is never the last word – it is not final. Even in the worst disasters we may know the presence of Christ. It is this faith that gives us the resources to hold on and to survive whatever may happen to us.

☐ *Thy truth unchanged hath ever stood;*
Thou savest those that on thee call;
To them that seek thee thou art good,
To them that find thee, all in all !   *Bernard of Clairvaux*

Friday March 26   Mark 13.24–37

None of us can accurately predict our own future or the future of the world in which we live; neither does our Lord offer us any encouragement to do so. The Christian faith is not characterised by fatalism, but by an open attitude to the future, the knowledge that we may be taken by surprise, the faith that whatever happens God is with us and his word will endure to the end (verse 31).

What Jesus does exhort us to do is to remain vigilant (verses 33–37). The reason for vigilance is twofold – we do not know when disaster may strike our lives, neither do we know the hour of Christ's coming. In other words, we have to be prepared for whatever comes. This is a warning against a spiritual indolence that finds us unprepared when a crisis comes, demanding of us all the strength and resources we can muster. It is also a warning against that spiritual indifference which fails to recognise the hand of God at work in our lives.

Those who sleep do not see the sun rise, do not hear the first songs of the dawn and have no time to gather their wits.

☐   *Pray for those living through a time of crisis;*
and for the Church, that it may be open to God's future.

Saturday March 27   Mark 14.1–11

In these verses are recorded two things that are remembered wherever the story of Jesus is told – the loving act of anointing, and the treachery of Judas Iscariot in betraying Jesus. Both stories mention money. The woman put a high price on her devotion, willing to spend what would have been a small fortune on the precious perfume that she brought. Judas set a price on his treachery, no doubt hoping to get the best deal that he could.

Money and what we do with it says much about the sort of people that we are. There is a generous use of money for others that reflects the extravagance of God's love for us. It may be in response to a need, or it may be out of gratitude, expressing the love that is in our hearts. There are also people who will do almost anything to make money. We do not know Judas' motives in betraying Jesus, but we do know that he did not decline the offer of reward. But this reward was the wage of sin, and this was finally paid out to the full for, as Paul tells us, the wage of sin is death (Romans 6.23).

Generosity and greed – they were both remembered. It should make us pause before we decide between the two.

☐ *Lord, keep me from ever calculating the cost of my love to you.*

For group discussion and personal thought
Read and consider Mark 12.28–34a. Who are the people today who are 'not far from the kingdom of God' (verse 34)? How should we present the Christian faith to them?

THE VICTORY OF THE CROSS

James and John had not been nicknamed 'Sons of Thunder' for
nothing. They seem to have been an aggressive and ambitious
pair. Their aggressiveness is shown in Luke's account of the
journey to Jerusalem when they wanted to raze an unwelcoming
Samaritan village to the ground (see Luke 9.51–56). Here, their
ambition drove out of their minds all remembrance of Jesus' repeated teaching about his kingdom not being a political kingdom
but one that must come through suffering and sacrifice, and
whose greatness lay in humble service. They boldly requested
key positions in what they imagined the new order would be.

Aggression and ambition are not, in themselves, bad things.
They are forms of mental vigour and energy, which were qualities Jesus must have wanted in his followers, for the task lying
ahead of them would require all the energy they could muster!
But aggression can be selfish and destructive or it can be unselfish and positive. Ambition can be self-centred and competitive or it can be a longing to fulfil a vision and a desire to be
obedient, come what may, to the call to win the world for God.

Which of the two kinds of aggression and ambition take
priority in our individual lives and in the life of our church?

☐   *Take me, whom thyself hast bought,*
    Bring into captivity
  Every high aspiring thought
    That would not stoop to thee.   *Charles Wesley*

Monday March 29   Mark 14.12–21

The events that are recorded in Mark's Gospel from this point
onwards are placed in the setting of the Passover. This was the
central religious observance of the Jews – the annual remembrance of their deliverance from slavery in Egypt.

Later, when Christians celebrated the death and resurrection
of Jesus, they thought of it as the *Pascha*, the Christian Passover.
Just as God had delivered the Israelites from slavery, leading
them through the waters of the Red Sea into freedom, so Christ
delivered his people, leading them through faith and the waters
of baptism into the freedom of the resurrection life.

We are now approaching Eastertide, the season of the Christian *Pascha*. For us there is no holier time in the year. It is not
simply a remembrance of events long past, but a present

celebration of freedom and life in Christ. Every year is given to us the renewal of our death and resurrection in Christ and the opportunity to renew our vows and commit our lives again to the way of the cross and resurrection.

☐ *Were the whole realm of nature mine,*
  That were a present far too small,
 Love so amazing, so divine,
  Demands my soul, my life, my all.

Isaac Watts

Tuesday March 30   Mark 14.22–31

The disciples could have little idea of the significance of Jesus' words as he took the bread and the cup (verses 22–24). Nor could they be expected to understand until the crucifixion and the resurrection had taken place, for only then would the bread and wine be the signs of the kingdom that Jesus was to bring through his dying and rising again (verse 25).

When we meet to celebrate the Lord's Supper we are not simply recalling the night when our Lord shared his last supper with his disciples. That was a night of prophecy, a meal in which signs yet to be fulfilled were set before the disciples. For us, as we meet around the Lord's table, the prophecy has become salvation history, the signs have been fulfilled. We do not come in sadness to remember the last hours of mortal anguish that our Lord spent on earth, but rather to celebrate the Christ who gives himself to us in broken bread and outpoured wine.

For us, the Lord's Supper is holy ground. It is a place of thanksgiving and joy, a place of communion with the risen Lord, a place where our vows are renewed.

☐ *O blest memorial of our dying Lord!*
 Thou living bread, who life dost here afford,
 O may our souls for ever live by thee,
 And thou to us for ever precious be.

Thomas Aquinas

Wednesday March 31   Mark 14.32–42

Some of the Christians of Mark's time were emphasising the divinity of Jesus at the cost of his humanity. In so doing it was as if they were detaching him from our flesh and blood, making him less than human, minimising the painful and mortal struggles that he shared with us and for us. Mark seeks to correct the balance. Here there is no pretence at being human (verses

34–36), no suggestion of someone immune from pain and horror pretending to experience them. The agony of Gethsemane was of a man, vulnerable to pain as are all humans, shrinking from violent rejection, and death in the abandonment of the cross.

Gethsemane is a place where Jesus kneels to pray alongside all those who feel abandoned, frightened and tormented by the dread of what is to come. We sometimes face situations and possibilities that make us sweat with apprehension. The fear is made worse by a sense of isolation, the knowledge that whatever has to be lived through has to be endured in the loneliness of our own bodies.

But when we come to that extremity we know that Jesus is with us, praying for us, bearing in himself our dread, scattering our loneliness by his presence.

☐ *Lord, when I face the future with dread, be with me, for you know what it is to live through such times.*

Thursday April 1   Mark 14.43–52

In the darkness of the garden Jesus was arrested. Even in the modern world the scenario is not unfamiliar – the arrest under cover of darkness, the act of betrayal, the weapons of intimidation, the atmosphere charged with fear. The scene has been re-enacted in our own times in countless ways. It reflects the methods of tyrants.

Even in books that we might normally associate with the young the imagery of darkness is used to represent the presence of what is alien and hostile. The forest in *Wind in the Willows* is full of menacing sounds and the scurrying of unseen enemies. In *Lord of the Rings* the night is inhabited by deadly riders on horses who swoop out of the darkness creating death and havoc.

Out of the night Jesus' pursuers came with their treacherous code-sign, their shouts and their swords and cudgels, representatives of priests, rulers and scholars who, thinking themselves honourable men, failed to recognise the darkness in their own hearts.

There are times for all of us when we are aware that the 'jungle' is never far from our ordered lives, menacing us, sometimes coming closer to us and threatening to engulf us.

Even at the edge of the most civilised lives the dark 'jungle' is never far away.

☐ *Lord, lead us not into temptation, but deliver us from evil.*

Already the illegality of what was taking place in the high priest's house was beginning to become apparent. Under Jewish law, the testimony of two witnesses was necessary for conviction. People prepared to testify against Jesus came forward, but no two of them could agree. At this stage, the trial should have been abandoned for lack of conclusive evidence.

The importance of truth when we speak about other people is one of the foundations upon which our life together rests. Those who came forward to condemn Jesus not only failed to observe the legalities of the law court, they also broke one of the ten commandments – 'You shall not give false evidence' (Exodus 20.16).

If false evidence in a court of law is perjury, then unfounded scandal and gossip about other people are sins. They are verbal assaults on the reputation and happiness of others, forms of verbal violence damaging the character and standing of their victims. Also it is just as much a sin to listen to false evidence, to want to hear the worst and be prepared to believe what is untrue. Jesus' enemies heard what they wanted to hear regardless of its falsehood.

☐   *Let us pray for truth in all our human dealings,*
       and for care in all our words.

Peter was one of the first to be called to follow Jesus. He was also a member of the 'inner circle', comprising himself, James and John, a group who had shared with Jesus in some of the deepest and most sacred moments of his ministry. He was given the name Peter meaning 'the Rock' – the strong one, the foundation-stone, the person upon whom so much else depended. He had listened to Jesus as he taught, he had seen him heal the sick. He had promised his loyalty to the end. Yet it took no more than the taunt of a maid for him to collapse and pretend that he knew nothing of Jesus.

We cherish hopes that one day we shall reach a point in our Christian lives where there is no longer any possibility of being disloyal or failing Christ at a critical moment. As our experience grows deeper, as we become more mature, so our sense of security increases and our assurance that nothing will be able to shake our faith or make us forsake it.

Such hopes are illusory. We do not know when we are going to stumble. As much as we know ourselves we may not know the weakness that could yet be our undoing. Our confidence should rest, not upon our growing strength in Christ but in his undying love to us. Peter denied Jesus. There was never a time when Jesus denied Peter.

☐ *Lord, when I fail you, forgive me, and lift me up again.*

For group discussion and personal thought

What did Jesus fear as he prayed in the garden of Gethsemane (Mark 14.32–42)? What do **we** most fear in our lives? How can we best prepare ourselves to meet the ordeals that life has in store for us?

Palm Sunday, April 4   Matthew 21.1–11*

THE WAY OF THE CROSS

Last Sunday we thought about the aggression and ambition of James and John. Today we may think about the aggression and ambition of Jesus! What could be more aggressive than a procession into the capital city in which he allowed his followers to shout acclamations to him as a king and to carpet the ground with palms? Surely that was something designed to bring about a violent reaction from the civic and religious authorities! And what could be more ambitious than to aim at establishing the kingdom of God by such an act? Further, according to the first three Gospels this was followed by other aggressive and ambitious acts and words – the cleansing of the temple, and the teaching in the temple.

There was nothing 'meek and mild' about Jesus. There was vigour, courage and a positive activeness in everything he did in that incredible week. But there was no hatred nor selfishness in it. It was the energy and anger of love that drove him on.

Let us have no pity for Jesus this week but only renewed amazement at his methods – his weapons and his way of the cross that led at last to the fulfilment of his ambition.

☐ *Ride on, ride on in majesty!*
In lowly pomp ride on to die;
O Christ, thy triumphs now begin
O'er captive death and conquered sin.   Henry H. Milman

Monday April 5   Mark 15.1–5

In the face of criticism, unjust accusations and mockery we do
not find silence easy. Our natural instinct is to retaliate by
pointing out the unfairness of the criticism, or putting right the
record or trying to cap mockery with mockery. We fear to let
facts speak for themselves.

In Mark's account of the trial before Pilate, Jesus uttered only
one rather ambiguous sentence (verse 2) and after that was
silent. The charges against him had mounted up, yet he made no
effort to deny them or to defend himself. He had preached, he
had healed, his whole life had been a witness to the embracing
love of God. If his enemies could still bring against him charges
of political aspirations, could still treat him as a common
criminal, then there were no words left to speak.

History has judged in favour of the accused and against the
accusers. Jesus' life spoke with an eloquence no words could
find. There are times when we need to tread the same path. You
cannot argue with silence.

☐   *By thy last silence in the judgement-hall,*
        By long foreknowledge of the deadly tree,
    By darkness, by the wormwood and the gall,
        I pray thee, visit me.

                                                    Jean Ingelow

Tuesday April 6   Mark 15.6–20

As the barrage of hostility grew louder and the physical brutality
more unsparing so the sense of abandonment was increased. No
one spoke a word in defence of Jesus. There was no kindness to
alleviate the blows and cuts that bruised and lacerated his body.
There was no compassion, no mercy, no justice, no decency. The
people in the narrative are portrayed as men caught in a whirl-
pool of violence as they descended into mindless hatred. And
Jesus became more isolated by each brutal act.

The price we sometimes have to pay for believing is that of
being isolated. Not for us the violence that tore at the body of
Jesus but the rebuffs of indifference and cynicism. People find it
hard to understand our faith and, more often, make no attempt to
understand. In their eyes, maybe, we are odd, different, we do
not conform to other people's lack of religion, we inhabit a
world of belief that they do not understand.

Loneliness, in these circumstances, can be painful. Jesus
entered into more pain than we can begin to imagine, but his

example stands for all of us. It was one of steadfastness, the refusal to break.

☐ *Lord, be with me when I feel cut off from others by my faith. Help me to be steadfast and true to you.*

Wednesday April 7   Mark 15.21–27

There are times in this Gospel when Mark seems to be referring to people whom he expected his readers to know. In verse 21 we have an example of this in his reference to Alexander and Rufus. The manner in which they are introduced into the narrative suggests that they were known as members of the early Church. They were the sons of Simon, the 'man who had carried the cross'. People would recognise them as the sons of an honourable man, a man who had had the supreme privilege of doing the one act of kindness that lightened Jesus' journey to Golgotha.

The example that all of us, as Christians, should seek to pass on to the generation that follows us is that of carrying the cross. Sharing Christ's cross is something that we are able to do every day of our lives, as we strive to express his sacrificial love, as we share his concern for others, as we co-operate with him in the work of his kingdom. The rare privilege that was given to Simon is available to us, whoever we are and wherever we are. It is for this, more than anything, that we would wish the Alexanders and Rufuses of the next generation to remember us.

☐ *Let us pray for faithfulness in our own generation;*
                        for willingness to carry the cross;
                        for an example left to those who follow us.

Thursday April 8   Mark 15.29–32

The taunts continued unabated. The Jews mocked Jesus, ridiculing him because he did not perform the miracle of coming down from the cross, jeering at his inability to do for himself what he had done for others. Blindness, leprosy, madness, disabled limbs, had given way to his powers, but it seemed that nothing could pull the nails from the wood. There he hung, helpless, dying, defeated, forsaken.

Had they but known it the Jews were witnessing the greatest miracle of all. A Christ who stepped down from the cross would be unremembered. The Christ who stayed there, held there not by nails but by love, is the Christ who is worshipped and followed by countless people in every generation and in every place. Jesus gave himself up for our salvation, he died for us, his love embraced us, bore death for us and would not forsake us although a thousand voices mocked him.

Redeeming love is always more powerful than self-preservation. The latter makes no difference to the world. The former sets others free and opens to them the kingdom of heaven.

☐ *Lord, we bless you that you did not come down from the cross, but stayed there for our sakes.*

Good Friday, April 9   Mark 15.33–39

In Mark's Gospel the life of Jesus in no way ends in victory. His last articulate words were the cry of a man feeling abandoned by God (verse 34). After this there was only a final, incoherent cry, followed by death.

Mark was writing for Christians facing persecution. He did not try to soften the blows that were to fall upon them. They, like Jesus, would know the mounting opposition of their enemies; they, too, would be mocked, insulted and, in some cases, arrested and put to death. Their experience might be the same as that of Jesus – the long path of suffering, the final loneliness, even, perhaps, the desolating feeling of being abandoned by God. This is how it might end, even for the most faithful. The death of Jesus offers no false promises.

Today we do not always have Mark's honesty. We want to hasten to the resurrection without experiencing the full depth of the cross; we want to reassure ourselves that Christians do not get hit as badly as other people. But they do. We have nothing less than faith and hope, but there may be times when we have to realise that we have nothing more, either.

☐ *Lord, help me to believe and to trust; there is no depth to which you have not already descended.*

Saturday April 10   Mark 15.40–47

For those who observe the liturgy of Holy Week, sharing with the Church in the remembrance of our Lord's last days and his crucifixion at Calvary, the time between Jesus' death and his rising again, is a time that subsides into peace. In Mark's narrative, it is a time in which some tenderness again appears. After the shouting of the crowds, we witness the quiet grief of the women (verses 40–41), after the political machinations that encompassed Jesus' death we are faced with a man who belatedly made a courageous stand and asked for the body of Jesus in order that it might be buried with dignity (verses 43–44).

Today, the day between Good Friday and Easter, is a day to remember all those acts of kindness and humanity that lighten darkness and bring peace in the midst of tumult. Tomorrow the alleluias will ring out and, in glory and beauty, the Church will proclaim her faith in the risen Lord. But in the quietness of today, we recall with thanksgiving those acts of kindness that have made grief more bearable for us and brought to our troubled lives a tranquillity born of compassion.

☐ *Lord, thank you for help in yesterday's suffering and for tomorrow's hope.*

For group discussion and personal thought

Make a meditative study of Mark's account of the crucifixion (15.21–39). In what sense was the death of Jesus a victory (see John 19.30)?

Easter Day, April 11   **Matthew 28.1–10***

THE RESURRECTION OF CHRIST

'He is not here,' said the angel. 'Here' was the tomb, the place of death, of apparent final defeat and of the end of the Jesus-movement that had been such a trouble to the authorities. 'Here' was where not only the body of the 'trouble-maker' had been buried, but also his teachings, his vision of a kingdom, the hopes of the disciples. 'Here' was a place to make his enemies crow with joy and his friends weep with despair, But – **'he is not here'**!

If he is not 'here', then where is he? He is on the path along which the women run. He is in Galilee where the disciples will meet him. He is alongside two travellers on their way back to their own village of Emmaus (Luke 24.13–32). He is beside the lake where everything began. In due course, he will be found – although invisible – wherever there are those who believe in him.

He, who once was limited in time and space, is now living in the hearts of those who love him. His teachings, his vision and

73

his energy are with us for ever. His kingdom continues for ever. This is the ultimate significance of Easter.

☐ *Then wake, glad heart, awake, awake!*
And seek thy risen Lord;
Joy in his resurrection take,
And comfort in his word.

John S.B. Monsell

STANDING ALONE FOR GOD

Selected readings from 1 Kings 12 to 2 Kings 2

Notes by Revd John H. Atkinson, MA

John Atkinson is Chairman of the West Yorkshire District of the Methodist Church. He has previously served in circuits in Yorkshire and North Wales, as a theology tutor in the West Indies, and as General Secretary of the Division of Social Responsibility of the Methodist Church in Great Britain.

Saul, David and Solomon ruled over all the tribes of Israel as one united nation. After Solomon's death, the kingdom was split in two. The southern tribe of Judah, together with the small tribe of Benjamin, became a separate nation centred around Jerusalem. The remaining tribes formed the northern kingdom which kept the old name, Israel.

Both kingdoms had rulers who disobeyed God's law. This was particularly true in the northern kingdom, where the rulers did not want their people to look on Jerusalem as the centre of true worship; it was, after all, in the rival kingdom of Judah.

1, 2 Kings focus on the prophets who constantly challenged the rulers, standing alone for God and his truth. God raised up several of these men of faith, the greatest in these selected readings being Elijah.

Suggestions for further reading

First Book of Kings and *Second Book of Kings*, both by Joseph Robinson, Cambridge Bible Commentaries on the New English Bible (Cambridge University Press);

The Hebrew Kingdoms by Eric W. Heaton, New Clarendon Bible series (Oxford University Press).

Monday April 12

Towards the end of the reign of King Solomon, one of his courtiers, Jeroboam, started a rebellion, encouraged by the prophet Ahijah. Solomon discovered the plot and Jeroboam had to run to Egypt to save his life. When Solomon died, his successor was his son and David's grandson, Rehoboam.

▶ Read I Kings 12.1–19.

It is often wise to listen to the voice of experience. Rehoboam, however, would not listen to the older men who had been his father's advisers. In many ways Solomon had been a hard and oppressive ruler. High taxes and forced labour were common in his time. Instead of reducing these, as the older men suggested, Rehoboam took the fiercer advice of the young courtiers. He decided to increase, rather than decrease, the oppression of the people. He would show them that he was king!

Before criticising Rehoboam, we should ask ourselves – even though we are not kings and have far less power – whether we make life hard for those over whom we have some influence or authority (for example, those in our family or at work). And we should make sure that when we are given advice which suggests that we ought to 'climb down' we do not resent it.

☐ *Quietly think whether you make life hard for others, and whether you resent advice to 'climb down'.*

Tuesday April 13

The ten northern tribes quickly accepted the rebel, Jeroboam, as their king. The tribes of Judah and Benjamin accepted Solomon's son, Rehoboam, as their ruler. Jeroboam, therefore, had far more land and people – and a much larger army – than Rehoboam. It would have been easy for him to have defeated his rival.

▶ Read I Kings 12.21–33.

Shemaiah was the first of a long line of prophets who had to stand alone and give unpopular advice. Jeroboam and his army could easily have conquered Judah and made the kingdom one again. But God's word to Rehoboam and his people through Shemaiah was: 'Don't fight! Go home.' And they obeyed.

Unfortunately, Jeroboam then made a great mistake. The temple was in Jerusalem, which was part of the kingdom of Judah. To stop his people looking to his rival's capital as their place of worship, Jeroboam decided to give his people worship-objects of their own – two golden calves (verse 28) and the hilltop shrines (verse 31).

Let us remember that, as Christians, the focus of our worship is not a place or an idol, but Jesus.

☐ *Think on the words of Jesus : 'Real worshippers will worship the Father in spirit and in truth.' (John 4.23)*

Jeroboam reigned over Israel from 922 to 901 BC. King Josiah, to whom the unnamed prophet refers, did not come to the throne of the southern kingdom of Judah until about 640 BC. So, in verse 2, the prophet was looking into the far distance, almost three hundred years away. By then the northern kingdom of Israel had ceased to exist – it fell to the Assyrians in 721 BC. But Josiah was able to extend his influence much further north than Judah itself and he fulfilled the prophecy in today's reading by rooting out the northerners' pagan religion and insisting that Jerusalem was the focus for their worship.

The prophetic message was confirmed by the paralysing of Jeroboam's hand when he stretched it out in protest – although the prophet successfully asked God to heal it. Jeroboam had to learn that it is not possible to stop God by holding out one's hand. What God says he will do, he does. That is true of his judgement; but it is also true of his mercies.

☐   *Faithful, O Lord, thy mercies are,*
    A rock that cannot move;
  A thousand promises declare
    Thy constancy of love.   *Charles Wesley*

God's men – which is what the prophets were often called – must obey him completely. The unnamed prophet, who had rebuked Jeroboam so bravely, now faltered. He was deceived by a false claim from another prophet to have had a message from an angel. On the strength of that claim, the prophet went back to the home of the false prophet. It was not the prophet who told the lie who was punished, but the one who turned back.

It was wrong of him to retrace his steps. It meant delaying his journey by at least several hours. Those who follow God – and that includes us as well as the prophet – must be 'all out' for him. We must have a sense of urgency and a determination to do God's work without delay. Jesus himself made that point vividly when he rejected those who offered apparently good reasons for delay in becoming his disciples (Luke 9.57–62).

☐   *I would not with swift-wingèd zeal*
    On the world's errands go,
  And labour up the heavenly hill
    With weary feet and slow.   *Thomas H. Gill*

During the war in Burma in 1943, some Burmese women were bayonetted to death. Just before they died, they said, 'If we must die, give us a moment to get ready.' As Christians, they used that moment to kneel in prayer. Two years later, the war was over and the first confirmation service was held in Rangoon Cathedral. Among those to be confirmed, the bishop recognised a prominent anti-Christian leader. He asked him how he came to be baptised. 'It was the way those women in the village died two years ago,' he answered. He realised that they had something he did not have.

King Jeroboam had a sneaking regard for the prophet Ahijah. He sent his wife in disguise to ask the prophet what would happen to his sick son. Unfortunately, Jeroboam did not go further and accept the prophet's faith, as the Burmese anti-Christian accepted the faith of the girls who stood firm. Their story is a reminder that when we stand alone for God, our example may well win others.

☐ *Lord, help me to stand firm for you, knowing that I shall thus do your will, and praying that others may turn to you when they see my faith, poor though it is.*

Saturday April 17

Four years before King Jeroboam of Israel died, King Rehoboam of Judah died. His reign was marred by an Egyptian invasion in which Jerusalem itself was plundered (1 Kings 14.25–26). He was succeeded by his son, Abijam.

▶ Read **1 Kings 15.1–15.**

Abijam ruled for only three years and was no better than his father, Rehoboam. But he was succeeded by Asa, who reigned for forty-one years. His rule was notable, not only for its length, but also for the fact that he was much wiser than the previous kings of Judah. Although he did not absolutely abolish all the pagan religion of his day – the hill-shrines were left untouched (verse 14) – he stamped out the rest of the idolatry which had disfigured the kingdom.

His wisdom was also shown by the way in which he offered so much of the wealth of his family to God (verse 15). We must make the same response – not merely in terms of any wealth we may have, but also in offering our thinking and our talents to God.

□ *Take my silver and my gold;*
   Not a mite would I withhold.
   Take my intellect, and use
   Every power as thou shalt choose.   *Frances R. Havergal*

For group discussion and personal thought
Read 1 Kings 12.1–14. Why did Rehoboam choose to give a
harsh answer? Many of us have some kind of power over other
people; how should we use it?

Sunday April 18   **John 6.35–40***
THE BREAD OF LIFE

Last Sunday was Easter Day. But Easter did not end at the close
of that day. The significance of the resurrection of Jesus will
continue until the end of time. For his resurrection means that
all the things he stood for, the teachings he gave, the promises he
made and the friendship he offered, are released from one time
and one locality into all times and all places. For the next four
Sundays we shall read and consider words attributed to Jesus in
John's Gospel. They express the certainties of the earliest
Christians who had known the Easter and Pentecost experience.

Jesus said, 'I am the bread of life.' According to John, he had
just been challenged to give a sign of his authority. His critics
reminded him that the authority of Moses had been proved by
his provision of manna for their ancestors in the wilderness –
'bread from heaven'. In effect, Jesus' answer was: 'That bread
sustained the ancient Hebrews for a while; but what I bring can
sustain a man for always.'

There is a hunger deeper than the physical hunger in man, a
hunger for the meaning of existence, a hunger for truth, for
love and for hope. In Christ that spiritual hunger is satisfied. For
in him we come near to God, the source of all truth, love and
hope. In Christ, we can taste something that is not subject to
change – **eternal life** (verse 40).

□ *'He took bread, gave thanks, and broke it; and he gave it to them*
   with the words: "This is my body." ' (Luke 22.19)

Monday April 19

While Asa reigned long and wisely in the south, Israel had a succession of kings. Eventually Zimri, a senior army officer, usurped the throne but his victory was short-lived. The army would not have him as king and replaced him with their commander, Omri, who reigned for twelve years, He was succeeded

ISRAEL
in the days of
ELIJAH

SIDON   Damascus
Zarephath
PHOENICEA   ARAM
Dan
Mt Carmel
Aphek
Jezreel
Brook Cherith
Samaria   Tishbe
ISRAEL
Bethel
Jericho
PHILISTIA
JUDAH   N
Beersheba   MOAB
To Horeb

by his son Ahab, who not only continued the pagan policy of his predecessors, but also married Jezebel, a Sidonian princess and Baal-worshipper. It was at this dark moment that the greatest of all the prophets who stood alone suddenly appeared on the scene. His name was Elijah.

▶ Read **1 Kings 17.1–16.**

God taught Elijah to trust in him – a lesson he would need in the lonely days ahead when he would challenge both king and nation. The ravens fed him and the miracle of the flour-jar and the oil-flask proved that God's power was with him. If we learn to trust God, we too need never be afraid.

☐ *Lord – I am trusting thee for power,*
Thine can never fail;
Words which thou thyself shalt give me
Must prevail.   *Frances R. Havergal*

Tuesday April 20

Once again, God gave Elijah power.
▶ Read **1 Kings 17.17–24.**

But Elijah was not the only one who had the courage to stand firm for God. Obadiah, one of the king's highest court officers – 'the man in charge of Ahab's household affairs' (1 Kings 18.3, LB) – held on to this faith, too.

▶ Read **1 Kings 18.1–6.**

It would not have been easy for Obadiah to keep his faith when surrounded by the court of Ahab and Jezebel. And it has often been hard for Christians to be true to Christ when all around them were those who denied him. One such Christian was the Roman soldier, Sebastian, who was promoted to the rank of captain in the emperor's personal guard. At great risk to himself, he used his position to save many fellow-Christians whom the Romans had condemned to death. He never neglected his military duties. Every day he prayed for his country, but he kept his faith in Christ and, in the end, preferred to die a martyr's death rather than break that faith.

☐ *Thank God for those fellow-Christians who help you to keep your faith. And ask God to help you to witness to that faith when you are with those who do not know Jesus.*

Wednesday April 21   1 Kings 18.7–24

It seemed that nothing could stop Elijah. No one even knew where he would be next. Obadiah was afraid that if he told the king where Elijah was, the prophet would be whisked off somewhere else when the king looked for him and Obadiah would be punished (verse 12). Even Ahab saw Elijah as a formidable opponent (verse 17). Yet God's man was outnumbered by nearly a thousand to one – Baal had 450 prophets and the goddess Asherah had 400. The final battle between Elijah and his enemies would soon come. But even that battle-ground did not favour Elijah. He met the pagan prophets on Mount Carmel, one of the high-places on which the Israelites had practised false worship for many years. Elijah was fighting on enemy ground.

Surprisingly, the people had not completely thrown in their lot with the pagan prophets. They were still hesitating (verse 21). Instead of commending them for their reluctance to worship Baal, Elijah told them to make up their minds either to follow God or to follow Baal. Often we need the same challenge. We may hesitate to turn our backs on God, but what we really need is firmly and decisively to make up our minds to follow him.

☐ *Quietly ask yourself if you have really made that decision; or whether you need to make it yet again.*

Thursday April 22   1 Kings 18.25–40

Elijah won a great victory on Mount Carmel. To us, it may seem very wrong that he followed it up by ordering the murder of the prophets of Baal. But he felt deeply the wrong they were doing to the people and to God. He decided that he had to put an end to them and their false, evil faith.

It seemed that single-handed he had defeated the massed hordes of pagan prophets. But the whole point is that he was not single-handed. God made the victory possible – 'the fire **of the Lord** fell'.

This story has often been seen as a symbol of God's dealings with us. Before Pentecost, for example, all the disciples could do was to wait for the gift of the Spirit, as Jesus had told them to do. That gift would come by God's power and in God's time. And on the day of Pentecost, the Spirit came – significantly, 'like flames of fire' (Acts 2.3). We can pray in faith and wait in trust, but we cannot fashion our own salvation. That is God's gift, which makes Carmel happen in our hearts.

☐   *O that in me the sacred fire*
    Might now begin to glow,
  Burn up the dross of base desire,
    And make the mountains flow!

  O that it now from heaven might fall,
    And all my sins consume!
  Come, Holy Ghost, for thee I call,
    Spirit of burning, come!

                                       Charles Wesley

Friday April 23   1 Kings 19.1–18

Despite the victory on Carmel, Elijah's life was in danger and he went to the desert to escape the queen's revenge. He was weary, too weary to want to live. But when he awoke from sleep, he found food and drink beside him – sure signs that God cared for him.

When our spirits are low and we seem almost too tired to go on, God does not forget us. But he does not always come to us in dramatic ways. We have to learn to catch the quiet sound of his coming. Elijah learnt that at Horeb. God was not in the tempestuous wind, the terrifying earthquake or the roaring fire, but in the 'low murmuring sound' (verse 12).

☐   *Open, Lord my inward ear,*
    And bid my heart rejoice;
  Bid my quiet spirit hear
    Thy comfortable voice;

> *Never in the whirlwind found,*
> *Or where earthquakes rock the place,*
> *Still and silent is the sound,*
> *The whisper of thy grace.*
>
> *Charles Wesley*

Saturday April 24   1 Kings 20.22–34

By all human and military rules, Ben-hadad and his army should have defeated Israel. The Aramaeans (Syrians) greatly outnumbered their enemy; they 'covered the countryside' while Israel 'seemed no better than a pair of new-born kids' (verse 27). The Aramaeans had also chosen the ground for the battle, making sure that it took place in a valley where their cavalry and chariots could wreak havoc (verse 25). And perhaps the Israelites, as well as the Aramaeans, thought that their God belonged to the hills rather than to the valleys (verse 28). But Israel won the battle and learnt two great lessons:

● Although they were few, they had untold resources because God was on their side.

● God was God of the hills **and** of the valleys. He was the God of the 'everywhere'. There was no place in which he would not be with his people.

Like Israel, we also may set narrow limits on the power and love of God. There is no end to what God can do.

☐ *Forgive me, Father, if my faith is small and I set limits on what you can do. Give me the confidence to know that you are every-where and that there is no end to your care.*

For group discussion and personal thought

God reveals himself both in dramatic events (1 Kings 18.17–40) and in times of quietness (1 Kings 19.1–18). In what experiences have *you* felt God's nearness? What can we do to make sure that we always recognise his presence and power?

Sunday April 25   John 10.7–18*
THE GOOD SHEPHERD

Sheep are notoriously helpless creatures. When they meet a car in the road, they either rush hither and thither in a bunch or stand stock still in fear. They wait for a wisdom and a will greater than their own to show them which way to go. In the Middle East in New Testament times, sheep had to face the terrors of wild animals and thieves at night. The shepherd had to put the sheep in the fold at nightfall and, if necessary, himself lie down to be the door of the sheepfold. On occasions he had to fight wild beasts and risk his own life. Hirelings would not take such risks. But the true shepherd cares.

In all these senses Christ is the shepherd of his flock for he is the good – the true – shepherd. And, reflecting his care, all church members are called to be shepherds. It is not just our fellow church members we are to care about but those 'other sheep' whom Jesus mentioned (verse 16) – people who may not come to church but are as much our concern as those who do.

☐ *A challenge to Christians:*

> *Men wander about like sheep*
> *in distress for lack of a shepherd.*   *(Zechariah 10.2)*

Monday April 26   1 Kings 21.1–14

Naboth valued his independence and did not want to sell the land which by Hebrew law belonged to his family for ever. Indeed, he seems to have been a respected figure in his community and was probably not alarmed when he was asked to sit at the top of the table (verse 12). Even so, his action in defying the king needed the courage of one ready to stand alone. It is noticeable that others lacked the courage – the city leaders timidly gave in to Jezebel's murderous plan and those who gave false witness against Naboth were probably his neighbours.

Of course, Naboth was not standing out for moral or religious reasons, but to protect his property and his position – and he was obviously right to do so. But no one would stand with him. All joined the conspiracy of lies, murder and theft.

There are times when people whom we know have to stand alone. Do we stand by them? Or do we become – as Naboth's neighbours did – the willing tools of those who would be unjust toward our friends?

☐ *Lord, help me to stand by those who stand alone. Grant that neither fear nor favour will ever lead me to betray my neighbour.*

Tuesday April 27   1 Kings 21.15–29

Naboth, who had dared to defy the king, was dead – just as

Jezebel had planned. Even then, Elijah did not flinch from going immediately to confront Ahab with the evil that had been done. His message was one which the Bible often repeats:

● **No one can defy God with impunity.**
● **We reap the results of our actions.**

At last, Ahab regretted what he had done and God decided that the punishment for Naboth's murder would not be exacted in Ahab's lifetime. Instead, disaster would fall on his son. This is hardly a less dreadful penalty. What man, given the choice of condemning his own son to death or of dying himself, would choose the former? Even to a man like Ahab, the thought that he brought doom on his son must have been a bitter punishment.

So Ahab learned that, despite his kingship and his apparent power to do what he pleased, there was a king above him – God. And he learned that those who will not stand for what is right – even if they have to stand alone – do not in the end have any ground to stand on at all. God sweeps them off their feet.

☐ *Lord, keep me on my feet. Help me to stand firm.*

Wednesday April 28

Some seventy years had passed since the death of King Solomon. Scarcely anyone could remember the days when Israel and Judah had been one nation. In their lifetime, the two nations had been neighbours, but not friends. They had never joined together against a common enemy. But now, at last, they seemed prepared to unite their forces.

▶ Read **1 Kings 22.1–14.**

Witch-doctors, wizards and magicians have been a common feature of many nations. Zedekiah, putting the iron horns on his head (verse 11), must have seemed more like a witch-doctor than a true prophet. He told the two kings what they wanted to hear – victory would be theirs. As often happens, there was no shortage of other court-prophets willing to echo the same welcome message. Elijah was not sent for – no doubt the kings could guess what he would say. But they did send for another prophet, Micaiah. And, like Elijah, he was prepared to be unpopular and to say what God told him to say, rather than what the kings wanted to hear.

Are we ready to be unpopular if necessary? Paul reminds us that we should not curry favour with men but wholeheartedly do the will of God (Ephesians 6.6). We must make sure that we do.

☐ *Ask yourself: 'Whom do I try to please – men or God?'*

The reward of the man who stands alone for God is that he sees heavenly visions (verse 19). A slap on the cheek does not worry Micaiah (verse 24). Neither does being thrown into prison with little food or water (verses 26–27). Micaiah was in gaol, partly as a punishment, but no doubt partly to keep his message from the soldiers' ears. He was not worried; he was sure that his words were God's words and would therefore come true. And so they did, despite an ingenious plan to cancel his prophecy by Ahab's decision to disguise himself.

The description of the king of Israel, mortally wounded, but propped up in his chariot, facing the enemy as he bled to death, is a picture of a brave warrior. But darkness fell, and death and defeat came. It was not courage the king lacked, but wisdom – wisdom to accept God's word. There is a time to play the hero. But it is **always** time to build our lives on the wisdom which God gives to the people who trust and obey him.

☐   *Happy the man that finds the grace,*
   The blessing of God's chosen race,
   The wisdom coming from above,
   The faith that sweetly works by love.

                                                            Charles Wesley

Friday April 30

Despite their defeat on Mount Carmel, the prophets of Baal still had many followers, not least in the royal palace. Even after the death of King Ahab his son, Ahaziah, still turned to them when he wanted advice.

● Read **2 Kings 1.1–17.**

By sending soldiers to order Elijah to come to him, Ahaziah did wrong in thinking that he could order the prophet and the God whom he served to do what he wanted. Even the phrase, 'man of God', which should be reverenced, was used roughly in the captain's command (verse 11). For this insult to God, the soldiers were destroyed. (We should remember that, in Luke 9.55, when James and John asked Jesus to punish similar rudeness in the same way, Jesus refused.) Another fifty men met the same fate. But the captain in charge of the third party approached the prophet humbly. He was spared and Elijah went with him to meet the king – but only to confirm the sentence of death.

So Elijah's struggle with Baal continued. Those who stand alone do not always reap at once the fruits of their triumphs – their 'Carmels'. We must learn to go on standing firm for God until, many victories later, his final triumph is won.

☐   *Stand up, stand up for Jesus!*
        Ye soldiers of the cross;
    Lift high his royal banner;
        It must not suffer loss.

    From victory unto victory
        His army shall he lead,
    Till every foe is vanquished
        And Christ is Lord indeed.   *George Duffield*

Saturday May 1

Elijah's life was drawing to a close. But God did not leave himself without witnesses. Elijah's last act was to commission his successor.

● Read **2 Kings 2.1–15a** (to 'settled on Elisha').

When Elisha asked for 'a double share' of Elijah's spirit (verse 9) he was asking for the portion which by Hebrew law was the share of the eldest son. His request was granted. When the waters of Jordan divided as Elisha struck them with Elijah's cloak, the watching prophets could see that he had indeed succeeded the great prophet (verse 15).

It is good for us to remember that we, too, are heirs of a great succession. From the first apostles and missionaries, through the dark ages when the faithful few kept the faith alive, through those who brought the good news to our own country and those who have bravely witnessed to it here and everywhere, we have a wonderful heritage. We rejoice that, down to our own day, God has never left himself without witnesses.

☐   *Thy hand, O God, has guided*
        Thy flock, from age to age;
    The wondrous tale is written,
        Full clear, on every page.
    Our fathers owned thy goodness,
        And we their deeds record;
    And both of this bear witness:
        One Church, one faith, one Lord.   *Edward H. Plumptre*

For group discussion and personal thought

Micaiah, like other prophets who stood alone, spurned popularity (1 Kings 22.14). Why? Must we do the same? Is it always wrong to be popular?

Sunday May 2   John 11.17–27*

THE RESURRECTION AND THE LIFE

A new quality of life was released into the world by the resurrection of Jesus Christ. People's longing for release from this 'poor, dying' existence on earth does not have to wait for the death of the physical body; it can happen here and now.

There is a spiritual death that many of us have experienced – a death of hope, love, faith, goodness when, defeated morally or exhausted spiritually, we feel lifeless and empty. But when we awake again to the truth of Christ's teachings and the reality of God's love shown in his death and resurrection then hope, love, faith and moral strength come alive in us again. It was surely this experience which led Paul to write: 'All I care for is to know Christ, to experience the power of his resurrection.' (Philippians 3.10) When we experience that, everything good comes to life again for us. All this is summed up in Christ's words: 'I am the resurrection and I am life.'

☐ *My faith burns low, my hope burns low;*
      Only my heart's desire cries out in me,
   By the deep thunder of its want and woe,
         Cries out to thee.

   Lord, thou art life, though I be dead;
      Love's fire thou art, however cold I be :
   Nor heaven have I, nor place to lay my head,
         Nor home, but thee.   *Christina G. Rossetti*

88

ROMANS 1–8

Notes by Revd Howard Booth

Howard Booth is the Superintendent of the Workington Methodist Circuit. Previously he was in Harrow, Middlesex. He is the author of several booklets and devotional aids including 'Prayer Tools for Health and Healing' (Grail Publications).

The issue which dominated the entire ministry of Paul was the relationship between Christianity and Judaism. At first Christianity was, quite naturally, a movement within Judaism. But the 'new wine' could not be contained in the 'old bottles'. While converts to Christianity were Jews plus a few proselytes (people who had accepted Jewish traditions and discipline), all was well. But when larger numbers of 'pagans' began to be converted, there arose a confrontation between the hard line Jews and those who, like Paul, felt that it was unnecessary and unwise to force Jewish ways and laws upon them.

In *Galatians*, Paul responded sharply to his critics; now in *Romans* he goes over the same ground in a more restrained and deliberate manner. Paul is hoping to go to Rome and he sets out the gospel as he understands it and as he hopes to proclaim it in their midst. The first eight chapters are theological: they are about how men get right with God – through faith and trust and nothing else!

The letter was probably written from Corinth about AD 56–58.

Suggestions for further reading

Good News in Romans by Joseph Rhymer, Fontana Books (Collins Publishers);

Wrestling with Romans by John A.T. Robinson (SCM Press).

Monday May 3 Romans 1.1–17

Paul has not yet been to Rome but when he arrives it is essential to establish good working relationships with the Christians already there. He takes an early opportunity to congratulate them on the quality of their faith. He also makes it clear that, when he comes, the learning process will not be one sided: he will benefit from their faith as they will benefit from his.

Concentrate your thoughts on verses 11–12 and see how they relate to ecumenical and inter-faith discussions today:

● Paul writes of **sharing spiritual blessing** (GNB) with the Christians in Rome. This is about a mutual experience. Relations between Christian denominations, and between Christians and other religions, are frustrated when one side expects the other to submit to their way of thinking. Out of honest sharing much good can come.

● **Helping** or **encouraging** each other will arise out of honest testimony. It is important to recognise our own bias and to be willing to be helped by those whose experience has come in 'packaging' different from our own.

☐ *Reflect upon the significance of verses 11–12 for mission. Are* **sharing** *and* **helping** *keywords for successful missionary activity? What do these two verses have to say to a minister undertaking a new pastoral charge?*

Tuesday May 4   **Romans 1.18–32**

These verses may seem to be a cruel and unyielding statement of God's attitude towards sinful people, but of course it is part of a whole. Paul is building up his case as every good advocate does. He now paints in dark and sombre colours the nature of life lived in deliberate opposition to God's will.

It is important to remember that 'divine retribution' (verse 18), or 'the wrath of God' (AV), does not describe the nature of God's attitude to man – which is constant love – but refers to 'an inevitable process of cause and effect in a moral universe' (C. H. Dodd). There are two sides to every coin and if the 'gift' of God is life, then the 'wage' of sin is death (Romans 6.23).

Concentrate on the vivid phrase in verse 18: **'stifling the truth'.** Think of ways in which we ourselves and the communities of which we are a part do just this. We are better at noting our virtues than acknowledging our failures – yet to admit to having fallen into lovelessness is one of the most positive ways of releasing the blockage and letting the love flow!

☐ *Ask yourself: Am I 'stifling the truth'?*

Occasionally, in pastoral work, I have had gently to take to task those who, from a high moral vantage point, condemn people whose only fault is that they do not do things in the way the self-styled moralist would like! Some members of the choir may say harsh things about another choir-member because she does not attend worship services as regularly as they do. They do not always inquire about the personal difficulties that person is facing. If they did they might be more understanding.

How easy it is to pass judgement upon others while at the same time we are grievously at fault! Jesus wanted to make his hearers think hard when he raised a smile by telling of the critic who pointed to a splinter in another's eye while he had a plank sticking out of his own! (Matthew 7.3–5)

Reflect today on verse 11: **'God has no favourites'**. This means that men and women are judged from the standpoint of where they began. Jews had the law, a special privilege – but privileges bring responsibilities. We also have privileges! How can we express our gratitude? Certainly not by condemning others – either near or far – but by trying to understand them.

☐ *Yes, you are favoured. God loves you. How are you going to express that awareness in your relationships?*

The followers of Jesus have a heavy responsibility. What other people understand Christianity to be is associated with the way we live. How faithful are we to the implications of the gospel? Nations which are predominantly Islamic or Buddhist look at the so-called Christian West and pass judgement upon what they see – and often that judgement is severe. They are disappointed with our preoccupation with material prosperity. The West seems to work always to **have**, whereas those who come from the East seem more concerned about **being**.

In today's reading the Jews are accused by Paul of not fully appreciating their heritage. They have received so much. The law was – and is – a precious inheritance; but they have become more concerned to obey the letter of the law than to discern its spirit. In so doing, while they may think they are obeying the law, they are in fact breaking it!

Read verses 28–29 slowly but instead of 'Jew' read 'Christian'. Consider each phrase carefully and examine your own heart.

Think about the difference between external behaviour and inward thought and experience. What we do depends upon what we are. How do we become those who are 'directed by the Spirit'? How do we become more concerned to have God's approval than to have man's esteem?

☐ *Reflective prayer helps us to discover more about* **'being'**; *then we are more likely to be able to* **'do'** *what God desires!*

Friday May 7 Romans 3.1–20

Paul was able to meet the Jews on their own ground and exchange argument for argument and quote text for text. The end result, so far as Paul was concerned, was always the same. The Jews were privileged; they had been given a marvellous endowment; some had made better use of it than others but, in the final analysis, they stood side by side with the Gentiles and the verdict was – guilty!

Those who have been born into Christian families and brought up in Christian homes are in precisely the same position. They may think that this gives them special privileges and that thereby they are secure in God's kingdom. Not so! There is no discipleship by proxy. There is only one way to find God for ourselves – that is to acknowledge our sin and failure and thrust ourselves on the mercy and love of Jesus.

Yet even this kind of understanding can harden into legalism and an insistence that only those who use a certain kind of religious language and adopt a particular theological stance are 'insiders'.

☐ *What is the ground of* **our** *faith? To trust God is to be like a child in a mother's arms – safe and secure. When this experience is at the heart of our faith we can choose the churchmanship and the theological position which best suits our thinking. But we must hold fast to Christ – and let this be the inspiration of our life!*

Saturday May 8 Romans 3.21–31

Try to put yourself inside Paul's illustrations:
● One is from the **law court**. This is always a place of high drama because people's lives and futures hang in the balance. Who can forget that trembling moment when the foreman of the

jury rises to deliver the judgement? No one who has ever been involved in a significant case can cancel out that moment from his memory. Here the verdict is 'not guilty' because we share in the victory won by Jesus.

● The other is from **slavery**. We are familiar with mortgages and debts. Young people buying their first home take on a heavy burden in repayments. What a sense of relief if someone steps in and settles the mortgage! It is like an elderly American black slave who, when he was told by his Quaker master that he was free, exclaimed: 'Oh goody, goody, I thought I should die a slave and now I shall die a free man!'

And what of life? God offers life of a higher order. The secret lies in the relationship we enjoy with him. Being 'justified' (verse 24) – 'put right' (GNB) – is surely what we all feel in need of at various stages in our lives.

☐ *Quietly go over the experiences outlined above – and be very thankful. 'Not guilty'; 'free'; 'alive with his life'. What makes it all possible? Grace! God's love in action! Rejoice!*

For group discussion and personal thought

Read and study Romans 3.21–26. How would you say that Jesus' death made it possible for God to forgive people's sins? Why couldn't God have accepted us as right in his sight without Jesus dying?

Sunday May 9   John 14.1–11*

THE WAY, THE TRUTH AND THE LIFE

The course of a person's life is often described as a **journey**. The most famous of such descriptions is John Bunyan's *Pilgrim's Progress*. Jesus described his life's work in terms of a journey to his Father.

Jesus' disciples were anxious. Not only did it sound as if they were going to lose him, but they felt, in their weakness and failure, that they themselves would never be able to make the journey successfully. We may feel the same. Our way of life seems so uncertain. We so often 'lose our way'. In crises, we cannot 'see the way ahead'.

Christ reassures his friends – and us. Through him, the way ahead becomes clear and there are places along it for our refreshment. More than that, he himself comes back to accompany us on the journey. Companionship with him is the way.

There are many ways by which people get an inkling of God's reality. But the way to the Father, to a full comprehension of the love of God with its assurance of forgiveness and hope, comes through Christ alone.

☐ *A song for a pilgrim on the journey of life:*

> *Hobgoblin nor foul fiend*
> *Can daunt his spirit;*
> *He knows he at the end*
> *Shall life inherit.*

John Bunyan

Monday May 10   Romans 4.13-25

Legalism is always creeping back into Christianity. Many years ago I felt deeply hurt when a brother minister refused to have me in his pulpit. In his opinion I was not orthodox enough in my beliefs. In a discussion I suggested to him that his understanding of 'orthodox' was 'one who agrees with me'. His reply was that he had to protect his pulpit from heretics!

To the orthodox Jews, Paul was a heretic. He had abandoned the law in favour of a religious faith which did not have clear-cut rules and regulations. Paul was delighted to be able to present to them Abraham, their spiritual father, whom Paul saw as the outstanding illustration of a person who simply trusted God. See what had happened over Sarah. She was barren and too old to give birth to a child; but God enabled just that to happen. And Abraham believed God when the promise was made.

So, today, vital faith arises out of an acknowledgement that we are helpless but that God can do for us what we cannot do for ourselves. Our faith is in Christ's resurrection power. This is what brings people to life. This is what makes possible our ability to love others.

☐ *Reflect upon your own Christian life. You are surrounded by God's love. The Christian life is a response to love. Enjoy it! Be grateful! A deep sense of indebtedness is the best motivating force for Christian service.*

Tuesday May 11   Romans 5.1-11

In his autobiography James Galway describes the stage in his life when he stopped worrying about the future but instead put everything in God's hands and decided to play his flute 'as homage to the creator'. He also asserts that the motor cycle which ran out of control in Lucerne and injured him seriously was, in some ways, a blessing in disguise. His disabilities were painful and limiting but he 'almost regarded them as a further spur to spiritual awareness'.

We do not go looking for troubles but there is no doubt that, when they come, our attitude towards them makes a great difference to our life. A creative attitude is the direct result of faith and trust. And where does this kind of faith come from? From Jesus. It was his death which was the guarantee that God cares.

An affirming attitude to life is the best one. So often we tend to look over our shoulders, half-afraid that something or other on the horizon will blight our lives. What a lot of nervous energy we waste in anticipating troubles which never come!

☐ *Think over your own problems and difficulties – for we all have them. Can they possibly be the means whereby you may gain in spiritual awareness? Ask God if today's reading has a direct message for you? If so, write it down on a slip of paper or in your Bible and read it again and again.*

Wednesday May 12   Romans 5.12–21

Adam was the first man – the representative man. It is this representative man whose story Paul tells. Trace it out and, if it helps you, write it down. Adam is the symbol of the fallen state of man. He failed; he sinned; he was guilty; he experienced death as the consequence of his sin. This is the Adam line.

Now we contrast Adam with Jesus. Jesus came as the result of grace – God's grace; he offered himself to die for all men's sins; after his death he rose and now he offers life to all who trust him. This is the marvellous, superb gift of God.

We are in a fortunate position; we can switch from the Adam line to the Christ line. If we put our trust in Christ we share his resurrection life.

☐ *There is the 'Adam' streak in all of us. We can so easily live selfishly and turn inwards – and the result is spiritual death. The alternative is to look to Jesus and to 'fly blind' with him. Sometimes we shall wonder where we are going but we shall always be conscious that the pilot we have taken on board can be trusted. If we choose Christ we are also choosing adventure!*

From the very first moment of our life we are dying. This sounds dramatic, yet it is true – we are born to die. But there is a fascinating possibility presented to us in this reading. We can discover how to 'die' creatively and we can experience 'resurrection' while we are physically alive. How can these things be?

When children grow up and prepare to 'leave the nest', parents feel deeply for them. Ours is a hard world full of dangers and pitfalls. So much so that some parents are reluctant to let their children go; they try to hold on to them. This is a mistake. It is far better for us to 'die' to one kind of relationship that our children may 'rise' to another.

Similarly, as people age so the limitations of life catch up with them. Some try to deny this and continue as they always have done. But this is not possible. It is far better to 'die' to our more youthful way of life and look for the 'new' possibilities that the later years can and do bring with them.

This **dying and living** process is symbolised in the sacrament of baptism. Think of it when next you share in such a service. Picture the drama of immersion (the practice in Paul's day) – the sinking down beneath the waters and the rising again – 'ransomed, healed, restored, forgiven' through faith in Christ (verses 3–4).

☐ *What are the 'dying' and 'rising' experiences which you can recall? Have you felt the tension of longing to remain at one stage of experience when the next is beckoning you on? Might it be that our little 'deaths' and 'resurrections' will have a vital bearing upon our attitude to our final parting with this life?*

Slavery was something Paul's readers were familiar with. Some of them had sold themselves into slavery in order to have a job and be paid wages. A slave had no rights of his own; he was owned body and soul by his master.

The new relationship with God made possible by knowing Jesus is the exact opposite. Paul's use of the phrase 'slave of righteousness' (verse 18) might seem to suggest something other than a free choice, but we know from the letter as a whole that was just what Paul rejoiced in – he had found freedom at last through Jesus!

We can share his sense of liberation but this does not mean that we can now please ourselves so far as our actions and attitudes are concerned. We are now controlled by love and this guides our thinking and our behaviour.

T. H. Robinson suggests a parallel with a modern footballer who is sold for a large fee. From the date of the transfer, although he has been sold with his own consent, his new club now 'owns' his loyalty. It must be complete and absolute; he cannot go back on the odd occasion and play for his old club.

☐ *Do you sometimes find yourself uneasy about possible alternative courses of action? This is quite normal and part of every Christian's experience. Remember that you belong to God because you have freely given yourself to him. He respects your freedom but expects you to live by the constraints of love.*

Saturday May 15   **Romans 7.1–6**

Like a scintillating diamond which flashes its light in various directions, Paul keeps on placing before his readers related ideas but in different ways.

Freedom from the Jewish law is what Paul wants to get across yet again. A married woman is bound to her husband in his lifetime. To go with another man while her husband is still alive is adultery. But if he dies she is free and can remarry. Similarly Christians are placed in a new position by their relationship with Jesus. They now want to obey a loving Father because they want to and not because they have to.

How many industrial problems could be solved given real attempts to understand what 'the other side' is thinking? Behind the welter of words often described as 'negotiations' there are entrenched positions on both sides of the table. It may seem naïve but a bit of honest loving could solve many tough industrial problems. Remember that love is not so much a sentiment as an attitude of life.

☐ *Think over your own attitude to some of the more complex relationships in which you are involved. Is religion just 'being kind to the tea lady' as someone put it, or is it applying gospel insights to work situations in more thoughtful and deliberate ways? One man who began to do this said that it was like being 'switched on' so far as his Christian life was concerned.*

For group discussion and personal thought

What did Augustine mean when he said, 'Love God and do as you like'? Does Paul's teaching in this week's readings support this idea? In what ways is legalism tending to creep back into modern Christianity? How can we regain our freedom in Christ?

Sunday May 16   John 16.12–24*

GOING TO THE FATHER

There are some who treat the Bible as a book of exact and detailed instructions upon every possible human situation. But this is not the right approach. We cannot find in what Jesus said direct answers to the complex problems of today. He lived at a particular time and in a particular place, and his words belong to that time and place. Even for his first disciples, there were situations to come for which he had not given them explicit instructions (eg, relations between Gentile and Jewish Christians). For us, there are situations arising from the complexities of twentieth-century conditions to which Jesus makes no reference at all.

But Jesus did promise the gift of the **Spirit of truth.** It is through prayer, honest examination and openness to the leading of this Spirit of truth that we may find the answers we seek – and they will not contradict the words Christ spoke. What we shall find is an interpretation of his words applicable to our situation. The Jesus who went away from the world came back as the Spirit of truth and never were the first Christians, nor Christians ever since, without his guidance.

☐   *The Spirit breathes upon the word,*
    And brings the truth to sight.

                                       William Cowper

Monday May 17   Romans 7.7–13

I was brought up in a rather strict home where rules had to be obeyed; if they were broken then there was a punishment to be borne. I felt that some of the rules were quite unfair. I used to break these and often got away with it – but sometimes I was found out and had to face the consequences. Paul says that in a sense rules and regulations have the effect of enticing us to break them!

Some rules are, of course, necessary, but the Jews of whom Paul was writing tended to obey the law for the wrong reasons. They thought that they were totting up 'righteousness'; they wanted to win a reward; to secure a prize. Thus they became guilty of spiritual pride.

Growing in grace means being delivered from stoical obedience to a set of rules. It is about becoming aware that we are loved and responding with the obligations of love. This was the deliverance Paul had found and which he wanted to share.

☐ *Think back to your childhood days. Did you enjoy breaking rules? What motivates your Christian life now? Obedience to a tradition? Loyalty to a particular church? Or is the basis of it all your love for Jesus? Think hard! Good things can so easily become perverted.*

Tuesday May 18   **Romans 7.14–25**

Paul here moves from the past into the present tense, a change which some scholars believe to be of considerable significance. The argument is that the previous section (verses 7–13) refers to the pre-conversion stage while today's reading refers to the realities of the Christian life. If this is so then it is a depressing picture which is painted, relieved only by the positive note in verse 25.

In looking for help in living our own Christian lives, we need to recognise that the debate about the part played by 'the law' does not mean as much to us as it did to those first century Christians who had been delivered from the bondage of an unrelenting legalism.

Nevertheless, we know that the Christian life is no bed of roses! For instance, we have to struggle with an inborn disposition towards lovelessness. But we do have Jesus and we do have the power of the Holy Spirit. The nearest 'bondage' parallels we have in contemporary experience must be those of drug addicts and alcoholics. To break free is almost impossible, yet when they reach rock bottom there is hope. Out of sheer desperation new possibilities can arise. Similarly, when we are most acutely aware of our own failures Jesus will draw near with his very special 'lifting power'. 'Who is there to rescue me?' cries Paul. 'God alone, through Jesus Christ our Lord!' (verses 24–25)

☐ *Acknowledge the reality of the 'downward pull' and then dwell on verse 25 and the experience which lies behind it.*

One of the most significant experiences in my life was when I became aware that God was on my side! Previously the Christian life had been a kind of challenge. There were so many opposing forces arrayed against me and God expected me to respond with courage and energy. The emphasis in my mind was on what God expected of me. It was a 'mini-conversion' when I realised that God was directly involved **with** me. He was not an onlooker but a participant, and he was – and is – working on my behalf. The thrust of life is in my favour!

What a difference it makes if you are a member of a team whose captain sets a cracking pace but who lifts you and strengthens you by the very atmosphere of hope and confidence his example creates!

In today's reading the realities of human experience are still acknowledged but the emphasis is on the liberating and energising power of the Holy Spirit. We are in direct contact and so have come 'alive with his life' (John 1.4). He is on our side and we are on his!

☐ *Just sit back and let verses 1–4 pour over you. Pick out your own keywords and let your mind and spirit be inspired by them. Who is your controller? Whose hand is on the tiller of your life?*

A small girl came to live with her new 'Mum and Dad'. She was 'in care' and never could there have been a more appropriate phrase. She had been without a sound and stable home base from her earliest years. In her new home she 'flowered' – she had been 'born again'. At first she was withdrawn and almost afraid. But now she is happy and content – although very much a little rascal!

How wonderful it is when we realise that God is our Father! He is concerned for our total well-being. Just as the two 'parents' were determined sensibly to 'love' their new daughter to life, so God wants us to realise that he is totally concerned about our development as members of the human family.

This kind of realisation can make a great difference to our prayers. In verse 15 Paul uses the local diminutive with which a Jewish child would address his father – 'Daddy' is the nearest we can get to it. But the emphasis here is not on cheap familiarity;

rather, it speaks of a deep sense of trust and dependence. The Father cares, loves, provides, encourages, stimulates, inspires.

☐ *A prayer for Ascension Day*

'Almighty God, as we believe your only-begotten Son, our Lord Jesus Christ, has ascended into the heavens; so may we also in heart and mind thither ascend, and with him continually dwell; who is alive and reigns with you and the Holy Spirit, one God, now and for ever.' (Methodist Service Book)

Friday May 21   **Romans 8.18–30**

God's salvation is experienced here and now. We know that we belong to him and he belongs to us. But we do not yet possess all our proper inheritance. There is much which remains for us in the future. Hope, for instance, helps to give meaning to life – and our hope is based on the surest foundation, Jesus Christ.

When Dietrich Bonhoeffer was in prison he hoped and believed that he would be freed. But in one sense he was more free than his custodians. They were slaves to false ideas of racial supremacy; he was 'in captivity to Christ' but his spirit was free. Even when he died, he was the victor! Those who killed him are remembered as evil men while he is remembered as a devout and faithful follower of Jesus and a creative thinker whose ideas have influenced theological development and made a difference to many people's lives.

God's Holy Spirit is always available and, from time to time, Spirit-led initiatives take place in our lives.

☐ *Fix your attention on verse 28 and work out if what it says has come true for you.*

Saturday May 22   **Romans 8.31–39**

These verses complete the first section of *Romans* and appropriately end upon a note of complete confidence. Bishop John Robinson describes these verses as the ending of 'perhaps the greatest chapter in the New Testament'.

To stimulate our minds and spirits we turn to some words from two hymns by Charles Wesley, who steeped himself in Paul's letter to the Romans and then expressed its central themes in sublime poetry:

□ *Not all the powers of hell can fright*
A soul that walks with Christ in light;
He walks, and cannot fall:
Clearly he sees, and wins his way,
Shining unto the perfect day,
And more than conquers all.

Stronger than death and hell
The mystic power we prove;
And conquerors of the world, we dwell
In heaven, who dwell in love.

For group discussion and personal thought

Romans 8.26–27 suggests that the Holy Spirit is 'on our side', always there to help us and to give us strength in our weakness. What difference should this knowledge make to us as we try to cope with all the problems and difficulties of life?

Sunday May 23   Luke 24.44–53*

THE ASCENSION OF CHRIST

Our reading describes what must have been one of the most significant moments the first disciples had ever experienced.

● It was a moment of **understanding**. In the risen Christ was the fulfilment of the hopes that had sustained the Jewish people through their turbulent history. The disciples' growing understanding of God and his ways reached its climax in Christ's triumph.

● It was a moment of **challenge**. They were to be the ones who should proclaim this message to the world, a message which was a call to men to change their minds and accept the forgiveness of God. It could have been a most frightening moment, but for one thing . . .

● It was a moment of **promise**. He told them they would receive 'power from above'.

Parting is often a time of acute sorrow. Not so with this parting. They returned to Jerusalem with great joy, with minds enlightened, with a clear task to carry out and with the assurance that they would receive all the resources they needed.

□ *Christ's task is still unfinished. Now it is our turn. We need not be afraid, for he has promised us his power.*

A DEVELOPING EXPERIENCE OF GOD

God – Father, Son, and Holy Spirit

Notes by Revd Donald H. Hilton, BA

Donald Hilton is minister of the United Reformed Church, Princes Street, Norwich, England. He has previously served in London and Hampshire, and was also Youth and Children's Secretary of the Congregational Church in England and Wales for six years. He has been President of the National Christian Education Council, and has written and compiled several books published by the NCEC.

The great Christian creeds affirm our belief in the Trinity. We believe in God the Father, God the Son, and God the Holy Spirit. When we make such a statement we are summarising the thinking of many years in which people tried to understand the character of God.

The Bible does not give us a precise statement about the Trinity; instead it offers us a record of the religious experiences out of which such a statement grew. We must constantly go back to those human experiences to understand the meaning of the idea.

'The highest knowledge,' said Albert Schweitzer, 'is to know that we are surrounded by mystery.' He recognised that our human thought is too shallow fully to understand the world around us, and that human language is too limited fully to express even what we do know. Schweitzer's attitude is urgently needed when, with our frail words, we try to describe God himself.

In the next two weeks we shall attempt to trace the way in which, thinking about their experiences and encounters, Bible authors describe the development of the understanding of God which led them to say: **Father, Son and Holy Spirit.**

Monday May 24   **Genesis 8.20 to 9.3**

From the beginning mankind had to come to terms with the created world. How vast the mountains! How deep the seas! How swiftly a horse runs, and how dangerous is a volcano! Creation is both awe-inspiring and frightening.

It is also beautiful. The setting sun speaks peace and the rippling pond induces a feeling of calm. The austere moorlands and the lush meadows each have their own appeal.

Further, creation sustains mankind. Birds and beasts become man's food. Tree and root provide crops; woods and caves give him shelter.

One of the themes in the Noah story is the belief that God looks after his people; he is steadfast and trustworthy. Creation is one of the means by which he shows this. The author of *Genesis* looks at the rhythm of the seasons, the pattern of days and months, and finds in them a clue about God's providential care and love. Here is an example of a constantly recurring human conviction: that creation is not arbitrary, nor dependent on chance, but that deep within the mystery of creation lies the eternal purpose of God's loving providence.

☐ *Recall any experience of your own in which the sight or sound of creation helped you to understand God better.*

Tuesday May 25   **Isaiah 48.12–21**

Think about this reading section by section and see the way in which the author's ideas progress from thinking about God as the creator of the world, to thinking of him as arbiter in the affairs of nations.

● *Verse 12* – God's unique nature is declared. He is the only one; first and last.

● *Verse 13* – God is the creator. Earth and sky came into being because God commanded it.

● *Verses 14–16* – God is in control of men and nations. He raises up those who will achieve his purposes. The prophet believes that the time has come for Babylon, captors of Israel, to be destroyed, and he sees the hand of God in this outworking of history.

● *Verses 17–19* – such activity by God demands a response from his people. Man's prosperity and success, indeed his very future, depends on his obedience to God.

● *Verses 20–21* – God acts decisively in human affairs. He cares for the oppressed, and ransoms his servants.

As we read these verses the thought about God develops from a providential God who provides food, to a God active in history, who calls for a response from mankind. Remember that although these verses are in the first person as though God is speaking personally, they are actually the writing of an author who, thinking about his nation's experiences, believes that he can now see, and in future will still expect to see, God at work.

☐ *God is working his purpose out as year succeeds to year.*
Arthur C. Ainger

Wednesday May 26   **Psalm 139.13–18, 23–24**

Try to find time to read the whole of Psalm 139. There is no better example of the conviction that God knows every person intimately. 'Intimate' is the right word. It is one thing to believe that God controls the movement of the stars and the rhythm of the seasons, or even to see his hand in the affairs of nations; but what brings us to our knees in awe – and perhaps in fear – is the conviction that God is nearer than our breath and closer than our heartbeat. He knows us through and through. He knew us before we were born; he will know us after we have died.

Most religions speak of a creator-God who made the universe but not all dare to show God as one who has a personal relationship with each individual. In our readings, therefore, we have moved from the idea of a providential God of creation, to a personal God who knows his own people. This Old Testament psalm is preparing the ground for the ministry of Jesus.

Jesus, my Lord – I know his name,
His name is all I trust;
and . . .
Then will he own my worthless name
Before his Father's face. *Isaac Watts*

☐ *Man – who climbs the peak of Everest or with a microscope magnifies a speck of creation a thousandfold, or steps on the moon – can say, 'God knows me.'*

Thursday May 27   **Psalm 103.8–18**

We find our most intimate relationships within family life: husband and wife, parents and children. As soon as mankind learned to speak of God with the intimacy suggested by yesterday's reading it could not be long before family relationships were used to describe this new understanding of him.

The prophet Hosea (see 2.14, 16a) was bold enough to describe the relationship between Israel and God in husband/wife language. This thought is taken up into Christian language, as when the Church is thought of as the bride of Christ.

In Psalm 103 the psalmist uses the parent/child relationship as a way of expressing his experience of God's loving care. He keeps it only as a simile, ie God is **like** a father; we have still to reach the stage where a man looks into the skies to cry, 'Father!' – but the pattern is developing.

Again, it is important to recognise that this is a human attempt to use weak, everyday words to describe strong, religious experiences. God is not a husband. He is not a father. It is simply that these everyday relationships offer us vivid and dramatic clues about the character of God and enable us to describe our deep spiritual experiences. It may be helpful to some people to think of the motherly nature of God.

☐   *'Can a woman's tender care*
    Cease towards the child she bare?
    Yes, she may forgetful be,
    Yet will I remember thee.'

William Cowper

Friday May 28   Matthew 6.7–15

Now we come to the central point in this part of our theme. We can look to the providential creator, the arbiter among nations, the intimate friend, and simply say, 'Father'.

There is an old story (probably apocryphal!) of a newly ordained minister who, with his theological college language still fresh on his tongue, led prayers in his new church by saying: 'Eternal, Almighty God, Creator and Omnipotent, Lord Omniscient and Omnipresent, Great Designer and First Cause, what shall we call thee . . .?'

The prayer was interrupted by an elderly member: 'Call him Father, laddie, call him Father.' Our necessary theological enquiry must never obscure the simplicity of our approach to God. We are children looking to the glad friendship of a Father.

The Lord's Prayer has been studied earlier this year (see January 18–23). Today, as you read it, notice the central plea: please give me the food which satisfies my physical needs and the forgiveness which answers my spiritual and emotional needs. These are the needs we experienced – and had fulfilled – in our family as children. It is the same needs that we put to our heavenly Father.

☐ *Say the Lord's Prayer slowly, phrase by phrase.*

It was Jesus who brought us to the place where 'Father' becomes the best way to describe our experience of God's care. He interpreted the ways of God so clearly to men, and lived out the same convictions in life and death with such persuasion, that his disciples began to ask new questions about him: 'Who is Jesus?'; 'What is the nature of this man who, by word and deed, brings us so close to God?'; 'How is it that his death and resurrection mysteriously release and renew us?'

It was not a sudden process. The New Testament – Gospels and letters – describe the mounting experiences which eventually led men and women to confess him as Lord and God. It began in simple ways. They met him by the seashore and discovered qualities of attractive friendship and dynamic leadership which caused them to leave boats, tax-collecting tables, and homes in order to be with him.

It has happened in a similar way for many of us. Our understanding of Jesus Christ has grown from admiration and the desire to follow his teaching, to a recognition that, in meeting him, we have encountered God himself.

Albert Schweitzer describes Jesus as 'coming to us as One unknown'. As we respond to his call through life's toils, duties and sufferings, we discover in our own experience who he is.

☐ *Our friend, our brother, and our Lord,*
    What may thy service be?   *John Greenleaf Whittier*

For group discussion and personal thought

Consider whether emphasis on God's closeness and intimacy reduces his stature to a point where he is no longer worthy of worship.

Whit Sunday, May 30   **Acts 2.1–11***

THE GIFT OF THE SPIRIT

For the Jews, Pentecost was a celebration of Moses' receiving the law on which their national life and faith was founded. For the first Christians, Pentecost was the time of receiving a new kind of law, what Paul called 'the life-giving law of the Spirit' (Romans 8.2). It was an inner energy, a power which enabled them to do the right.

Further, for the Jews, Pentecost was a harvest festival. For the Christians it was the beginning of a new kind of harvest, what Paul called 'the harvest of the Spirit – love, joy, peace, patience, kindness, goodness, fidelity, gentleness, and self-control' (Galatians 5.22–23a).

On that first Whit Sunday, a new understanding of the Spirit of God dawned. In the Old Testament, the Spirit was known as that power who created the world and empowered rulers and fighters. But now the disciples saw a deeper significance in his activity. He was the Spirit who broke down national and racial barriers, who worked in the lives of ordinary people, who renewed men and women and was, indeed, the very presence of Jesus at work in all times and places.

☐   *Away with our fears,*
   Our troubles and tears :
   The Spirit is come,
The witness of Jesus returned to his home.   Charles Wesley

Monday May 31   2 Corinthians 5.11–21

Jesus was a man – flesh, blood and bone – just like them: there was no doubt about that in the disciples' minds. And they should know. They had lived, ate, walked and talked with him for three years. He was truly human.

And yet . . . he was different. God became real as Jesus lived alongside the disciples. He spoke with an authority they had never known before. His life lifted their lives to a new level and called out from them resources of strength and power they did not know they had. In Jesus they could see all the human qualities of love and leadership – but also those extra, indefinable gifts that gave life dimensions they had not encountered before.

In the early days of the Church they struggled with this awareness. The manner of his death, and their experience of his presence after his death helped them more than anything else. They found they no longer wanted to 'live for themselves' but sought to 'live for him'. Their love for Christ gave them a sense of unity with him. Life is different, they said, 'a new order has already begun' (verse 17).

But how do you express your ideas about the man who caused all this to happen? Paul, the great New Testament thinker and writer, put it into these words: 'God was in Christ' (verse 19).

☐ *Jesus was human – and yet different. Recall incidents in the Gospels which you think might have led the disciples to become aware of the difference.*

Tuesday June 1   John 20.19–29

Thomas was not present when Jesus appeared to the other disciples in the upper room. Returning, he heard what had happened and faith and doubt mingled in his mind. Clearly, he longed for the same experience but, serious and honest man that he was, he laid down his conditions. He must be absolutely sure that it was the same Jesus he had known for three years – the Jesus whom he had seen hanging on the cross with pierced hands and wounded side.

But death and resurrection had disturbed Thomas. When flesh and blood die, that is the end. Resurrection? – that puts other thoughts into Thomas' mind. They reached their climax and fulfilment when, convinced that the risen Christ truly was the Jesus he knew, Thomas made his confession of faith: 'My Lord and my God!'

This was more than the dawn of one man's faith. John, writing long after the event, includes this story in his Gospel as a summary of the way the conviction grew in the early Church that Jesus Christ is both man and God – flesh and Spirit. What John expresses in story-form later generations would express in the formal language of the creeds.

☐ *'I believe in one God the Father Almighty, maker of heaven and earth . . . And in one Lord Jesus Christ, the only-begotten Son of God . . . God of God, Light of Light.' (The Nicene Creed)*

Wednesday June 2   Galatians 5.13 to 6.2

The word 'spirit' was long used to describe the activity of God. The order which came after the chaos in the creation of the world was attributed to the Spirit. When prophets spoke and kings ruled wisely, men claimed that the Spirit was leading them.

On the day of Pentecost a group of men and women were dramatically welded into a vital community, strongly motivated to proclaim Christ as Lord. The power they felt was reckoned to be the work of the Spirit.

Paul uses fluid, changing language to explain this, referring sometimes to the 'Spirit of God', sometimes to the 'Spirit of

Christ', or simply to 'the Spirit'. But the different words describe essentially the same spiritual experience – the direct interplay of God's action and human liveliness.

To summarise: mankind has emerged from some experiences speaking of a providential creator whose love is so constant that **'Father'** is the only way to describe him. At other times, mankind has enjoyed mysterious experiences of encounter and inspiration, in which **'Spirit'** has seemed the best word to use. And for one short period in the human race, a man walked through Palestine. He was flesh and blood – and yet? He was ordinary, like us – but . . .? **'Son of God'** best fits the experience.

Are there three different gods communicating with us? No! There is **one** God, only **one: God is God.** But in our human experience we encounter him in three varied ways.

☐ *Come, Holy Ghost . . .*
   Teach us to know the Father, Son,
   And thee, of both, to be but one.

                                                              Anon

Thursday June 3   John 14.7–14

John's Gospel, the last to be written, represents long reflection and thoughtfulness about the life of Jesus. If it is possible to speak of God in three different ways – Father, Son and Holy Spirit – how does the idea of 'God the Father' link up with the idea of 'God the Son'? John gives the answer to this question in a conversation between Jesus and Philip.

● Jesus is thought of as a picture of God. Philip wants to see God. John makes it clear that seeing Jesus is the same as seeing God; and knowing Jesus is the same as knowing God.

● Jesus is the agent of God – speaking God's words (verse 10) and doing God's deeds (verse 11).

● An even greater truth is presented. The relationship between the Father and the Son is expressed in close, intimate terms. The Son is 'in the Father', and the Father is 'in the Son' (verse 10); their relationship is one of complete unity. God is the invisible God who cannot be seen by human eyes; Jesus our Lord is the 'image of the invisible God' (Colossians 1.15).

☐ *Isaac Watts wrote of God's boundless love :*

   See where it shines in Jesu's face,
   The brightest image of his grace ;
   God, in the person of his Son,
   Has all his mightiest works outdone.

Friday June 4

In talking about God we are trying to put deep and abiding human experiences into words. This is especially true as we talk of the Trinity.

'God the Father' accurately expresses our experience of a loving God who lives in mystery, beyond human life. 'God the Son' brings immediate and refreshing pictures of the Jesus of history. But Jesus is the ascended Lord and can no longer be seen or touched, and God the Father is beyond our reach, invisible. How then do we explain those inner spiritual compulsions and consolations we still feel, today? Who is the cause of our search for truth and spiritual awareness? How do we explain the God who prods our conscience and also heals and comforts us?

▶ Read **John 14.15-21.**

Verses 15-17 express John's answer to such questions as those above. 'The Advocate' or the 'Comforter' (AV) is John's way of speaking of the God who still stands alongside us. He continues the ministry of Jesus and leads us into greater spiritual awareness and truth. Mysteriously, he links us with the Godhead and draws us to Christ (see verses 19b-20).

Here is a mystery: the believer finds a unity with the God whom we experience as Father, Son and Spirit.

☐   *... none can guess its grace,*
     Till he become the place
  Wherein the Holy Spirit makes his dwelling.

                           Bianco da Siena

Saturday June 5   **Matthew 28.16-20**

As Matthew reaches the end of his Gospel, the story of the life of Jesus is complete. He has told us of his birth, his teaching and healing work, his death and resurrection. Drawing on both his personal memory of Jesus and his experience in the life of the early Church, Matthew acknowledges the authority of Jesus and the charges he gave to the Church to proclaim the gospel to the ends of the earth (see verses 19-20). These verses are:

● **A statement of faith.** The complete trinitarian conviction is expressed; the Church has its creed. God has been described in the way which best does justice to our spiritual experience.

● **A challenge to mission.** The Church has a task; all nations are to hear the gospel.

● **A promise of companionship.** The Church will not be alone. Christ himself will be its guide and sustainer until time itself comes to an end.

☐ *Almighty God, to thee,*
Be endless honour done,
The undivided three,
And the mysterious one ;
Where reason fails with all her powers,
There faith prevails, and love adores.

Isaac Watts

For group discussion and personal thought

Would you agree that when we speak about God as Father, Son and Holy Spirit, we are simply trying to describe how we experience God? Discuss this in the light of the past two weeks' readings.

Trinity Sunday, June 6   Acts 2.22–24, 32–36*

THE CHURCH'S MESSAGE

The day of Pentecost was the birthday of the Christian Church. So for the next five Sundays our readings and notes are concerned with various aspects of the Church's life and work. To read what it was like to be a member of that very first group of church members is to enter a world both exciting and challenging. We, too, are members of the Church, but we live in a world very different from that of the first century. Our ways and our words are inevitably different from theirs. Yet the fundamental facts of their faith, life and mission remain for all time the essentials of any fellowship of people who call themselves the Church of Christ. To examine the life of these early church members is a means by which we may examine ourselves with humility and repentance.

The Church's message was simple and direct: **'Jesus is Lord.'** He was the long-awaited Messiah; he was the conqueror of death; the power shown in his Spirit-filled life was now available to all people. That message needs to be proclaimed in the modern world and applied to social, economic and political affairs as well as to the lives of individuals.

☐ *Pray for preachers and teachers known to you who will be communicating the Christian message today.*

RUTH; JONAH

Notes by Elaine V. Wake, MA

Elaine Wake, an Anglican, is a part-time co-ordinator of English teaching for immigrants. She has been a Religious Education teacher, a community worker for the Birmingham Council of Churches, and a social worker in a psychiatric hospital.

These two very different books have a common theme: the extension of God's care to people of all nations. We do not know the author or date of composition of either book, but it seems likely that they reached their present form in the years after the Jews returned from exile in Babylon, when they were tending to become narrowly nationalistic in their religion.

Ruth is a story about the doings of an ordinary Israelite family and of the Moabitess who came into it. It is concerned with the feelings and relationships of ordinary people, particularly of women; yet those ordinary people were of great significance for Israel, for Ruth was the ancestor of the great King David.

Jonah tells of a prophet who was called by God to preach to the people of Nineveh, but who did not want these foreigners to hear God's message and be saved. The book is really a caricature of the opinions of many of the Jews of that time.

Suggestions for further reading

Books of Ruth, Esther, Ecclesiastes, The Song of Songs, Lamentations: The Five Scrolls by Wesley J. Fuerst, Cambridge Bible Commentaries on the New English Bible (Cambridge University Press);

Joel, Obadiah, Jonah, Nahum, Habakkuk and Zephaniah edited by John D. W. Watts, also in the Cambridge Bible Commentaries series.

Monday June 7   **Ruth 1.1–14**

Elimelech and his family left Israel to stay for a while (the Hebrew verb shows that they did not intend to settle permanently) in Moab, to the east of the Dead Sea. The Moabites had often been hostile to Israel, and the law excluded them from the worshipping congregation (see Deuteronomy 23.3–4). It has been suggested that the book of *Ruth* was a protest against such discrimination.

When Naomi decided to return to Israel, she tried to persuade her daughters-in-law to stay in their own country with their parents. According to the custom of Levirate marriage (set out in Deuteronomy 25.5–6) the brother of a man who died childless married the widow, and the first child of the union was regarded as the heir of the dead man. Naomi told Ruth and Orpah that they could not hope for such a marriage, since she was unlikely ever to bear another son.

Notice how Naomi saw the death of her husband and sons as the work of the Lord (verse 13) but still kept her faith in him. Throughout this book we see the conviction that nothing happens by chance; in the affairs of men and women we trace the action of God.

☐ *Lord, help me to believe and trust in you even when I am unhappy and everything seems to be against me.*

Tuesday June 8

Many people are brought to God not primarily by an interest in religion or by rational argument, but through their love for someone who is a believer. What begins as a human desire to share with the loved one in all activities can become a true faith.

Ruth had been brought up in the Moabite religion, but her love for Naomi was such that she wanted to share in her religion, and she even took an oath by Naomi's God never to leave her.

▶ Read **Ruth 1.15–22.**

When the two women arrived in Bethlehem, Naomi was recognised by the women of the town (the men would have been out in the fields gathering the barley harvest). She told them not to call her Naomi, which means 'pleasant', but to call her Mara – 'bitter'. The play on words is brought out in Moffatt's version of verse 20: 'Call me *Mara*, for the Almighty has cruelly *marred* me.'

Notice how in verse 22 Ruth is described as 'the Moabitess'. The author is anxious to emphasise that the woman whose fortunes we are following is a foreigner, yet she is under the care of the God of Israel.

☐ *Lord, help me to live in such a way that I may bring those who love me to believe in you and love you.*

Naomi and Ruth were fortunate to return to Bethlehem at harvest-time, for they were able to take part in one of the very few activities by which a poor woman could make a living. The custom of gleaning – picking up the grain which the reapers had missed – is referred to in Deuteronomy 24.19–22, where it is said that even if the reapers forget one of the swathes or sheaves of corn, they must leave it for 'the alien, the orphan, and the widow'.

Ruth, the younger and more able-bodied of the two women, went out to glean and came to the attention of Boaz, presumably either because of her beauty or because she was obviously a foreigner. What he had learned of her history made Boaz well-disposed towards her, and he was more generous than the law commanded. He let her share in his servants' food and drink, and told them to let her glean among the sheaves (instead of waiting until the reapers had removed them), and to drop corn for her to pick up.

Boaz was led by compassion and interest in Ruth to go beyond the minimum requirements of the law. It was easy for the Jews to think that they had done all that God required by obeying the letter of the law. But the lesson they had to learn was the lesson of love, which was ultimately taught by Jesus.

☐ *Do I help others grudgingly, or do I freely show them the generosity of our loving Father?*

By dint of her own hard work and Boaz' generosity, Ruth gleaned more than she could have expected, and even had some of her lunch left to take back to Naomi.

Naomi was delighted to hear that the owner of the land where Ruth had been gleaning was Boaz, their 'next-of-kin' (NEB). This was an important concept for the Jews, referring to the relative whose duty it was to act as *go'el* or redeemer for someone in trouble. A particularly important function of the *go'el* was to redeem land which had been sold in time of poverty. The Jews believed that the land belonged to God, and that they were his tenants, so that they must never sell it except in time of real necessity, and then the first opportunity must be taken to buy it back, either by the person who had sold it, or by his 'next-of-kin' or 'redeemer'. In the book of *Ruth* it seems that the next-of-kin also took over responsibility for his relative's widow, in an extension of the idea of Levirate marriage.

Naomi saw Ruth's meeting with Boaz as a manifestation of God's continuing love and care for the family. The reference to 'the living and the dead' in verse 20 means that God's care for Naomi and Ruth was a fulfilment of his care for Elimelech and his sons.

☐   *Give thanks to the God of heaven,*
    for his love endures for ever.

                                                               (Psalm 136.26)

Friday June 11

Now that the harvest was over, Naomi thought of a plan to bring Ruth once more to the attention of Boaz, who was obviously attracted to her.

▶ Read **Ruth 3.1–18.**

Threshing was the process of beating the corn to separate the grain from the chaff. Afterwards came the winnowing, throwing the corn into the air so that the chaff was blown away and the grain fell back to the ground and could be stored. The threshing-floor was an open place, away from the town, where a good breeze could be obtained. Boaz was doing his winnowing in the evening, when there was a suitable breeze, and was sleeping on the threshing-floor to guard his grain.

When Boaz woke in the night, Ruth asked him to spread the skirt of his robe over her. This act was a sign of protection, especially associated with marriage. Boaz was glad to do so, and admired her family loyalty (verse 10) in choosing him rather than a man of her own age, who might have been thought more attractive.

The word translated 'skirt' in verse 9 is the same as that used for God's 'wings' in Ruth 2.12. Ruth had placed herself under God's protection, and now Boaz was to become a partner in God's blessing of her.

☐   *Lord, help me to share in your care of others.*

Saturday June 12
                                                         Ruth 4.1–22

Boaz went to the city gate, where all legal business was transacted, to discuss Ruth and the land with the next-of-kin, in the presence of witnesses. The other man was not willing to marry Ruth and was happy to let Boaz take over the position of next-of-kin.

When they had performed the legal formalities, the witnesses hoped that Ruth would be as fruitful as Rachel and Leah (Jacob's two wives from whom most of the tribes of Israel were descended).

The son born to Ruth was deemed to be the heir of Ruth's dead husband and therefore Naomi's grandchild. Thus she who 'returned empty' from Moab had a child to care for in her declining years, to give her the love and companionship she needed.

Now comes the amazing part of the story. We learn that this baby, the child of the Moabitess, was the grandfather of David, the king who symbolised the greatness of Israel. For the Christian reader, the last few verses recall the first chapter of Matthew's Gospel, where we read that Jesus, too, was a descendant of this lowly foreign girl.

☐ *Let us remember that God can use the small and humble, and the outcast, to fulfil his purpose for men and women.*

For group discussion and personal thought

What do you think was involved when Ruth chose to accompany Naomi to Bethlehem (Ruth 1.16–17)? Was she being disloyal to her own family and people? When must even family love give way to a greater loyalty?

Sunday June 13   Acts 2.37–47*
THE CHURCH'S UNITY AND FELLOWSHIP
We should note carefully the events in the experience of these new church members. We may sum them up in this way: there was conversion, growth in Christian education, constant communion with their fellow-Christians, sharing in a ritual that helped them to remember and encouraged their spiritual growth, a development of their prayer-life, and a practical expression of love to others.

We are church members. All the above elements are to be found in various measure in our modern experience of churchmanship. But we need constantly to ask ourselves if we are weak or slack in any one of them.

● **Conversion.** Have we personally accepted Christ?

- **Growth in Christian understanding.** Is our understanding of the faith deeper than it was, say, ten years ago?
- **Rituals.** Do we understand the purpose and value of these or have they become a mere habit with us?
- **Communion with fellow-Christians.** How genuine is it within our church – and with members of other churches?
- **Prayer.** Have we really learned the art of praying?
- **Practice.** How concerned are we about those in need?

☐ *Lord, help us to ask these questions with honesty and to act courageously upon the answers you give us.*

Monday June 14

The vocation of a prophet was a frightening responsibility. We read in the Old Testament of several prophets who were afraid or reluctant to preach the message God gave them, but only Jonah tried to escape his call by fleeing the country.

▶ Read **Jonah 1.1–6.**

There was a historical prophet called Jonah, mentioned in 2 Kings 14.25, who lived in Gath-hepher, near Nazareth. The author of the book uses him as the basis for a story which teaches about the dominion of God and the role of Israel. It has been suggested that Jonah is a symbol for the nation.

God called him to go to Nineveh, the great Assyrian city to the far north-east of his home, but Jonah went south-west to Joppa and embarked for Tarshish, probably in Spain – the furthest place he could go from Nineveh.

The sailors did not know God, but were ready to call on him in case he might be able to help them (verse 6). Jonah knew him, and knew that his dominion extended over all nations, but foolishly tried to escape from him.

When God calls us to do something we do not like, we may try to avoid it, but he will call us back to the task – not by a storm, but by inner turmoil and the pricking of conscience.

☐ *Lord, help me to hear your voice, to understand what you want me to do, and to obey gladly.*

Tuesday June 15

God is not only the Father of all people, but the maker and ruler of the world of nature. The Jews feared the sea, and often used it as a symbol of evil, but they had to learn that it was under the control of God.

▶ Read **Jonah 1.7–17**.

The sailors were Gentiles and Jonah was not interested in preaching to them. However, under their interrogation (verse 8) he could not help revealing the truth about God, who had made the sea, and was therefore responsible for the storm. Despite himself, he was preaching to Gentiles.

The sailors' response to God, unlike that of Jonah, was simple and direct. They recognised his work in the stilling of the storm, and worshipped him.

Jonah now knew that he could not escape from God by sea, yet he still seemed prepared to drown rather than preach to the Ninevites. God did not let him drown, however. The author tells how he arranged for a sea creature to swallow him and keep him safe. We do not need to speculate about what the creature was, or how Jonah stayed alive. Rather, the writer is using a well-known legend to demonstrate God's sovereignty and the working out of his will for men.

☐ *Lord, help me to see you at work in all your creation.*

Wednesday June 16   Jonah 2.1–10

We have seen God as Lord of all nations and of nature; now he is shown as the Lord of life and death. *Sheol* ('hell', AV) was the Jewish name for the abode of the dead – a shadowy realm, a pale reflection of earthly life. In the earlier part of their history the Jews believed that to dwell in *Sheol* was to be cut off from God (compare Psalm 115.17). It was only gradually that they learned of the extent of his dominion over the living and the dead.

When the people of Israel were exiled in Babylon they went through an experience that seemed like a kind of death. They felt cut off from God's presence and deprived of his love. God had rescued them from their desolation, as he had saved Jonah from drowning. Now they had to understand what work he had for them to do.

We sometimes use the metaphor of drowning to express the guilt and depression that can overcome us. Yet, however deep we sink, God can rescue us.

☐ *'I am convinced that there is nothing in death or life . . . nothing in all creation that can separate us from the love of God in Christ Jesus our Lord.' (Romans 8.38–39)*

When God called him a second time, Jonah behaved as a prophet should, and obeyed at once. The period of forty days (verse 4) is often used in the Bible to denote a time spent in fasting or retreat from the world. It was a long enough period for the people of Nineveh to repent of their sins.

Like the sailors on the ship, the people of Nineveh reacted at once to God's word, and showed their penitence by mourning in sackcloth and by fasting. The whole population of the city, both human and animal, joined in the expression of grief and repentance. It was not merely a ritual response to Jonah's message; they also turned from their wicked and violent ways (verse 8).

In verse 10 we read how God 'repented', changed his decision about the fate of the Ninevites, in response to their penitence and change of heart. The word 'repent' here does not mean that God was sorry for wrong. The Ninevites had shown that they were turning from sin to follow the way they knew was right, and God responded to them.

It often needs the threat of some great disaster to make us see the error of our ways; but it is better if we can live always remembering God's presence and behaving as he has shown us we should.

☐ *Make the thought of the last paragraph the theme of your prayers.*

Friday June 18

We might expect that Jonah would rejoice at the repentance of the Ninevites and the demonstration of God's mercy and love. Instead he behaved in what was almost a childish fit of sulking.

▶ Read **Jonah 4.1–5.**

Jonah, as a prophet, had an insight into the nature of God: he knew what God would do, but he did not agree with it. Ironically the words Jonah quoted in verse 2, from Exodus 34.6–7, show how God's loving and forgiving nature was the basis of the covenant with Israel. Jonah was jealous of this privilege of the Jews and did not wish it to be extended to other nations.

It is very tempting to keep one's good fortune for oneself instead of sharing it with others. The Jews did not wish to see God's love shared with other peoples. Often we find it hard to be glad when someone from outside the church as we know it experiences God's grace. Although we have the teaching of Jesus about God's forgiveness, we often find it hard to accept in practice.

☐ *Forgive us the wrong we have done,*
as we have forgiven those who have wronged us.

(Matthew 6.12)

Saturday June 19   Jonah 4.6–11

In these verses we see how irrational and childish Jonah really was. He was joyful when the plant grew up to give him shade, and he then plunged into the depths of despair when it died. His petty care for the plant is contrasted with God's loving care for the great city and its inhabitants. Notice that the book ends with a question: the Jews needed to understand and accept God's concern for everyone in the world, but would they do so?

We accept intellectually that all men are God's children, but it is hard to realise that everyone in our town, or even everyone in our road, is a unique being, made in the image of God and under his care. The keener we are as church members, the easier it is to be involved with our own concerns and shut out those outside our circle. Outsiders often see a church as an enclosed group cut off from the rest of the world by a barrier of smugness and indifference. But if we really follow the teaching of the Bible we shall be open to all and show the love of God to everyone.

☐ *What can we do to work God's work, to prosper and increase*
The brotherhood of all mankind, the reign of the Prince of peace?
What can we do to hasten the time, the time that shall surely be,
When the earth shall be filled with the glory of God as the
waters cover the sea?   *Arthur C. Ainger*

For group discussion and personal thought

Read again Jonah 4.1–4. Why was Jonah angry when the people of Nineveh repented? Contrast his attitude with that of Jesus toward repentant sinners, and consider how we can overcome the temptation to feel as Jonah did.

Sunday June 20

THE CHURCH'S CONFIDENCE IN CHRIST

Today's notes are in the form of two short dramatic acts:

Act 1 *Scene – the high priest's house in Jerusalem. Time – Passover. Jesus has been arrested. Peter is sitting by the fire among members of the high priest's household.*

Serving-maid This man was with him too.

Peter Woman, I do not know him.

Another You also are one of them.

Peter No, I am not.

A third person Of course this fellow was with him. He must have been; he is a Galilean!

Peter Man, I do not know what you are talking about.

Act 2 *Scene – the same high priest's house in Jerusalem. Time – about two months later.*

▶ Now read **Acts 4.5–12.***

Same man, same place, same powerful rulers. But the contrast in Peter's demeanour and behaviour – in a few short weeks – is almost unbelievable! What has happened? What had previously seemed to be the defeat of his Master is now recognised as victory. The significance of Jesus' teaching, acts and death has come alive, and he is actually there with Peter bringing power and serenity.

☐ *Pray that the Church today may discover that her risen Lord still reigns – and will reign for ever and ever.*

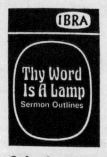

ACTS 18–28

Notes by Revd Michael J. Quicke, MA

Michael Quicke is minister of St Andrew's Street Baptist Church, Cambridge. He has previously ministered at Blackburn, Lancashire, and also served as Secretary for Student Work in the Baptist Union of Great Britain and Ireland.

These last chapters of *Acts* continue the exciting story of Paul's missionary journeys – and exciting it is! Paul dominates events. We see him in riots, before judges, in prison and in a shipwreck; teaching, encouraging, healing, confronting and always using every opportunity to preach the good news.

The constant opposition from Jews, because Gentile Christians were entering the Church through Paul's ministry, forms a backdrop to some vividly described drama. This opposition forces the final, eventful journey to Rome.

As we read this, not only will our understanding of a great Christian missionary be deepened, but our life and witness today will be challenged.

Suggestions for further reading

The Acts of the Apostles by William Barclay, Daily Study Bible (Saint Andrew Press);

Acts of the Apostles edited by J.W. Packer, Cambridge Bible Commentaries (Cambridge University Press).

Monday June 21

'Half-way' Christians are people who know only enough of Christ to make following him an effort rather than a joy. As Paul travels to strengthen converts he meets several 'half-way' Christians.

▶ Read **Acts 18.23 to 19.7.**

Apollos and the Ephesians have three things in common:

● **A defective faith.** At first they knew only the baptism of John the Baptist, which spoke of just half of the Christian experience. This baptism stressed repentance from sin without the accompanying power of Christ's forgiveness and the Holy Spirit to live the new life.

● **A complete experience.** When Apollos and the Ephesians have the Holy Spirit explained to them, they make a full commitment. Note their different responses. For Apollos there does not seem to be the 'speaking in tongues' of the Ephesians. There is always a rich variety to Christian experience.

● **A proclaimed faith.** Lastly, all of them declare the good news. Their spiritual experience is no private matter. So often we confuse what is personal with what is private. Although faith is always personal, it should never be private. Through the boldness of Apollos and the Ephesians the story goes on. Apollos becomes a leader in Corinth, and about Ephesus we shall hear tomorrow.

☐ *Lord, grant me in my personal faith **fullness** and in my public witness **boldness**.*

Tuesday June 22   Acts 19.8–20

Ephesus was to prove an important missionary base but, as usual, Paul's ministry begins with strong opposition. Note the two completely different levels of opposition:

● There is **human opposition** which forces Paul to abandon the synagogue as the place for preaching. Instead he begins to hold open meetings in a lecture-hall belonging to a local philosopher, Tyrannus.

● There is **spiritual opposition.** There is the Christian world of the miraculous where, in the name of Jesus Christ, extraordinary things are accomplished. The unusual tokens (verse 12) are reminiscent of Jesus' cloak (Luke 8.44). But there is also the dark realm of magic which had considerable power in Ephesus as is evidenced in the value of books burned – equivalent to a well-paid man's annual salary.

It is most disquieting to learn of the rise of occultism today. Recently the Church of England has emphasised the need for trained exorcists to help people disturbed by the occult. Some careful research concludes that in nine cases out of ten those dabbling in magic and spiritualism are harmed physically, mentally or spiritually.

☐ *Today's missionaries continue to face opposition – right where we are!*

This description of the riot in Ephesus is a piece of first-rate journalism. Written racily and yet full of accurate facts and personalities, it gives real colour to the drama.

Ephesus was an important religious centre with its temple of Diana or Artemis – one of the Seven Wonders of the World. We can easily picture events beginning with the rabble-rousing of Demetrius and concluding in the town clerk's brilliant leadership.

We should take special notice about the cause of the riot. Was the anger of the crowd caused primarily because Christianity was threatening their religion or their economics? There seems to be a good clue in verse 27 where Demetrius is concerned first and foremost about his business, and only as an afterthought about the goddess! The truth is that they had made a god of their standard of living.

Unfortunately, the application is all too close to home. In his book *Rich Christians in an Age of Hunger*, Ronald Sider concludes that 'the majority of affluent "Christians" of all theological labels have bowed the knee to mammon'. Jesus said: 'Where your treasure is, there will your heart be also.' (Matthew 6.21)

☐ *Is our treasure material or spiritual?*

Today's reading has the vivid realism of a travel-diary. Verse 5 shows that Luke joins the team and now he writes 'us' instead of 'them'. The firsthand reporting gives not only names and places but eye-witness details like the many lamps burning (verse 8).

Note how two different elements combine in these verses:

● **Common sense** determines that Paul should avoid the Jews who are plotting his death (verse 3). Although Paul sometimes received special guidance, he never dispensed with using basic common sense to avoid unnecessary trouble. God gives us minds that we might use them!

● The **miraculous** intervenes as Eutychus is taken up alive after his fall (verses 10, 12). This story is deliberately included by Luke to show that the kind of miracle in the Old Testament, as when Elijah revives the widow's son (1 Kings 17.17-24), can happen again.

The Christian continues to live in a world where alongside common sense there must always be room for God to act.

As Corrie ten Boom asserts: 'God raises the level of the impossible.'

☐ *O Lord of surprises, grant me not to be lazy in thought nor narrow in expectation.*

Friday June 25

Saying a final goodbye concentrates the mind. In his urgent compulsion to reach Jerusalem, Paul makes time to say goodbye to a group who have to travel some thirty miles from Ephesus to hear him. Strangely, this is the only occasion in *Acts* when a direct speech by Paul to Christians is recorded.

▶ Read **Acts 20.13–24.**

There are two intense themes embedded in this first part of Paul's speech:

● There is **suffering.** Preaching the gospel has brought him suffering in the past and will probably do so in the future. The greatest saints have always seemed to have suffered. Sadhu Sundar Singh, the missionary to Tibet, travelled backwards and forwards from India through the mountains on foot. Once, when he was desperately ill, he collapsed on the mountainside. A companion bent over him to find him smiling and saying in a low voice: 'I am so happy: so glad to suffer for my Master.'

● There is **selflessness.** Verse 24 is the true Christian response to the Master who calls his followers to deny themselves, take up their cross and follow him.

☐ *Christ of the upward way,*
   My guide divine,
Where thou hast set thy feet
   May I place mine.

Walter J. Mathams

Saturday June 26   Acts 20.25–38

At heart Paul was a pastor, and his deep pastoral concern for people is reflected in these words to the Ephesian church leaders. He sets before them two things:

● A commission to be shepherds (verse 28), to oversee their flock amidst threats from outside and inside. Unfortunately, sheep are all too apt an analogy for people. Sheep are not noted for their cleverness, individuality or character; we say 'silly sheep', 'sheeplike', 'sheepish'! Sheep need care and attention, just as we do.

Juan Carlos Ortiz, in his book *Disciple*, tells of an old woman to whom he was introduced in Argentina with a family beginning with six children and thirty-six grandchildren. He calculated its expansion could reach 216 great-grandchildren, and 1,296 great-great-grandchildren. He posed the question how this lady could manage such a large family to which he received the reply: 'I didn't. I just took care of the six. And each of them took care of their own six.' That is the kind of shepherding principle the Church needs.

● **An example of leadership.** Paul underlines his purity of motive in preaching the gospel (verses 33–34) and the quality of his self-giving. Just how good an example Paul was is best seen in the deep emotion and sadness at his leaving.

□ *Pray for church leaders as they shepherd God's flock.*

For group discussion and personal thought
Study Paul's speech to the Ephesian elders in Acts 20.18–35. This shows his great pastoral concern for his people. How can we become better 'shepherds' in our own church community?

Sunday June 27 Acts 8.26–38*
THE CHURCH'S MISSION TO THE INDIVIDUAL
The communication of the gospel was, and is, the Church's task. It is done at two levels:
● Through its public proclamations, evangelical campaigns, sermons and addresses, radio and television programmes;
● Through the private witness of individuals to individuals.

Both have their place, but many of us could testify that the latter is the more effective of the two. Many a man has entered into a meaningful experience of Christ as a result of a quiet conversation with just one other person with whom he has been able to explore his own particular needs, doubts and hopes. Today's reading is about such an event.

The man was an Ethiopian – and so a Gentile, but a Gentile adherent of the Jewish faith. He was a eunuch – and such were excluded from the community of Israel (see Deuteronomy 23.1). He therefore had special problems. Philip was able to offer him the Christ who fulfilled the hopes and removed the hindrances of the faith he held.

☐ *A thought about Christ:*

Whose mercy is divinely free
For all the fallen race and – me.

Charles Wesley

Monday June 28

How do we know what is the right thing to do when we are faced with a difficult choice? Henry Drummond said there were two classes of people in the world of Christians:

● Those who have God's will in their character;
● Those who have God's will in their career as well as in their character.

▶ Read **Acts 21.1–14.**

Pressure to stop Paul's journey to Jerusalem builds up from spiritually-sensitive people; first, from the Christians at Tyre, and then from those at Caesarea. Even Agabus, who foretells Paul's suffering in Jerusalem in symbolic action just like the prophets of the Old Testament, fails to dissuade Paul. The truth is that suffering is part of Paul's mission, and he will not shrink from going to the place where his Master died. In spite of contrary well-meaning advice, Paul had the 'secret whispering of God in the ear'.

For the spiritually mature that inner voice overrides all others. No wonder Paul wrote: 'The sons of God are those who are guided by the Spirit of God.' (Romans 8.14, Moffatt)

☐ *Guide me, O thou great Jehovah.*

William Williams

Tuesday June 29

Acts 21.15–26

False accusation is one of the toughest tests of Christian maturity. Slander can so easily provoke angry defiance or bitterness. But with the utmost maturity, Paul deals with the malicious rumour that he has become lax about the Jewish law. When James and the elders in Jerusalem confront him with the charge and suggest a course of action, Paul accedes humbly. He joins some poor men and pays for their Jewish ceremony. This was considered an especially pious act which would show Paul's critics that he is still a good Jew.

Why does Paul do this so readily? In part it is because as a great missionary he is concerned to break down every possible barrier and to be conciliatory for the cause of Christ. He sums it up: 'While working with the Jews, I live like a Jew in order to win them.' (1 Corinthians 9.20, GNB)

Hudson Taylor, the renowned missionary to China, found his western dress was proving to be a barrier and resolved that he must transform himself into a Chinese, pigtails and all. As well as adopting Chinese dress, his sandy hair had to be died black and plaited. He records that the effect was immediate; his preaching was more readily acceptable.

Of course, Paul was a Jew all the time, but he went out of his way to allay rumour for the sake of the gospel.

☐ *How careful and mature we have to be as missionaries for Christ!*

Wednesday June 30   Acts 21.27–39

Here is stark tragedy. After the mature attempt at conciliation, about which we read yesterday, Paul is suddenly in danger for his life. The charge against him is deadly serious – that he has taken a Gentile into the inner parts of the temple and so defiled the sacred place. This grave accusation will change Paul's life and lead him through imprisonment and trials to Rome.

But the evidence is pure assumption. Because Paul has been seen with a Gentile in the city someone has jumped to the conclusion that they have been in the temple. From this piece of unfounded gossip springs a riot so serious that Paul is thought by the arresting commander to be a dangerous Egyptian terrorist.

No one engaged in Christian work for long will have avoided the tragedy of opposition and misunderstanding from sincere people who are sincerely wrong. It is part of the picture of the spiritual battle in which the Christian should put on the whole armour of God (see Ephesians 6.10–17).

☐ *Fight the good fight with all thy might;*
Christ is thy strength, and Christ thy right.
Lay hold on life, and it shall be
Thy joy and crown eternally.   *John S. B. Monsell*

Thursday July 1   Acts 21.40 to 22.16

Paul's life is in danger, and this speech is a matter of the utmost importance. See how two characteristics clearly emerge:
● **The hallmark of the preacher.** Paul is making his defence before Jews and no one knows his audience better than he does. Specifically he addresses them. He speaks in Hebrew, the

Jewish language. He mentions Gamaliel, his famous Jewish teacher. He underlines his zealous Jewish past, and name-drops the best possible Jewish witnesses – the high priest and Council (verse 5)! He also emphasises the respectability of Ananias as a Jewish leader. Good preaching always begins where the people are.

● **The hallmark of the Christian.** Soon Paul comes to the heart of the matter – how Christ has met him and changed him. This is the single most important moment in the whole of his life and it must be told.

The Christian's greatest gift to the world is the news that Christ has met him and changed him. Of course our experiences will all be different, but that meeting with Christ will be central to them all. It is the hallmark of the Christian.

☐ *O Lord, help me put the risen Christ at the centre of my life.*

Friday July 2

There is an old story about a negro who tried to gain admittance to a white church in the United States of America and was told to pray for guidance. After two weeks he returned saying how the Lord had told him not to worry because he could not get into that church either! The sad truth is that people can so easily exclude others because of their race or colour. It is only when Paul mentions the Gentiles in his speech that the crowd again erupts in fury.

▶ Read **Acts 22.17–29.**

Even the mention of Paul's part in Stephen's death does not diminish the hatred of this Jewish crowd. Their anger is based partly on fear that their in-group will be threatened by outsiders. Fear rules so many of us. It is fear, too, that grips the Roman centurion and commandant as they realise how near they have come to breaking the law that forbids the flogging of a Roman citizen.

Look at the huge contrast. On the one side, the fear that makes the crowd so bitterly exclusive, and the fear that disturbs the authorities. On the other side there is Paul, calm, dignified and seemingly liberated from fear. But then, that is exactly the promise for the Christian: 'Perfect love banishes fear.' (1 John 4.18)

☐ *Faint not, nor fear; his arm is near;*
He changeth not, and thou art dear.   *John S.B. Monsell*

Saturday July 3

Oliver Cromwell made a famous comment to his portrait-painter: 'Mr Lely, I desire you would use all your skill to paint my picture truly like me, and not flatter me at all; but remark all these roughnesses, pimples, warts, and everything as you see me, otherwise I will never pay a farthing for it.' The only valuable picture of a man is the honest one. Luke gives us just such a portrait of Paul.

▶ Read **Acts 22.30 to 23.11.**

Two things are revealed here about Paul:

● His **quick temper** which bursts out in strong language (verse 3). This was part of Paul's temperament and is indicated elsewhere, for example Acts 15.39.

● His **quick wits** which leads to the dubious strategy of setting the Jewish Council at each other's throats. One of the deepest divisions between Pharisees and Sadducees concerned the resurrection of the dead, which the Sadducees rejected. When Paul deliberately mentions this doctrine he succeeds in stirring up such hatred that the Pharisees are prepared to acquit him to spite the Sadducees.

☐ *Saints are made out of flesh and blood as we are. These weaknesses in Paul only make his abiding qualities more remarkable.*

> *The saints of God began just like me,*
> *And I mean to be one too.*

Lesbia Scott

For group discussion and personal thought

Read Acts 21.18–26. Why do you think that Paul decided to join these four men in their vow? Is it sometimes right to compromise our principles? When? Consider some particular instances.

Sunday July 4   Acts 11.4–18*

THE CHURCH'S MISSION TO ALL MEN

The intense exclusiveness of the Jews is understandable in the light of their history. Swept away into exile in a foreign country centuries earlier, their unique faith in the one, good God had been in danger of becoming contaminated by pagan superstition. Therefore, when they rebuilt their nation, they highlighted the Jewishness of their faith and put up barriers against non-Jewish practices. Christianity had to break through these barriers if it was to fulfil its conviction that Christ was for all men.

The problem which the Jews faced – their relations with people of other faiths – has taken a strange twist for Christians in our time. With a deeper understanding of other world religions, the question arises: What is to be our attitude to other faiths? Many Christians no longer feel able to dismiss them as 'heathen', for all faiths are paths along which people are seeking God. Nevertheless, we believe that if we follow the Christian path truly and share our insights humbly, in the end they, too, will come to acknowledge the Lordship of Christ.

☐ *Jesus the Lord said : 'I am the Light,*
The one true Light of the world am I.'

Anon

Monday July 5

After the uproar in the Jewish Council, Paul is taken to governor Felix at Caesarea for further trial. There he is kept in prison for two years until a new governor Festus is appointed.
▶ Read **Acts 25.1–12.**

Paul's case has become political. What happens to him is important for Jewish-Roman relations. In cowardly compromise Festus delays justice and suggests the Jewish plan for a further trial in Jerusalem.

J. F. Clarke claims: 'Conscience is the root of all true courage.' Certainly Paul's integrity and clear conscience are evident, and courageously he presses for justice. And finally, to resolve the issue, he claims the right of any Roman citizen to be tried by the highest power in the land – the emperor.

Aida of Leningrad was a young Russian girl sent to prison for her religious beliefs in 1968. Michael Bordeaux writes that in her trial and imprisonment perhaps the most remarkable feature was her utter integrity of character. In her final trial speech she said: 'I'm not a heroine. I love freedom and would very much like to be free now with my family and friends. But I can't buy freedom at any price; I don't want to act against my conscience.'

☐ *Lord, give me courage to be true to him who is the truth.*

Tuesday July 6

Acts 27.1–12

Luke's travel-diary gives great detail as Paul begins his voyage to Rome. Obviously, the wind was the dictator of any progress –

or the lack of it! But glowing among the facts is the kindness shown by Julius, the Roman centurion. Not only does he allow Paul to meet his friends at Sidon (verse 3), but we may assume that he asks Paul – an experienced traveller – for his judgement as to whether they should stay or continue the voyage (verse 10). Although Paul's advice is eventually rejected, he clearly enjoys the special relationship that kindness makes possible. What a difference that must have made to the whole journey!

Sir Wilfred Grenfell, the famous Labrador doctor, tells of the very first time, as a young doctor, that he boarded a vessel bound for the deep-sea fishermen. When he arrived at Yarmouth he saw the small craft in the darkness and felt his courage fail him. Suddenly a cheery, welcoming voice on deck called out to him and, encouraged, he went aboard to begin a lifetime's service as a medical missionary. Looking back on that kind voice he later wrote: 'What big things hang on a smile and a cheery word no man can ever say!'

☐ *Christians especially should know all about kindness. It is a fruit of the Spirit that should be growing in us all.*

Wednesday July 7   Acts 27.13–26

The perilous drama of the storm is so vivid that we can almost feel the sea-spray! The favourable wind was replaced by a devastating north-easter. Corn ships could be large – up to 43 metres long and 11 metres wide (140 feet by 36 feet). In a storm they were cumbersome; there was no rudder but only two paddles on either side under the stern. There was only one mast and an unwieldy, square sail. In this bad storm they could only drift helplessly, undergirding the ship to reduce leaks and lightening the load.

In all the terror the prisoner Paul emerges as the man for the hour. With great courage he speaks words of encouragement, not borne of vague optimism but grounded in a fresh revelation of God.

☐ *Let us remember today's travellers on the seas:*

> *Eternal Father, strong to save,*
> *Whose arm hath bound the restless wave,*
> *Who bidd'st the mighty ocean deep*
> *Its own appointed limits keep,*
> * O hear us when we cry to thee*
> * For those in peril on the sea.*

William Whiting

Thursday July 8

Perhaps you have heard it said: 'If you can keep your head when people all around are losing theirs, then clearly you are out of touch!' But the truth is that a special kind of leader often emerges out of a crisis where others panic. Paul was just such a man.

▶ Read **Acts 27.27–44.**

Note Paul's leadership qualities:

● He has **great practical sense.** Paul's alertness and incisive comment (verse 31) prevent the sailors from abandoning the ship. He also insists on the crew and passengers having something to eat. It is understandable that appetites were poor but strength would be needed for beaching the boat, and Paul leads the way.

● He has **a deep spiritual sense.** Paul makes the meal a kind of communion. In the midst of the raging storm he gives thanks to the God who would not abandon them.

As the ship runs aground the stature of Paul is so high that it saves the other prisoners from death (verses 42–43).

Many great Christians have had such qualities of leadership. For example, it was said of John Wesley: he 'had a strangely warmed heart allied to a strangely cool head'. Certainly Paul had a cool head as well as missionary zeal!

☐ *Lord, grant me a cool head and a warm heart.*

Friday July 9   Acts 28.1–15

The final lap of Paul's long journey to Rome has several interesting points. In particular, note the two kinds of welcome that he receives:

● **The native welcome in Malta** is especially kind, from the common people right through to the chief official, Publius. Again, Paul is right in the centre of the action as he helps to make the fire, and amazes the onlookers when he calmly shakes off the snake before it can bite him. Incidentally, some commentators note that the verb 'cured' (verse 9) actually means 'received medical attention'. Could this suggest that Luke himself helped as a doctor – the first recorded medical missionary?

● **The Christian welcome** as he nears Rome. Roman believers came as far as Appii Forum (43 miles from Rome) and Tres Tabernae (33 miles from Rome) in order to welcome Paul. The fellowship of believers goes the 'extra mile' in that further dimension that belongs to the Christian family. When Christians greet one another it should be much more than natural hospitality – for it is the welcome of a brother or a sister! No wonder Paul feels encouraged.

☐ *Blest be the tie that binds*
Our hearts in Christian love.   *John Fawcett*

Saturday July 10

What would you like to see in this last section of Paul's story: what happened when he appeared before the emperor; or how his life ended?

▶ Read **Acts 28.16–31.**

Are you disappointed at this ending? At first sight it may seem a very unsatisfactory conclusion to some thirty years' story. And yet there are two great themes which symbolise the whole story:

● **'to the Jews first'** was always Paul's strategy. Even in Rome after the tragic hostility of the Jews, Paul still wants to tell Jewish leaders the good news (verse 17).

● **'then to the Gentiles'** always followed in Paul's mission plans. Paul sums up the rejection by the Jews as he quotes (in verses 26–27) from Isaiah 6.9–10. Yet this tragedy is used by God in the fulfilment of his purposes, as Paul blazes the pioneer trail of new churches amongst the Gentiles.

While he waits in Rome he loses no opportunity to pass on the gospel message. As well as writing to new churches like the Philippians, Ephesians and Colossians, his home becomes another mission base for preaching. We do not know what happened to him, but the most important thing is that the triumph of Jesus Christ which he preached will never end.

☐ *The story continues right on – to you and me.*

Christ for the world! we sing :
The world to Christ we bring
With fervent prayer.   *Samuel Wolcott*

For group discussion and personal thought

Paul received hospitality in many places throughout his long missionary service for Christ (for example, see Acts 28.1–2,7). He urges the giving of hospitality upon other Christians in Romans 12.13. Why is it so important? How could we practise it more?

THE NEW MAN

There is a phrase used by some Christian writers today which seems to sum up the basic thought of today's reading. It is: **'Become what you are.'** Paul's letter to the Ephesians is largely devoted to a description of the characteristics of Christians as they are ideally, and an appeal that they should live up to that ideal. In Christ, says Paul, warped human nature is restored to God's original plan for it – namely, made in his image and likeness (see Genesis 1.26). We human beings are the children of God, made by him to be reflections of his own character. Christ came to tell us this. We may well believe it, but unfortunately we do not always rise to our high destiny!

This is a timely warning to all Christians, for it has to be admitted that Christians, as much as non-Christians, can show some nasty traits at times. Who of us can honestly say that we never display in ourselves falsehoods, grudges, harmful speech, destructive anger or selfishness? The 'old human nature' is always on hand to oust the 'new nature'. So Paul's simple instructions to the Christians of Ephesus are important for us, too. Yes, we do love Christ; but every new day we need his help to become what we are – to put on our true nature.

☐ *Think on this phrase from verse 24: 'Put on the new nature of God's creating,' or as the GNB translates it: 'You must put on the new self, which is created in God's likeness.'*

BIBLE
storytime

*For children up to
seven years old*

A series of six books each containing twenty Bible stories retold in simple language. Includes related activies and prayers. Also available on cassette.
Ask your IBRA group secretary for details or write to the appropriate address on the back cover.

PRAYERS OF THE BIBLE

Notes by Revd Howard Rady, BA

Howard Rady is minister of Whetstone United Reformed Church and headmaster of a boys' preparatory school. Previously he taught in London and Dorset.

Prayer is the way in which we set aside time to experience God so that we may be aware of him at all other times in our lives. Sometimes the way of prayer seems easy, at other times it is hard and grey. Indeed, many of us will probably have tucked away in the 'bankrupt corner' of our bookshelves various 'helps to prayer' which have long since 'gone dead' for us.

This section on *Prayers of the Bible* is not one more attempt to help us to pray better – although it may conceivably do that. Rather, it seeks to confront us with some of the men and women of the Bible turning to God in prayer. And as we watch them in our imagination and listen to them offering their praises and petitions, we may find new encouragement to continue exploring the way of prayer for ourselves.

Suggestions for further reading

Praying the Psalms by Leslie E. Stradling (SPCK);

The Prayers of the New Testament by Donald Coggan (Hodder and Stoughton).

Monday July 12   **Psalm 139.1–12**

It is quite a severe shock the first time we become truly aware that God really **does** know everything there is to know about us; yet God's knowledge of us is the basis of all prayer. The experience is both a thrilling and an alarming one and we may find ourselves reacting in conflicting ways:

● **We may want to escape.** To have to face this all-knowing God is the last thing we want to do and it is highly disturbing. But, as Paul Tillich wrote in *Shaking of the Foundations*, 'A man who has never tried to flee from God has never experienced the God who is really God.'

● **We may want to rejoice.** After all, if God's interest in us is as personal as the psalmist says it is, then we need never again feel lonely or afraid. His is a love that will not let us go; and even when we lose our hold upon him, he still holds us.

The poet Francis Thompson likened God to the 'Hound of Heaven' who tracked him down even into his own personal hell and pit of despair in order to win his love. It is well worth pondering these lines which reveal why Thompson was so long in responding to the divine love:

☐   *For, though I knew his love who followed,*
            Yet was I sore adread
      Lest, having him, I might have naught beside.

Tuesday July 13

Asked what had struck her most on her return to Britain after several years in Papua New Guinea, a missionary replied, 'The pace of life.' She had noticed how lacking in peace and tranquillity her country had become since her last furlough.

▶ Read **Psalm 131.**

A small baby feeding at his mother's breast will complain if his wants are not satisfied. But when he is weaned he becomes less demanding, enjoying his mother for what she is and not for what she gives. How frequently we resemble a fretful babe-in-arms when we pray, complaining to God about one thing after another! How much we need to be weaned from our self-centredness and to be calmed by him!

Within the wider Church there is often something approaching fretfulness in our continual demands for unity. Where can we find guidance on how to pray?

▶ Read **Psalm 133.**

Unity is something which has to permeate the atmosphere like the subtle fragrance of the oil with which the high priest was anointed. The harmony among those who work together for God ought to have the same effect on the rest of the community as dew has upon parched land.

☐   *'Lord, grant me the serenity to accept the things I cannot change, the courage to change the things I can, and the wisdom to know the difference.' (Reinhold Niebuhr)*

Wednesday July 14   Psalm 19

The vicar of a Cornish farming parish, distressed that the only service attracting a large congregation was the Harvest Festival, used the occasion to deliver the following rebuke: '. . . and as I shall have no other opportunity, may I wish you all a happy Christmas and joyful Easter!'

Some people's religion is almost unashamedly 'nature worship'. They feel a genuine dependence upon the one who sustains the universe, but they want no other revelation of God. Nature tells them all they need to know. But does it? Or was Emil Brunner right when he said that, when confronted with the wonders of creation, men are like dogs in an art gallery – observing the pictures but failing to 'see' them? For beautiful though the 'book' of nature is, we need a far more clearly written book before we can adore God for what he is.

The Jews believed they had such a book in the *Torah* (the law of the Lord) – the instructions which came from God through the utterances of priests and prophets. They treated it as absolutely dependable and better than anything money could buy. Christians believe that God has much to teach them through the inspired writings of the Bible, but to them the final revelation of God himself is the 'Word made flesh' in the person of Jesus Christ.

☐   *The voice that rolls the stars along*
     Speaks all the promises.   *Isaac Watts*

Thursday July 15

Many people resent talk about sin and guilt because they are suffering from a childhood hangover connected with naughtiness and punishment. This, however, does not mean that there is no such thing as a genuine 'conviction of sin'; there is, and it can lead us to the very throne of grace.

▶ Read **Psalm 51.1–17.**

No one had to prove to the psalmist that he had sinned. Like Saul Kane in Masefield's poem *The Everlasting Mercy*, he was conscious of 'all the harm I done in being me'. He was sure there was something wrong deep down in his personality and that only God could remedy this. But besides seeking forgiveness he asked for a new attitude towards life – something we need to pray for when we have failed as Christians:

● A **willingness** to learn more of the truth about ourselves.
    Sincerity and truth are what you require;
    fill my mind with your wisdom.   *(verse 6, GNB)*

139

- A **desire** for greater stability and loyalty to God (verse 10).
- A **longing** for a new spirit of joy which will enable others to find their way back to God (verses 12–13).
- A **confidence** that God does not reject the prayer uttered in humble self-honesty (verse 17).

☐ *'The forgiveness of God is, in my opinion, the most powerful therapeutic idea in the world.' (Leslie Weatherhead)*

Friday July 16   Psalm 107.1–16

A mother and her small son on a train journey got into conversation with an old gentleman. When he produced a bag of sweets the mother was acutely embarrassed by the way her son filled his mouth without a word of thanks. 'What do you say, Johnny?' she challenged. 'More please!' came the sticky answer.

How like us this is in our individual approach to God! We forget to thank him sufficiently for past blessings and concentrate on asking for more. And in our corporate worship it is very much the same: various groups of people are prayed for in public, but very rarely do we hear them offering thanks.

Today's psalm may have been used in some annual thanksgiving service in the temple, during which representative groups – such as desert travellers and prisoners – expressed their gratitude in a great litany of thanksgiving.

Is there any way in which present day Christians can be given greater opportunity to give thanks publicly during worship? Would a service structured on this psalm provide a suitable framework?

☐   *Ponder anew*
      All the Almighty can do,
He who with love doth befriend thee.   *Joachim Neander*

Saturday July 17   Psalm 72.1–19

Christians have a responsibility to pray for their country and its government (see 1 Timothy 2.1–4). We must recognise that, without some temporal ordering of society, life for most people is going to be 'nasty, brutish and short'. Nor should we be afraid to aim high in our prayers and, following the psalmist's example, ask for:

- **Justice for all** (verses 1–4). To champion the just cause of those in need is one of the fundamental tasks of government.

This is why we must pray that our leaders are taught of God, the fount of all justice.

● **Prosperity for all** (verses 15–16). Firmly fixed in the minds of the men of the Old Testament was the view that people and land belong together and that the welfare of the soil depends on the conduct of those it supports. There is a basic truth here; for the more governments concentrate on the conservation rather than the exploitation of natural resources, the greater will be the prosperity of present and future generations.

☐ *The powers ordained by thee*
   With heavenly wisdom bless;
  May they thy servants be,
    And rule in righteousness.

William W. How

For group discussion and personal thought

Why do we so often neglect to give thanks to God for his past goodness? Read the whole of Psalm 107 and make your own list of blessings for which you want to give God thanks. Then consider whether such thanksgivings should be included in public worship as well as in private prayer.

Sunday July 18   **Romans 8.1–11***

THE MORE EXCELLENT WAY

In his argument, Paul refers here to different kinds of law. Human nature has been corrupted by 'the law of sin and death' so that we are cut off from fellowship with God. The Jewish law of Moses was useful in enforcing good behaviour, but it cannot by itself bridge the gap between us and God since it does not cure our sinful human nature. But if we will let Christ enter our lives, the 'life-giving law of the Spirit' sets us free from 'the law of sin and death'; with him there is forgiveness and new hope.

There are also two different levels of living, according to Paul: 'the level of our lower nature' and, in contrast, 'the level of the spirit'. The former spells death, the latter brings life and peace.

What Paul is saying is that in Jesus, God has offered us his love, forgiveness and power which can transform us and give us lives filled with victory, peace and love – a more excellent way indeed!

□ *My Saviour ! how shall I proclaim,*
How pay the mighty debt I owe ?
Let all I have, and all I am,
Ceaseless to all thy glory show.

Paulus Gerhardt

Monday July 19   **2 Chronicles 6.12–21**

Some present-day Christians question the need for having special buildings set apart for worship. They argue that the church is made up of people, and that where there is a strong sense of fellowship the surroundings hardly matter at all. It is therefore relevant to notice the purpose behind the erection of the first permanent building dedicated to the worship of God: that it might be the place where God 'set his name' (verse 20, RSV). In other words, it was intended to be a visible witness to the supreme majesty of the invisible God.

And what of the witness of the prayers we use in public worship? Do they speak to the congregation of God's wonder and sovereignty? Modern man's fascination with 'unidentified flying objects' and films like *Star Wars* suggests that he is beginning to think of the universe as a potentially hostile place. When, as Sir Frank Catherwood warns, the popular imagination transforms the twinkling friendly star into a menacing spaceship, then it is high time to reaffirm that God is greater than the whole universe (verse 18). Indeed, we can hardly do better than make this a constant theme in all our worship.

□ *Praise, glory, worship, thanksgiving, honour, power and might, belong to our God for ever and ever !*

Tuesday July 20

The writer Anatole France once complained that certain scholars had ink in their veins instead of blood and that they never looked out of a window. This popular picture of the man of wisdom is quite out of keeping with the biblical view which joins theoretical thought with its practical application. Thus to be complete persons we need both the ability to judge and test ideas and the skill to convert them into effective actions. This is precisely what Solomon sought when he prayed for 'wisdom and knowledge' (verse 10).

▶ Read **2 Chronicles 1.7–12.**

The most striking feature of Solomon's prayer is his meekness – his willingness to be taught and disciplined by God. We are told that as a consequence he would receive many of the material blessings he had not asked for. Nor should this surprise us. For Jesus himself taught that the rewards of meekness are very great indeed: 'Blessed are the meek, for they shall inherit the earth.' (Matthew 5.5, RSV)

☐ *'O God, by whom the meek are guided in judgement, and light riseth up in darkness for the godly, grant us, in all our doubts and uncertainties, the grace to ask what thou wouldest have us do, that the Spirit of wisdom may save us from all false choices, and that in thy light we may see light, and in thy straight path may not stumble.' (William Bright)*

Wednesday July 21   Judges 13.1–13

Married couples, anticipating the birth of a longed-for first child, are often filled with a sense of their inadequacy. Manoah and his wife were no exception. But in their case the sense of inadequacy was reinforced by an awareness that theirs was to be a very special child, a 'Nazirite', that is someone consecrated for special service to God. Their plea for help and guidance (verse 8) was met by the assurance that, although they felt unfitted for the responsibility, nevertheless God could work wonders (see verse 19).

Not long after the end of the Second World War an ex-Royal Marine, playing with his small son, tuned in to a Sunday morning radio sermon entitled, *I can't cope but God can.* As he listened he knew the task of bringing up his son was too great for him; and that evening he set out for the nearest church. 'I've come,' he said to the steward at the door, 'to learn everything you can teach me about God.' Within a few months he had confessed Christ in baptism and had discovered one who could enable him to cope with tasks beyond his own strength and understanding.

☐ *Grant those entrusted with the care*
Of precious life from thee,
Thy grace, that worthy of the gift
And faithful they may be.   *Albert F. Bayly*

Thursday July 22   Jeremiah 20.7–18

Today's reading lays bare the inmost struggle in the life of one of God's greatest servants. Jeremiah had been attempting a task which threatened to overwhelm him, and here he is giving voice to his doubts about being called to the prophetic ministry. In particular, he believes that God's earlier promises to him (see Jeremiah 1.6–10) were but a deceitful bait, luring him to undertake a work beyond his resources. He simply cannot understand what God is doing.

There is always the danger that we shall not be open and honest in our prayers, attempting to hide from God any grievances we may think we have against him. To some extent this reveals just how prone we are to treat God as someone who can be kept in the dark about our feelings; but it also suggests how uncertain we are about his capacity to accept us as we are. God's greatest saints have never been inhibited in this way. Indeed, Theresa of Avila went as far as to tell God that it was not surprising he had so few friends if he treated them all as he was treating her. Even so, like Jeremiah, her obedience and loyalty remained utterly firm. Not to know what God is doing but to trust him just the same – that is a rare kind of faith.

☐   *In my frustration make me sure*
     That thou, my God, art he
     Who buildest something to endure
     From what seems loss to me.   *Leslie D. Weatherhead*

Friday July 23   Nehemiah 2.1–8

Nehemiah's split-second prayer – 'I prayed to the God of heaven' – in the midst of his interview with King Artaxerxes has attracted the attention of many preachers and writers. Rightly they have bidden us use the 'arrow prayer' or 'holy telegram' whenever we are in urgent need of divine wisdom and guidance. What they have not always added is that the instantaneous cry for help is no substitute for a disciplined prayer life. In Nehemiah's own case he had thoroughly prepared himself by prayer and meditation for whatever lay ahead of him (see Nehemiah 1.4–11). No doubt his 'telegram' was the more effective because he was already in the right frame of mind to receive the guidance he prayed for.

Few, if any, of us are likely to have to bear a responsibility as great as Nehemiah's, but we can still find opportunities for the arrow prayer. It oftens helps, for example, to look heavenwards while we wait to get a connection on the telephone, or as we write or go to post a letter. Maybe we shall find we have to replace the receiver, or tear up the letter. A better way of saying what has to be said will have come to us.

☐ *Prayer is the burden of a sigh,*
   The falling of a tear,
 The upward glancing of an eye
  When none but God is near.   *James Montgomery*

Saturday July 24

There is a proper place in the life of the Christian for dreaming dreams; and it can sometimes be the way in which we discover what God is asking us to do.

King David, convinced that it was wrong for him to live in a fine palace while the ark of the covenant was meanly housed in a tent of skins and drapery, began to dream of building a magnificent temple. He consulted the wisest man he knew, the prophet Nathan, and found him in full agreement. But Nathan had spoken out of turn without divine authority, and was to find that when the word of the Lord came to him it was to forbid David to go ahead with his project.

▶ Now read **1 Chronicles 17.15–27.**

How are we to react when our dreams of taking up some new and exciting piece of Christian work come to nothing – when God says 'No'? How are we to pray when the bottom seems to have fallen out of our world? David's prayer is a model of acceptance. He sat in the presence of God reflecting on his goodness and recalling the promises he knew he could count on. He woke up to the fact that being known and loved by God was far more important than anything he could possibly do for God. Can we, like David, extract a blessing from our disappointments?

☐ *'God has more to teach us from his denials than from his permissions.' (Alan Redpath)*

For group discussion and personal thought

'Lord, give me what you are requiring of me.' (St Augustine) In the light of the prayers you have been reading this week would you want to echo this request? Do you agree that the object of prayer is not primarily to obtain answers but to be in union with God? How would you reply to criticism that 'prayer doesn't work'?

THE GIFTS OF THE SPIRIT

People are not all alike. But differences need not lead to competition or jealousy. Rather they should be seen as individual gifts, all of which are necessary for the enrichment of the whole community. Using the metaphor of the human body (verse 12) Paul describes the rich diversity of Christian activity as existing for the upbuilding, not the breaking up, of the Church.

Let us widen Paul's thought and think of the Christian Church as it is today. One denomination excels in its understanding of liturgy; another in Bible exposition; another in charismatic endowment; another in the recognition of the 'inner light'. All are the gifts of the same Spirit. We are learning that the various branches of Christ's Church may gain greatly from one another's insights and traditions and we thank God for that.

Let us widen Paul's thought still further. The world consists of many different cultures, systems of government, racial characteristics. One day, by the grace of God, we shall see these not as points of tension but as means of mutual enrichment. We shall not cease to cherish our own race, our own nation, our own culture, but we shall have learned that we are all part of the one family of man, to whose welfare all our various gifts and cultures may contribute.

☐　*Bind us together, Lord, by your Spirit of love.*

Monday July 26　　　　　　　　　　　　**Luke 2.25–35**

Simeon was one of the 'Quiet of the land' – a small group of Jews who waited in quiet, faithful expectation for the day when God would reveal his Messiah to them. We notice two striking things about him:

● **His attitude.** Because he was waiting upon God, he saw what others missed in the peasant girl and her baby. Whereas others of his advanced years might have been content to dwell on the past, he kept his mind open and receptive, sure that God's best was yet to come.

● **His prayer.** He spoke of:

A fulfilled promise (verse 29). Although God may appear to delay beyond the time we hope for, he never breaks his word.

Enlightenment (verse 32). Whenever Jesus is brought into any situation, there is a dispelling of the darkness and a broadening of our horizons.

Deliverance (verses 30–31). The gospel is more than enlightenment; it is, as Donald Coggan wrote, 'a divine rescue operation directed to man in his need' (see Matthew 1.21).

☐ *Waiting upon God 'is more than putting up with things and keeping quiet until they improve . . . it is the using of a time for waiting to prepare for what is coming, and so to grow in faith' (Leslie Stradling).*

Tuesday July 27

Peter and John had been summoned before a special court to answer the charge that they had healed a man by invoking a name other than God's. Although a large crowd had seen the miracle take place, it seems that no one was willing to give evidence against the apostles, so all the court could do was to let them off with a caution. The reaction of the infant Church was to pray.

▶ Read Acts 4.23–30.

The structure of this prayer is interesting. Notice:

● **The words used to address God** (verse 24). There is no one correct way to call upon God. It is often helpful to use a title which encourages us to look for definite help from God in our particular circumstances.

● **The use of Scripture** (verses 25–26; see Psalm 2.1–2). The occasional use of biblical quotations in our prayers can remind us of others who have previously found support in God.

● **The petitions themselves** (verses 29–30). The disciples left their enemies to God; asked courage for themselves; and prayed that their witness might be accompanied by signs of divine blessing. The crisis they had been through served to concentrate their minds on the true priorities.

☐ *Strong Son of God, when we are timid or uncertain, help us to take our stand on you, the rock of our salvation.*

Wednesday July 28   Acts 9.10–19

Prayer involves learning to live in time and eternity; and, at its best, it brings us into a close companionship with God himself. Ananias' intimate relationship with God enabled him to 'talk through' his doubts about the genuineness of Saul's conversion. There is ample evidence that Ananias was a Christian who listened as well as spoke to God.

In one of his books the Swiss psychiatrist, Paul Tournier, tells how he came to make a great discovery. He used to visit a saintly old pastor who always prayed with him before he left. What struck Tournier most was that the old man's prayer seemed just a continuation of an intimate conversation he was always carrying on with Jesus. This led Tournier to make Jesus the centre of his devotion and his travelling companion in life.

People who talk as if they have a 'hot line' to heaven come in for a good deal of criticism, particularly when they claim they **always** know exactly what the Lord is telling them to do. While resisting any exaggerated claims we should be equally careful not to devalue the possibility for ourselves of a close companionship with God.

☐ *Lord, give me the open ear which is –*
   Alive and quick to hear
      Each whisper of thy word.   *James D. Burns*

Thursday July 29   **1 Corinthians 1.1–9**

It is easy for our prayers of thanksgiving to turn into mere statements of gratitude for the material benefits we receive from God. In today's reading Paul reminds us that what marks out Christians from other worshippers is thanksgiving for the **spiritual blessings** which are ours through Jesus Christ.

● There is the **wonder of 'grace'** (verse 4) – that gracious acceptance and forgiveness which not only puts the sinner 'right with God' but is also the source of all that enriches his life as a Christian.

● There is the **fact of spiritual growth** – something which shows itself in the believer's growing grasp of the implications of the gospel (verses 5–6).

● There is the **phenomenon of 'gifts'** (verse 7, literally 'gifts of grace') which are given to individual Christians to equip them for service.

● Finally, there is the **promise of God's power** to keep the believer firm and true during his earthly life and safe on the day of judgement (verse 8).

☐ *'We bless thee for our creation, preservation, and all the blessings of this life; but above all, for thine inestimable love in the redemption of the world by our Lord Jesus Christ; for the means of grace, and for the hope of glory.' (The General Thanksgiving)*

148

God has chosen Christians to be agents in reconciling the world to himself through Jesus Christ. Such a task would be altogether impossible were it not for the amazing resources put at our disposal. Even so, our use of them is scant – which is why we cannot be too familiar with the prayer that comprises our reading today. In it Paul asks:

● That the Holy Spirit will strengthen his readers in their **'inner being'** (verse 16) – a phrase meaning the control centre of their personalities. Paul believes that when our thinking, emotions and will are energised by the Spirit, then there is no knowing what may happen.

☐　*Direct, control, suggest, this day*
　　All I design, or do, or say.   *Thomas Ken*

● That the living Christ will make his home in their hearts **'through faith'** (verse 17). The more a person trusts Christ, the more he will think Christ's thoughts and see life through his eyes.

☐　*May the mind of Christ my Saviour*
　　Live in me from day to day.   *Kate B. Wilkinson*

● That they may become more fully aware of the limitless dimensions of God's **love** (verses 18–19). For this is the only environment in which spiritual growth can truly take place.

☐　*Come, fill our hearts with inward strength.*   *Isaac Watts*

We read this great prayer as a fitting conclusion to our series of readings on *Prayers of the Bible*. Its principal petition is that we may be 'made perfect' (verse 21) or, to put it more crudely, 'mended' – ie reset like a broken bone or repaired like torn fishing nets (see Mark 1.19). How much we need to make this prayer our own! We limp along in our devotional life and the holes in the net of our service are all too obvious. Yet no matter how hard we try to put things right ourselves, we shall not succeed. It is the God of peace and healing, whose power raised Jesus from the dead, who must do the work in us.

And so we come to the word most frequently used in Christian devotion – *Amen*. Hebrew in origin, it was a kind of holy 'Hear! Hear!' which bound those who used it to follow up what had been said or prayed in their presence. When understood in this way, the saying of Amen helps us to be sincere in our own prayers and it frequently reminds us that we must start living differently when we rise from our knees.

☐ *Lord, teach us to pray. Amen.*

For group discussion and personal thought

Acts 4.23–30 has been called an early example of a prayer meeting. Do you think that the decline of special meetings for prayer has led to the weakening of church life and witness? What is their particular value? Why have they lost their appeal? Is there a way they could gain a more central place in your local church's programme?

Sunday August 1   2 Corinthians 6.1–10*

THE WHOLE ARMOUR OF GOD

Paul's battle was one against evil and ignorance and prejudice. He writes of the weapons he used – 'the weapons of righteousness' (verse 7). Notice what they are: 'steadfast endurance' (verse 4), 'the innocence of our behaviour', truth, patience, kindliness, love and spiritual gifts (verse 6).

But are such 'weapons' enough in the world of today? Christians have sometimes been tempted to give the world a taste of its own medicine, to use violence and persecution, to try and buy over the opposition. But these will not work, Satan cannot cast out Satan. The only weapons a Christian is permitted to use are the weapons of righteousness.

The world tends to laugh at the Christian's powerlessness, his apparent defeat (verses 8–10). But, behold a paradox! Every now and then the world recognises the truth that Christians claim, the life, joy and wealth they really possess. How envious unbelievers sometimes feel in the quiet, serene presence of a true Christian! They know in their heart of hearts that **he** is on the winning side and that they are still among the defeated.

☐ *Single, against hell, earth, and sin,*
  Single, yet undismayed, I am:
  I dare believe in Jesu's name.   Charles Wesley

HEBREWS

Notes by Revd William Loader, BA, BD, Dr theol

William (Bill) Loader, a New Zealander, is a minister of the Uniting Church of Australia and at present is lecturer in New Testament studies at Perth Theological Hall.

The author of the letter to the Hebrews, who remains unknown, was probably writing to a group of churches who had to face a growing problem. On the one hand, official government in their part of the Roman empire seems to have decided to clamp down on Christians and some might have had to face death. On the other hand, it is likely that a good number of these Christians had been Jews and knew that the old faith was a 'legal' religion allowed by Julius Caesar. Would it not be better to practise Christian faith within the framework of Judaism? In its more tolerant years Judaism had allowed the practice provided the law was obeyed. However, some 50 years after Jesus' death, return to Judaism meant much stricter adherence to that faith.

This letter works on two fronts:
● It argues that the old covenant is obsolete; yet it acknowledges the value of the old in that it points to the new.
● More directly it helps Christians to understand what they confess about Jesus and to see that he is the source of their help and has faced the same kind of pressures as they do.

Suggestions for further reading

A Letter to the Hebrews by John H. Davies, Cambridge Bible Commentaries on the New English Bible (Cambridge University Press);

The Epistle to the Hebrews by F. F. Bruce, New London Commentaries (Marshall Morgan & Scott).

Monday August 2

Living in the first century was living in uncertainty. All around were forces and powers – economic, social, political, spiritual. Tomorrow one might be a refugee; one might not have food;

or one might be set free from slavery. The powers that be were thought of as coming from angels, good and bad.

▶ Read **Hebrews 1.1–14.**

Being named 'Son of God' meant more than being given a title. It was the name once given to Israel's king as God's vice-regent. It meant being installed to power and authority. God's Son was proclaimed King of the powers of the universe only after he had struggled with them in his life on earth.

It must have been hard to say, 'Jesus is King', when the Romans had just imprisoned your son or daughter for being loyal to him. It was just as hard to believe in God when Jesus was dying on the cross. It is also hard today to say, 'Jesus is Lord', in the midst of injustice and oppression. But God has spoken his word of promise in the Son right in the midst of the struggle. By way of the cross God promises ultimate victory.

☐ *For the suffering, dying Jesus is the Christ upon the throne,*
And the travail of our spirit is the travail of his own.

Henry Burton

Tuesday August 3   **Hebrews 2.1–9**

How easy it is to slip back into old familiar ways! The readers of *Hebrews* were in danger of that. Not that the old ways were evil. They were good enough once: they were given by God.

But, through the Son, we are called to embark upon a new way – the way that he took! He became the true man. What the psalmist said of mankind (Psalm 8) is true first and foremost of him. God 'had regard to him' (verse 6) precisely because he entered into the thick of human struggles and suffering. And now the 'world to come' is subjected to him.

It must have been with real pain that the author wrote that we do not yet see 'all things' subject to him (verse 8). Imagine how insensitive it would have been to shout triumph when human rights were being violated or poverty was decimating large communities. But beside this pain is the joy of what we do see – Jesus who has been through it before us. Because he has travelled the path before us we can set our sights on him and keep on course.

☐ *O generous love! that he, who smote*
In man for man the foe,
The double agony in man
For man should undergo.

John Henry Newman

Death is camouflaged for the comfortable. In many countries only a few see actual dying. It happens behind the sterile walls of a hospital, and often under a mental veil of sedation. Hidden by flowers or soft music the dead come and go in secret. The anaesthetic against feeling and facing up to death in the company of our friends can also make us insensitive and apathetic to the dying and suffering in so many parts of the wider human community. Not facing our own pain, we often do not face the pain of others.

God is not like that. Jesus travelled the road of suffering. He faced gruesome death, with all its demonic power, head on. Full flesh and blood, he died a real death. He burst open the experience by entering it fully. And out of death God brought him to life.

We can spend our lives running away from death – busy, hurrying, filling our moments, fleeing the silence, avoiding close contact with ourselves, afraid to venture inside our inner temple, where life's deepest fears are represented.

But inside that temple death, as a great dragon, lies slain; and Jesus, our High Priest, will meet us offering liberation. He does not free us from suffering and death, but he frees us from the **fear** of suffering and death and he frees us to respond to the suffering of others with love.

☐ *O great High Priest, grant me freedom to feel pain without fear, to feel joy without apathy.*

Thursday August 5

The tribal meeting-house of the Maori people of New Zealand is built to represent the body of the tribe's founder. One enters under the carved outstretched arms, through the door (the mouth), into the body. Looking up one can see the backbone and from it come the ribs, painted with traditional designs. But along the walls on either side are other carved figures. Each represents a story of a famous ancestor. When the tribe meets in that building it knows itself to be part of one people stretching back over many generations. In a similar way we may know ourselves to be part of a great house.

▶ Read **Hebrews 3.1–11.**

God is the founder of our tribe and Jesus is its head. Moses is not its head; but he is one of its heroes. The author of *Hebrews* wanted to make Moses' place clear. To be a member of God's house is not to say that all that matters is the present. It is to enjoy being one with the faithful of all ages. Their stories are our stories. We all belong together in the community of the Church, the body of Christ. But this also means that each new 'today' we must hear and obey his voice anew.

☐ *Fain would we thy word embrace,*
Live each moment in thy grace,
Think, and speak, and do, and be
Simply that which pleases thee.   *William Bright*

Friday August 6   **Hebrews 3.12 to 4.13**

Israel's hope for a promised land in which to settle is a symbol of the deep hope that is in us all. We cannot always say what it is we hope for. Some think of a place to live; others of food and shelter; others of power or wealth. As a crying baby wants something but cannot say what, so the cries of the human heart have been expressed in strange and diverse ways, without the true need being identified. But behind the cries is a deep hope. In the community of faith we have confidence that God will not disappoint our inner yearning. Our yearning will find rest not in a land, but in God's own rest and fulfilment.

'Rest' in Psalm 95.11 has reminded the author of *Hebrews* of the seventh day on which God 'rested' after creation and of the seventh day, the Sabbath, observed by Jews as a day of worship. True fulfilment of man's hope is being with God. It is also doing what we do on the day of worship – praising him.

God's 'rest' is not armchair rest! He is active in love for his creation. In his 'rest' all human needs are taken seriously. To have faith is to live with the vision of his 'rest' and to live for it.

☐ *'Our hearts are restless till they find their rest in thee.'*
(Saint Augustine)

Saturday August 7   **Hebrews 4.14 to 5.14**

The path we tread has been trodden before us. Jesus has gone ahead of us, clearing the way. The goal of this path can also be described as the temple of God, so that we see our journey leading us right into 'the Most Holy Place', its innermost sanctuary, right into the intimate presence of God.

As High Priest Jesus has paved the way for us, having entered thoroughly into our human situation (see August 3). Just as in Old Testament times high priests were chosen who were as human as anyone else, so God made Jesus High Priest after he had travelled the path of human weakness. Jesus did not sin. Rather, when faced with persecution, suffering and death, he held firm, and so came to know what it is like to remain obedient when the going is tough.

Jesus' hopes and prayers were not disappointed. He was perfected – attained his goal – and was appointed High Priest. This means that he can help us on the way to salvation, if only we keep to the path. But we need the strength of sound teaching if we are to make the journey. Even in New Testament days it must have been easy to be distracted from the path if one did not learn to think critically about what other people said.

☐ *O God, our minds are bombarded by advertisements, sellers of new things, offers of new paths. Help us to persevere on the path of your Son.*

For group discussion and personal thought

What is the 'rest' referred to by the writer of *Hebrews*? (See especially Hebrews 3.15 to 4.11.) How can we obtain this rest?

Sunday August 8   **Galatians 6.1–10***

THE MIND OF CHRIST

'Fancy – and him a church-goer!' That is how people talk when they hear of a Christian who has had a moral lapse. Church-goers themselves can be equally surprised and condemnatory if a fellow-Christian does something wrong. Paul was neither surprised nor condemnatory. He knew that fallible human nature is not made perfect even in the most devoted Christians. The sudden temptation, the flaring up of desire, the outburst of anger – who of us has not experienced it or succumbed to it? At such times the burden of guilt and shame can be heavy indeed and we may torture ourselves with the question: 'Why did I, a Christian, do this?' We may even wonder if we ought to leave the Church.

Perhaps the Church has tended to stress too much the ideal of moral perfection and not enough the law of forgiving love. The Christian community is a fellowship of sinners who believe in the loving forgiveness of God. Our task is to help our fallen brother up again, bear with him the burden of his self-hatred (verse 2) and never, never smugly compare our rectitude with his weakness. If you want to do any comparing, writes Paul, compare yourself with yourself – what you are with your ideal self – then you will not feel so smug (verse 4)!

☐ *The mind of Christ is that of a redeemer.*

Monday August 9   Hebrews 6.1–12

At first glance we might think that today's reading is saying that anyone who becomes a Christian and then sins is lost for ever and will never be allowed to be saved again. But that is not what the reading means. Rather, the readers are being encouraged to do some solid building on the foundations of their original Christian experience. In contrast verses 4–6 take a side glance at trouble-makers who used to be Christians and are now probably bothering the readers. They have not just sinned – they have totally given up Christ and joined the way of those who killed him. In their situation it is a hopeless task trying to re-convert them. But the author is also warning his readers: 'Don't you be like them!'

Perhaps the threat of coming persecution could drive some of his readers to disown the faith. Another escape route would be to go (or go back) to the Jewish faith, which was a 'legal' religion in the Roman empire of that day. Lazy thinking was in danger of making them stay immature. But having a good grasp of what we believe strengthens us to follow the path of Jesus without being side-tracked or forced to give up.

☐ *What religious 'escape routes' from persecution are tempting Christians today? Pray for courage and strength to be loyal to Jesus.*

Tuesday August 10   Hebrews 6.13–20

Abraham is another hero in the house of God. He is a prime example of faithfulness because he believed in the promise God had given him, even though it seemed impossible for it to be fulfilled. Hebrews 11.8–12 tells the story.

Today's reading draws attention to the way God's promise was given to Abraham: it was with an oath as well as with the promise itself. These two things are also present in Psalm 110.4, words which the author understands that God applied to Jesus in appointing him High Priest: 'The Lord has sworn and will not change his purpose: "You are a priest for ever, in the succession of Melchizedek." ' These words are the basis of our hope; for Jesus is our forerunner. He is in the temple of God; he has been appointed High Priest. That means he has not only pioneered the way; he also offers us the kind of timely help (Hebrews 4.16) which we need along the way.

Holding on to this is like having a good anchor and having it in the right place! It will help us weather any storm; and when we take up the slack in the rope we shall find ourselves there with Jesus in the presence of God.

☐ *O God, when in the storm we cannot see for the driving rain, and feel hurled about by the world around us, we thank you that the rope holds and the anchor remains sure.*

Wednesday August 11   Hebrews 7.1–14

What does it mean to speak of Jesus as a priest of the order of Melchizedek? In today's reading the author selects details from the story of Melchizedek as recorded in Genesis 14.18–20. He also probably drew on some popular thinking about Melchizedek, such as we have in the community of Jews who wrote the Dead Sea Scrolls around the time of Jesus. They saw in Melchizedek a person like an angel. This explains why Jesus' priesthood could be compared to his, even though Jesus is superior to angels. Both Melchizedek and Jesus are priests of the heavenly king, whereas the Jewish priests operate on earth and only on a temporary basis.

The author of *Hebrews* pictures heaven as a great temple with priests and worshippers praising God, Jesus being the High Priest. The main focus of attention is not primarily Melchizedek but Jesus and the superiority of the new way of salvation. At best the rites and rituals of the past point beyond themselves to the One who can bring us through to the goal where man's deepest religious yearning finds rest: Jesus, who as one of us has been permanently installed as our High Priest and Saviour.

☐ *With joy we meditate the grace*
  Of our High Priest above;
  His heart is made of tenderness,
  And ever yearns with love.   Isaac Watts

The old temple system, with its way of dealing with man's basic needs, was inadequate. Now that the new priesthood had come the old system should be abandoned. Christians should not return to the fold of Judaism as an escape from persecution. That would be surrendering the One whom the Old Testament was ultimately pointing to – Jesus Christ, who has been installed as High Priest of a better way. There need be no more replacing of priests who have died, or keeping daily sacrifices going, or the annual 'coming and going' from the Most Holy Place. Jesus is there in the **true** 'Most Holy Place', and there for ever, having completed all he needed to do on the way. This means that he is free to pray for us as we travel the uphill road and thus to help us onward toward our goal.

We do not need to be distracted with religious 'busy-ness' – trying to win God's approval. For, through Jesus, God has declared his love for us once and for all. We are set free from having to justify ourselves to God.

☐   *Lord, it is coming to ourselves*
When thus we come to thee;
The bondage of thy loveliness
Is perfect liberty.

Benjamin Waugh

Turning to Christ means entering a new way, but it does not mean throwing away as rubbish everything we once lived by. The author of *Hebrews* is sensitive about the past. Although he leaves no doubt about the failure of past ways, he does explore them carefully to discover the light that shines in them. The temple with its system of priesthood was evidence of something much deeper and more profound.

This may be true of many human attempts to set up ways of worshipping the divine. It is as though people have caught a glimpse of reality and try to reproduce it in some shape or form. It is like trying to put true love into words. Words fail, but if you listen closely enough you will see the deeper reality to which the words point. This is how *Hebrews* understands the worship system of the Old Testament: it points to the deeper reality 'above' which is in the priesthood of Christ. Similarly, the words of the prophet Jeremiah (31.31–34) which are quoted in verses 8–12, contrast deep inner patterns with external rules.

The new covenant, the new contract God offers people, goes to the very heart of reality.

☐ *O God, help me to be aware of the work your Spirit is doing anonymously among people in all parts of the world.*

Saturday August 14   Hebrews 9.1–10

It seems probable that some Christians had already come to think of Jesus as being like a priest in the heavenly temple. In Revelation 1.13 he is pictured wearing the garments of the High Priest. The author of *Hebrews*, having reinforced the idea that Jesus as our great High Priest prays for us, begins in chapter 9 to develop a new way of thinking of Jesus as High Priest which includes his earthly ministry and death as well.

The existence of the old temple with its two sanctuaries and the fact that only the high priest could enter the Most Holy Place, and then only once a year, on the Day of Atonement, suggests in itself that the old temple system was inadequate. It points beyond itself to something deeper. But to understand what this is we need to understand that the temple was saying two things:

● **God is holy.** He is not something we conjure up or something there to make us feel warm and comfortable. He is the Holy One, the centre and source of all being.

● **To become at one with him matters above all else.** That means our sin which blocks us from him must be dealt with and taken seriously.

☐ *Most Holy One, within the innermost sanctuary of my being I worship you; for there I know myself in the innermost sanctuary of all being – at one with you and at one with all.*

For group discussion and personal thought

Read again Hebrews 7.23–25. What does the 'priesthood' of Jesus Christ mean for us as we seek to follow him and live by his standards day by day?

THE SERVING COMMUNITY

The Philippian church was going through a period of persecution and distress. Yet they had remembered their beloved Paul who was languishing in prison, and sent him a gift by the hand of Epaphroditus. The letter was written to thank them and to encourage them to stand firm in their troubles. Notice how Paul refers to their shared experience of suffering: 'You all share in the privilege that is mine' (verse 7). Privilege! Paul sees his imprisonment and their troubles as an opportunity to deepen their love – that is the privilege they share.

Read verses 9–10 again. They mention some of the elements to be found in real love. Love is not a sentimental feeling, a genial goodwill, an easy sympathy. Loving is effective when it shows **knowledge** of the other's situation, background and need; **insight** into the nature of the other's real problems; **true discrimination** between what is fundamental and what is superficial in the other's distress. When we say we love other people we should always test the genuineness of our love by these standards of knowledge, insight and discrimination. Loving is not easy; it demands mental energy, attention, ability to **hear** what the other person is really saying and to get behind his problem to his real need.

☐ '*Love is patient. There is nothing love cannot face.*'

(1 Corinthians 13.4, 7)

On the Day of Atonement the blood of a slain animal was taken by the high priest and sprinkled over the sacred box, called the ark of the covenant. This act 'atoned' for the sins of the people – put things right between God and his people. Some remember the meaning of 'atonement' by reading it as 'at-one-ment', restoring us to be 'at one' with God.

Jesus is compared with two aspects of the ancient ritual. He is the High Priest; but he is also the one slain, the sacrifice. Bringing these two ideas together for the first time, the author of *Hebrews* describes Jesus as having taken on flesh and blood, his body, sacrificed it, and then proceeded into the temple of heaven to stand before God.

Jesus' atoning act was his death. That is why in the Lord's Supper when we hear the words, 'This is the blood of the covenant' we think of it not as something Jesus is continually offering in the heavenly temple, as if his work was not finished, but as something which remains after he once and for all completed the atonement. Forgiveness is now open to all who will receive it.

☐ *Jesus, the Lamb of God, hath bled,*
    He bore our sins upon the tree;
  Beneath our curse he bowed his head;
  'Tis finished! He hath died for me!   *Charles Wesley*

Tuesday August 17   Hebrews 10.19–31

The writer here draws some practical conclusions of his teaching. Because we can be absolutely certain of forgiveness and that the way to God has been opened up by Jesus, there are things for us to do!

First of all, Christian faith is not just a private affair between each individual and God. We are a household, a community; and community fellowship and worship are essential. We need to help each other.

The alternative amounts to abandoning the path of life and choosing the way of death. Christians will stumble and fall from time to time, just as in marriage we are always on the way to **becoming** good husbands and wives. But there is a world of difference between wronging your partner or acting out of harmony with the marriage and then 'making up', and opting out of the marriage relationship altogether. It is the latter kind of action that is in mind here. It is possible to point back to a time when we 'became a Christian' while we may have long since opted out of the relationship.

☐ *In marriage, changed situations mean that we often need to re-*
  think and renew our vows so that the marriage continues to
  grow. How would you renew your 'vows' for your relationship
  with God today?

Wednesday August 18   Hebrews 11.1–16

If a handful of iron filings or iron sand are spread out on a piece of paper and a magnet is brought near them, then they will be drawn into a pattern. Having a goal or purpose in life works like this. We may see it illustrated when someone prepares for marriage. Every aspect of life – money, time, clothing, and so on – come to be looked at and handled in the light of the marriage. Having a single goal for the whole of life is a way of giving unity to our lives.

In *Hebrews*, faith means fixing our eyes on the goal and living life faithfully in the light of it. It could be said that the Christian goal is to be where God wants us to be. Ultimately that means being in the intimate fellowship of his presence, sometimes called 'heaven', although for many that word has come to mean something plush and lazy.

The old temple system was a very inadequate reflection of true worship but it had hints of the real thing. Even so the faith of Old Testament heroes could only dimly see the goal, but behind the hopes of people like Abraham was the yearning for the ultimate goal of God's presence. Thus their faith is an example for us.

☐　*Faith lends its realising light,*
　　　The clouds disperse, the shadows fly;
　　The Invisible appears in sight,
　　　And God is seen by mortal eye.

Charles Wesley

Thursday August 19   Hebrews 12.1–17

Besides the great examples of those ahead of us on the path of faith we have the greatest example of all – Jesus. But he is more than an example. He is the one who pioneered the way to begin with and he is the one who through his prayers for us can help us travel on, even when we face the same kinds of assaults on our faith as he faced on his. We fix our eyes on him both to know that we are aiming in the right direction, and because his life offers us the pattern of discipleship.

Exalting Jesus to the throne is another way of saying that God has raised Jesus up as the true image both of who God is and of how man is to live and is to be. It is not about knowing everything. Nor is it about success, or being able to boast of performing fantastic miracles, or of having the most extraordinary high spiritual experiences. True human living is to follow the path of love and self-giving; and that may well mean suffering. It is the way of the cross.

☐　*When was the last time you experienced conflict because to follow Christ meant a less popular, more difficult way ?*

Here the author points out in yet another way the contrast between the old covenant and the new covenant. He paints the
events at Mount Sinai, where the law was given to Moses, as
frightening and confusing. Not that he wants to deny that God
was involved. He was involved – but it was like catching only a
back-stage glimpse of a drama rehearsal. In contrast, we are invited to behold the full spectacle on stage. The scene is of a new
Jerusalem. Within it is a community of angels and people including the heroes of chapter 11, who have finally been brought
to their goal – 'made perfect'. In the centre is Jesus and his
blood, and with him is God. In the silence one voice is heard:
not shrieking for vengeance like Abel against Cain, but gently
offering forgiveness and life.

The scene as a whole says two things:
- Here is love and belonging. Here is community.
- But also: if you set your trust on other things to give you
security, such as your achievements, your possessions, even
your closed belief systems, beware! In the final shake-up of
reality when the drama reaches its climax, only what this scene
shows will remain. It is only God's kingdom that is indestruct-
ible.

☐ *Rejoice, the Lord is King!*
  Your Lord and King adore . . .
 His kingdom cannot fail,
  He rules o'er earth and heaven.   *Charles Wesley*

Fixing one's gaze on Jesus (12.2) is not something we can do
from an armchair or a comfortable seat in the stalls. Going the
way of Jesus involves us in action.

In stressing hospitality (verse 2) the author is probably thinking of Abraham's experience in Genesis 18.1–8. Christian action
also means concern about people who are tortured and imprisoned (verse 3), especially those who suffer because they
share the goals of Jesus. Such people have often been accused
of getting involved in politics. Sadly many Christians appear to
want to avoid such suspicion at any cost. But when we offer the
hope of the kingdom of God we cannot help but be understood
to say that any government or order of society fails to be the
kingdom of God, no matter how much good it might do. Thus

some governments will see Christians, who live out their faith, as a threat.

The true follower of Jesus can never truly belong 'in the camp' whether of Jewish religious values or of the value systems of the modern world. We cannot be truly at home where there is injustice, poverty, oppression and greed.

☐ *O God, keep me from comfortable religion, passionless piety, and heartless hypocrisy. May my life-style become 'good news for the poor' and a sign of the kingdom of your Son.*

For group discussion and personal thought

Hebrews 13.3 urges us to show our love by remembering those who are in prison as if we were in prison with them. Think of different kinds of imprisonment and consider how we might do this.

Sunday August 22 Acts 17.22–31*

THE WITNESSING COMMUNITY

The Court of Areopagus was a Greek court whose function may have been to exercise control over moral and religious matters in Athens. Before this interested and learned audience, Paul bore witness to the Christian faith.

All Christians are called to witness for Christ; but it is something which demands tact, sensitivity and preparation. In his speech, Paul displayed two qualities that we do well to note. They were **courtesy** and **knowledge.** His words in verse 22 were not insulting or derogatory (as the AV translation, 'Ye are too superstitious,' suggests). Rather they were a compliment on the serious religious awareness of the Athenians. Paul had obviously taken pains to get to know something of their religion and culture. He even quoted one of their own poets in verse 28. His aim was to lead them on from what they believed to a fuller understanding; thus he presented Christ to them.

Our task as Christians in this matter of Christian witness, is not to destroy but to fulfil.

☐ *Paul wrote: 'Let your conversation be always gracious, and never insipid; study how best to talk with each person you meet.' (Colossians 4.6)*

THE MESSAGE OF THE BIBLE

IBRA Centenary theme

Notes by Revd A. Gordon Jones, BD

Gordon Jones is an active supernumerary Methodist minister at Papworth, Cambridge. Previously he worked with the Richmond Fellowship for Mental Welfare and Rehabilitation.

For a hundred years the IBRA has been helping people across the world to read the Bible as a daily act of devotion, leading to greater understanding of its message and its relevance to life. Those who founded the Association – notably Charles Waters – and those who have directed it through the years, have believed passionately that God still speaks through the pages of Scripture; and that his word is of fundamental importance to us if we are to discover the full meaning and joy of life.

What is the word that God speaks? How does the Bible communicate it to us? As we follow these 'centenary' readings we shall seek to answer these questions. Also, as we read, let us remember in our prayers our fellow-members around the world.

☐ *Father, we thank you for the message of the Bible and for your word which comes to us through all its words – a word of faith, hope and love, a word translated at last in a human life, a word which has power to save the world. We pray for your blessing upon the work of the IBRA as it moves into its second century of service to God's people throughout the world. Guide those who write notes, those who edit and prepare them, and those who put these notes into the hands of the people in so many different localities. May those who write and those who read together discover afresh your word for our time.*

THE CONTENT OF THE MESSAGE

Monday August 23   **Psalm 119.97–112**

GOD'S LAW IS A LIGHT

The psalms are poetry; and the sentiments expressed in them spring from deep feelings. Psalm 119 is a sustained shout of joy about God's law. God's law is not the list of narrow rules and regulations against which Jesus protested. It is the revelation of his whole gracious purpose and loving character given through the law of Moses, the priests and the prophets. The law revealed that men are in a relationship of love with God which speaks both of his care for them and their responsibility to him. In our reading, this relationship is spoken of under these terms: law, commandments, instruction, precepts, word, promise, decrees, statutes.

The psalmist shouts for joy as he contemplates this law. He calls it a 'lamp' and a 'light'. This is the message of the Bible: there is a purpose in life and a way to live – a loving purpose, a loving way. To believe in the purpose and to be obedient to the way is to find fullness of life. We read the Bible in order to understand increasingly what the word of God is.

☐   *That blessèd law of thine,*
      Jesus, to me impart;
   The Spirit's law of life divine,
      O write it in my heart!

                                                        Charles Wesley

Tuesday August 24   Deuteronomy 6.1–15

ONE GOD TO BE LOVED

We read the Bible in order to discover the 'word of God'. That 'word' will take more than a lifetime for us to fathom fully. It needs continuous exploration, interpretation and application to our own circumstances. But the message of the Old Testament may be summarised thus: **There is one God who is to be loved.**

The Old Testament consists of the laws, prophecies, hymns, poems, wisdom and history of one nation, a nation which was destined to be different from her neighbours. The difference was to lie in her understanding of God and her attitude to him. Other nations had their gods – projections of their own passions and desires – and they feared or tried to exploit them. Israel's profoundest minds came to see that there is but one God, creator, separate from nature, holy, trustworthy, changeless. Further he is to be loved – not treated as an enemy to be appeased.

We can only love God when we trust him and know that he loves us. The message of the Old Testament is that he cares deeply for his people and our response to him must be to love him with our whole being.

☐ *'We love because he loved us first.' (1 John 4.19)*

166

CHRIST – THE FULFILMENT OF GOD'S PURPOSE

We cannot do without the Old Testament, for it provides the background for what followed. But it is in the New Testament that God's message – God's word – finds completion in the life, character and achievements of Jesus Christ. The Gospels tell us about his doings and teachings; *Acts of the Apostles* records the story of the early years of the Church he founded; the letters deal with the practical and theological implications of his existence; *Revelation* tells of the hope of his final triumph. In short, the message of the New Testament is that Christ is the fulfilment of God's purpose. That message is stated in today's reading.

● People feel enslaved by sin, depression and fear, but Christ is our **rescuer** (verse 13).
● People are bewildered about the nature of God or whatever reality lies behind our existence; but Christ is the **revealer** of God's nature (verse 15).
● People feel alienated from one another, from themselves and from God; but Christ is the great **reconciler** (verses 20–22).

In Christ is to be found the key to the mystery and mastery of our lives.

☐ *Read and meditate on verse 19.*

THE AUTHORITY OF SCRIPTURE

Central to the advice given here to Timothy is the insistence that, in days when the Christian faith was being doubted and overlaid with false doctrines, the Jewish Scriptures should be constantly brought to mind. Interpreted with Christian insights, these Scriptures contain the true way of salvation. For today's Christians, the 'sacred writings' include both Old and New Testaments and are indeed regarded as 'inspired' (verse 16).

The Bible is a whole library of books, written over many centuries by men with varying degrees of spiritual insight and knowledge. It is not to be regarded as all 'on one flat plane of uniform literary quality, religious significance or inspiration' (F.C. Grant). The Bible is to be read in a spirit of intelligent research and always awaiting the enlightenment of the Holy Spirit. Its authority lies in the fact that it is the literature of a people who were most open to the leading of God's Spirit.

With the Bible as our source-book, an openness of mind and a heart humbly awaiting the guidance of the Holy Spirit, we too shall find in it a developing and continuing word from God.

☐ *Come, divine interpreter,*
  Bring us eyes thy book to read.   *Charles Wesley*

Friday August 27   John 5.31–47
WORDS THAT POINT TO THE WORD

Jesus' opponents knew their Scriptures in detail. Yet they were missing the real message of those Scriptures. For what we find in the Bible is largely determined by the spirit that we bring to our reading. The opponents of Jesus looked for, and found, austere lists of rules and regulations, or fierce nationalistic details. If they had come to their Scriptures with unprejudiced and teachable minds, they would have seen that Moses and the prophets were pointing to a God and a grace which were identical with Christ's God and the grace portrayed in his own life.

There is a certain danger in calling the Bible 'the word of God'; for it may lead us to view the Bible merely as a book of rigid rules or a kind of *Old Moore's Almanac* foretelling exact dates. The true **Word of God** is the loving personality of Christ; and a humble, critical, open-minded reading of the Bible finds in it pointers to that Word who was made flesh.

☐ *Divine instructor, gracious Lord,*
  Be thou for ever near;
  Teach me to love thy sacred word,
  And view my Saviour there.   *Anne Steele*

Saturday August 28   Jeremiah 36.1–8, 21–32
THE WRITING OF THE MESSAGE

This reading gives us an insight into the fascinating and complex way in which the message of the Bible has been, and continues to be, passed on from generation to generation. Early oral traditions were written down, collected and edited by priests or prophets in order that they might be preserved for future generations. The words of the prophets, delivered on a variety of occasions, would be remembered and written down on scrolls. In today's reading we have an example of the writing down of a prophet's words and of how the angry reaction of an offended king could not destroy them.

Similarly with the New Testament, oral traditions of the actions and teachings of Jesus were carefully gathered together by writers like Luke, and letters from church leaders were collected and preserved.

It is a story that continues to this day. At this moment, you have beside you the Bible – a book which speaks of the labours of faithful and careful translators and scholars who knew that this message must be preserved and proclaimed at all costs, because in it is the key to mankind's salvation.

However, in the end, the written message has to be translated into the faithful living of those who believe it. The words that proclaim the Word live on in Christian lives.

☐   *Lord, speak to me, that I may speak*
        In living echoes of thy tone.

                                                            Frances R. Havergal

---

For group discussion and personal thought
When we speak of the Bible as 'the word of God' what do we mean? In what ways does the 'inspiration' of Scripture depend upon our approach to it?

Sunday August 29   Acts 20.17–35*

THE SUFFERING COMMUNITY

Paul, hurrying to Jerusalem with a gift of money for the poverty-stricken Christians there, invites the elders of the church at Ephesus to meet him at Miletus. Some might say that his fare-well speech has a note of complaining in it. Certainly there is self-defence for Paul has had to suffer the hostility of envious rivals. There is also a note of stern realism in it. He foresees more suffering for himself and no doubt for the Ephesians. Finally, there is a placing of responsibility squarely upon the shoulders of the Ephesian leaders for the future spiritual health of their church.

Perhaps we become too dependent upon great and much loved leaders. When they die we feel bereft; we think that things will never again be so good, that decay is bound to set in. But it is at this point that we, with thanksgiving for the past, have to assume their role and realise that now **we** are the ones to whom others will look for help, guidance and inspiration.

☐ *Rise up, O men of God!*
        The Church for you doth wait,
   Her strength unequal to her task;
        Rise up and make her great.   *William P. Merrill*

THE COMMUNICATION OF THE MESSAGE

Monday August 30   **Psalm 65**

THROUGH POETRY

The Bible is not one book but a library of books in which the
word of God is communicated through the various types of
literature. Before one begins a reading it is always helpful to ask:
To what type of literature does this belong?

The psalms are poetry or hymns; and hymns are used to
express our feelings in relation to God. They may express
thanksgiving, awe, longing, suffering, bewilderment – even
anger and depression. But always they seek after a deeper understanding of God and his ways. The language of some of the
psalms may seem harsh to modern Christian readers, but this
only serves to show how completely free the writers felt to express their feelings in the presence of God.

Psalm 65 is a hymn of thanksgiving, in which both the
spiritual and the physical gifts of God are set forth. You might
call the author of this psalm the 'Wordsworth' of the Bible – a
poet who sees in nature so much that calls forth thanksgiving and
self-dedication.

☐ *A poet's feelings about nature*

   To me the meanest flower that blows can give
   Thoughts that do often lie too deep for tears.

                                          William Wordsworth

Tuesday August 31   **Deuteronomy 8.1–18**

THROUGH HISTORY

Since the present and the future are largely the result of what
has happened in the past, the study of history should always be a
fascinating and valuable activity. We speak of 'the judgements of
history', or 'the lessons of history', indicating in these phrases
that what has happened in the past is never meaningless.

For the Hebrews, history was entirely meaningful, for they
saw it as God's activity. It has to be conceded that their account

of history – as, for example, in the books of *1, 2 Kings* – is selective and seen from one particular angle, namely the religious dealings of God with Israel. But, then, all written history is selective and depends largely on what the writer considers to be significant among the multitudinous events that have happened. The Hebrews saw the hand of God in all events – as in today's reading. They saw God allowing or directing events in order to humble, test, educate, discipline, guide and encourage them.

'**Remember**' – that is the key word in Hebrew history. We may learn from the Hebrews' approach to their history to look at our own nation's history, or our own individual history, in a similar way, in order to discern the hand of God and to apprehend the word of God. Thus, with humble gratitude, we shall learn more of his grace and wisdom and what he requires of us.

☐ *'Christianity is thoroughly committed to the view that God reveals himself in and through history.' (C. H. Dodd)*

Wednesday September 1   Amos 7.1–17

THROUGH PROPHECY

It was through the prophets that the Hebrews' understanding of history was worked out in detail. They interpreted events in terms of the will of God. 'Thus says the Lord' prefaced much of what they said. They were speaking to their contemporaries during a period of tremendous political turbulence, when small Israel (or Jacob) and Judah were being tossed about on the ocean of great world events. People asked: 'As God's people, where do we fit into all this?' The prophets watched, meditated and prayed – and then uttered their words of encouragement, denunciation or warning.

To grasp the significance of what they were saying, we need to know, as far as is possible, the occasion which brought forth each particular oracle. Remember that what they said refers to their own time and situation. Nevertheless, because they were in intimate touch with God whose purposes are changeless, we find statements leaping out of the local context and bearing meaning which we find fulfilled in Christ.

Today's reading gives us an example of the sincerity, courage, insight – and unpopularity – of some of the prophets. Amos saw the judgement of God falling upon Israel because of her disobedience to his laws. Are there any prophets like Amos today?

□ *Give us the insight, Lord, to recognise the evils that are ruining our society; give us the courage to denounce them; and give us the love to help people to overcome them.*

Thursday September 2 Luke 1.1–4
John 20.30–31; 21.24–25

THROUGH THE GOSPELS

The four Gospels do not constitute four attempts at a biography of Jesus Christ. They comprise his remembered sayings and actions which circulated orally in the early Church. After a period of years, the need for a written record was recognised. First Mark, then Matthew and Luke and, lastly, John produced their accounts of 'the gospel'.

Notice, there is only **one** gospel – the good news of God's action in the life, teaching, death and resurrection of his Son. That good news was variously interpreted in different churches. Thus we may say that:

● *Mark* represents the gospel cherished by Christians in Rome – a simple, clear statement of Jesus as God's Son;

● *Matthew* is the gospel cherished by Christian Jews – Jesus is the fulfilment of messianic hopes;

● *Luke* represents the gospel as understood by Gentiles – Christ the Saviour of the world;

● *John* presents the gospel in philosophical and theological terms.

So the one gospel comes to us 'according to' Mark, Matthew, Luke and John. With their differing emphases, their four books were written with the purpose of encouraging, inspiring and strengthening faith in Jesus Christ. Together, they give us a consistent portrait of a real, living and strong personality – the Son of God in whom we see all that was finest in Jewish hopes and the fulfilment of all that is noblest in human aspiration.

□ *Thank God for Jesus Christ, the Word of God, who comes near to us today through the words of the Gospels.*

Friday September 3 Colossians 4.1–9, 14–18

THROUGH LETTERS

We learn much through reading other people's letters! In letters to friends, there is an informality, freedom and self-revelation that gives us more information about the writer than any formal history or biography. Letters written by famous people can be very enlightening, not only in respect of the writers, but also of the characteristics of the age in which they lived.

Through the letters in the New Testament we catch vivid glimpses of the characters of Paul and others, of the problems faced by the young churches and, above all, of the living experience of Christ which was the very life-blood of the first-century Christian community. Nowhere in the Bible is its message more clearly revealed than in the New Testament letters. In them we have the earliest Christian literature, for many of these letters were wittten before the Gospels.

Today's reading is an extract written from prison. It encourages and advises its readers; it mentions friends and fellow-workers affectionately, and it contains greetings. Notice that Paul asks for it to be read not only in Colossae but also in Laodicea. Verse 16 hints that he had also written to Laodicea. Clearly, then, Paul wrote letters other than those preserved in the New Testament.

☐ *Do you know anyone who might like a letter from* **you**? *What about writing it today? God may use it to speak to your friend!*

Saturday September 4   Acts 8.26–35

BY WORD OF MOUTH

Perhaps the most effective means of communicating the message of the Bible is by word of mouth. Histories, letters, poems are all of tremendous importance; but to be face to face with a person who talks with you and answers your questions, is to open up channels through which the word may swiftly and vigorously run. We read the words of Jesus, but how much more must they have meant to those who heard his voice, saw his face as he spoke, caught the glint of humour or anger or compassion in his eyes! Paul could write vigorous letters, but *Acts* tells us what an immediately moving effect his speaking had.

The written word often needs explanation. Philip was needed to interpret a prophet's writing. Sermons will never become out-moded for they are the gospel taught through personality.

Personal testimony is worth a dozen religious tracts! We may shrink from this for, so often, it appears that the voluble Christian advocate is the least effective and, sometimes, the most offensive. But in this matter of Christian witness, many words are not required. Listen first, try to understand the need

173

of your companion, then speak with grace and humour (see also Colossians 4.6) and remember that it is your **everyday conversation** that communicates – or hides – the Spirit of Christ.

☐ *Pray for preachers who tomorrow will be communicating the gospel.*
Pray for yourself: May 'the words of my mouth and the meditation of my heart be acceptable in thy sight, O Lord, my rock and my Redeemer' (Psalm 19.14, RSV).

For group discussion and personal thought

In the Bible God's message is communicated in many ways – through history, poetry, words and acts of prophets, the parables and deeds of Jesus, and through letters. Think of some of the ways in which efforts are made today to communicate this message. How effective are these ways? Have you any other suggestions?

Sunday September 5   1 John 4.15–21*
OUR NEIGHBOUR

There has been one man – Jesus – whose life and death have spoken most convincingly of God's love. It is not so much what he said that convinces us as the love he actually showed to his fellow-men. **He** loved his **neighbour** – and so we know that **God** is **love**. And if our recognition that God loves has come through Jesus' love of his neighbour, God's recognition that we love him comes through **our** love of neighbour. There is, indeed, no other way of loving God than through loving our fellow-men.

This is the most obvious and the best understood of all Christian teaching. If asked, 'And who is my neighbour?' we unhesitatingly reply, 'Every man, woman and child is my neighbour.' But we must stop and ask ourselves:
● Are we sure of the implication of what we have said?
● Are there some people we would overlook in that apparently all-embracing answer – classes of people whom we exclude from the term 'neighbour'; people whom, through prejudice or fear or revulsion, we overlook and despise – perhaps people of another race or culture, or some whose life-style offends us?

☐ *For a moment or two search your own heart and mind on these questions and ask God to show you the answer.*

MISSIONARY APPEAL

Roy Chapman, the General Secretary writes on behalf of the **International Work of the IBRA**

'We could use three or four thousand more copies of *Light for our Path* daily notes,' said the IBRA Secretary in Ghana. 'Please can you send us more IBRA *Notes* and children's material,' said the IBRA Secretary in Nigeria. These were just two requests made to me on my visit to Ghana and Nigeria in 1981.

In Ghana, the IBRA car has almost fallen to pieces, but if we could provide a motor cycle this would be invaluable for local distribution in the large towns. In Nigeria, the IBRA headquarters is just one room which has to serve as office, storeroom, meeting-place and library. The government has given a plot of land on a rent-free 99-year lease but a considerable sum of money is needed to erect even a modest bungalow-type office.

These are just two of the items we would like to be able to provide in addition to maintaining the day-to-day distribution of IBRA notes. Everywhere I went in both Ghana and Nigeria I kept thinking how much more we could do, **if only we had the money.** Our international help goes to many more places, too, so the story can be repeated over and over again – **if only . . .**

IBRA members have been more than generous during the past year. Gifts large and small have come to Robert Denholm House – many with messages of encouragement – and all have been welcomed and put to good use. Dare I ask for even more during this Centenary Year? Yes, I dare – because I have seen for myself how much IBRA means to Christian people in two of the countries helped by the Missionary Fund.

For many of us it is easy to obtain IBRA books and to have their help in reading the Bible. Will you give a thank-offering to God and thereby help others to have this help too? There is so much we could do if only we had the money. Help us not to have to say, **'If only . . .'**

● *An envelope for your gift will be found between the pages of this book. Please hand it to your IBRA secretary or send it direct to the IBRA Missionary Fund.*

THE CHRISTIAN LIFE

Selections from Matthew

Notes by Revd James Martin, MA, BD

James Martin is a minister of the Church of Scotland at High Carntyne, Glasgow. As well as revising Willliam Barclay's 'Daily Study Bible', he has himself written several books, including 'A Plain Man in the Holy Land' and 'People in the Jesus Story' (Saint Andrew Press).

While all four Gospels tell us about Jesus, each has its own emphasis. Matthew's Gospel is sometimes referred to as the teaching Gospel because it gives us considerably more of the teaching of Jesus than the others. This teaching material is to be found particularly in chapters 5 to 7 – usually called the *Sermon on the Mount* – and in the large number of parables which the Gospel includes.

The readings selected for the next two weeks are taken from these teaching sections and are intended to focus attention on some features of the kind of life that Jesus wants his followers to lead.

Suggestion for further reading

The Gospel of Matthew (Volumes 1 and 2) by William Barclay, Daily Study Bible (Saint Andrew Press).

Monday September 6   **Matthew 5.1–12**

One of the many 'special' places the Christian pilgrim in the Holy Land is taken to see is the Church of the Beatitudes. Set on the crest of the hillside towards the north end of the Sea of Galilee, it looks down through its cloisters upon the waters of that lovely lake. It was in this location, so tradition says, that Jesus preached his *Sermon on the Mount*.

It is unlikely, however, that Jesus gave this teaching all at once. The Sermon on the Mount is almost certainly a collection of teaching that Jesus gave at different times. Its opening verses, which form today's reading, are called the *Beatitudes* and have been described as the 'Charter of Christian Living'.

I once heard a man declare: 'As long as you live by the *Beatitudes* you do not need to accept all that stuff about Jesus being God and Saviour.' That man was missing the point and the point is that the *Beatitudes* are counsel for Christians. It is for those who have accepted Jesus as Saviour and Lord. It is an outline of the way the Christian believer is meant to travel; and the fact is that unless we are willing to let Jesus assist us along that way, we will not have much success in following it. We need the help Jesus alone can provide if we are even to approach the standards he sets before us here.

☐ *Lord Jesus, we really would like to attain the qualities you describe in the* **Beatitudes.** *But we realise our own strength will not be enough for the task; and so we ask you to help us day by day.*

Tuesday September 7   Matthew 5.13–20

In our twentieth century society, salt is a commodity which most people can obtain easily and cheaply. It was not always so. There was a time when salt was so precious that it was used as an offering to the gods, and men have fought wars to gain possession of salt springs.

In Jesus' day no one was likely to forget the value of salt, for it performed an important double function. In the hot climate of Palestine salt was necessary to keep food from going bad, and it was also used to make food tastier. Jesus wants his followers to exercise a similar double function of preventing corruption and adding flavour to the life of the world around them.

This is to seek to do for the world at large the very things Jesus has done for us. He has saved us from our sins and has added a new relish to our lives. We are called by Jesus on the one hand to uphold the best values everywhere, his values; and never was this more important than now. The world in many ways is going bad and only the 'salt' of Christianity can save it from corruption. Also we are called by Jesus to show the world that Christianity is a joyful thing. We are meant to make the world a happier place and the lives of others more joyful because of our Christian faith.

☐ *Grant, O Lord, that someone today may find life a richer thing because of me.*

● **Offering the left cheek** (verse 39) was more significant than it might seem. If a right-handed man stands facing another and strikes him across the right cheek, he must do so with the back of his hand; and this was to convey a great insult. Jesus is saying that even if someone deals us a terrible insult, we should not resent it or retaliate. It is sad that nevertheless we are often quick to take offence.

● **Giving a man your coat as well** when he sues you for your shirt (verse 40) also has a point of its own. Even the poorest man would possess two shirts and the law permitted you to sue for possession of one of these. Most Jews, however, would have only one coat (the outer garment used as a robe by day and often as a blanket by night) and the law insisted that no man could have this taken away from him. Jesus is really saying here that no follower of his should be unduly concerned about standing on his rights.

● **Going the second mile** (verse 41) is an illustration taken straight from the fact that in Jesus' day Palestine was occupied territory. The Roman authorities had the right to compel any Jew to carry baggage for a distance of one mile. Jesus is saying that his followers are not to be content merely to give the service that duty demands, but of their own free will should give as much again.

☐ *O Lord, may we never be content with doing only what strict duty demands.*

Thursday September 9   **Matthew 6.1–15**

Jesus says here that the Pharisees are frequently guilty of two grave faults when they say their prayers. They often make a public show of them and just as often they fill them with empty phrases.

Some people in Jesus' day made a habit of saying their prayers in as public a place as they could find. Jews were supposed to pray three times a day – at 9 am, 12 noon and 3 pm. Since they said their prayers standing up, it was very easy for someone to make a spectacle of his set times of prayer. Such a man was saying his prayers to impress his fellow-men rather than to be heard of God; and Jesus says that that kind of prayer is no good at all.

Very often the same man would fill his prayers with well-sounding but meaningless phrases; and Jesus declares that this kind of prayer is also useless.

I once read about a busy housewife and mother who at times used to throw her apron over her head and for a few snatched moments say, 'Lord, Lord, Lord,' over and over again. The Pharisees might not have counted this as very much of a prayer but she was communing with God; and in Jesus' eyes that is what counts most of all.

☐ *Help us, O God, to avoid making our prayers either a mere show or a lifeless formality.*

Friday September 10   Matthew 6.19–34

What might be termed the keynote phrase in this section is found in verse 34 – 'So do not be anxious about tomorrow'. Jesus is urging his hearers to lay hold of the eternal values to be found in him. When a man does this, he need no longer be anxious about anything.

The AV translation, 'Take no thought for the morrow', has sometimes given people the idea that Jesus is saying it is wrong to plan ahead or make any provision for the future. Jesus, however, is not counselling us against prudent forethought; he is counselling us to have our trust so firmly based on him that we may face the future and all its uncertainties with the confidence that, come what may, the things that matter most are safe in his keeping.

In *The Pilgrim's Progress*, John Bunyan tells how Mr Little Faith, full of anxiety about what might befall him on his journey, had his fears realised when he was attacked and robbed in Deadman's Lane. But when he recovered consciousness he discovered that his jewels were still intact. The Christian need never be unduly anxious; for his eternal 'jewels' are always safe in Jesus' keeping.

☐ *Strengthen our faith, loving God, so that with our hand in Jesus' hand we may be serene in heart, knowing that whatever the future holds Jesus will be there beside us.*

Saturday September 11   Matthew 7.1–11

Misjudgements, sometimes harsh and hurtful, are commonly made. William Barclay quoted a dramatic instance. During the First World War, two young men in civilian clothes were lunching together in a London restaurant when a woman handed each of them a white feather – the badge of cowardice, intended to rebuke them for not being in the armed forces when the country was at war. In fact, one of those men was convalescing from severe injuries received with the Royal Flying Corps while the other had that very day been decorated for gallantry by his king.

For Jesus' sake we are meant to look as kindly as possible upon other people and their actions. If we were more aware of our own faults, says Jesus with characteristic humour (verses 3–5), we would be more tolerant towards the faults we see in others. The trouble is that most of us are much better at noticing faults in others than observing the very same faults in ourselves. A minister once preached on the theme of gossip. After the service the district's most notorious gossip said to him, 'That was a fine sermon. It fitted Mrs So-and-so to a T.'

☐ *Help us, Lord, to be more concerned about the weeds in our own garden than about those in our neighbour's garden.*

For group discussion and personal thought

Seeking revenge, worrying and being harsh in our judgements are ways in which we do great harm to our growth as Christians. Why? How can these faults be overcome? Consider Jesus' teaching in Matthew 5.38–40; 6.25–27; 7.1–5.

Sunday September 12   1 Peter 3.1–9*

THE FAMILY

Your first reaction to these verses might be unfavourable for, at face value, they seem to assume the now-outmoded concept of the superiority of the male over the female. But Peter's aim was to advise **Christian** women on how they should behave in the hope of bringing **pagan** husbands into a Christian experience. Women, who had become Christians in that predominantly anti-Christian world, might have been tempted to leave home, to separate themselves from their family, to despise the relationship they had had with their husbands and to look for fellowship with kindred souls outside the home. Peter says: Beware of this for it is not by creating a rift, but by the gentle continuance of your traditional wifely role, that you will be showing true Christian love – and maybe thus you will win your husband, too, for Christ!

But note this, too: Peter includes a word of advice to husbands.

His words in verse 1, in the light of his understanding of the marital relationship of 'sharing together in the grace of God' (verse 7), cannot have in them any hint of domestic tyranny. In the family, and in the wider context of all relationships, the Christian way is one of mutual affection, kindly and humble-minded.

☐ *Help us, Lord, in our most intimate relationships, to show the respect, courtesy and love that we show to friends outside our family.*

Monday September 13   Matthew 10.1–13

You may sometimes hear a man say, 'Of course, I am not the religious type.' This is usually intended to explain, or even excuse, his lack of commitment to Christ and his way of life. The fact is, however, that people are not divided by nature into religious and non-religious species: it is a matter of personal choice.

If any proof is required of the truth of this statement, we need look no further than the list of the twelve men whom Jesus chose to be his disciples (verses 2–4). They were such a varied group, differing widely in background and temperament; and yet to each and every one Jesus extended the same invitation, 'Follow me.'

Toyohiko Kagawa, that great Japanese Christian, once said, 'There are no frontier lines in the realm of the Spirit.' Jesus Christ calls everyone without exception to his side. Whether they respond or not is their own decision. For those who do respond there is a great challenge but there is also a rich reward.

☐ *Jesus calls us! By thy mercies,*
    Saviour, make us hear thy call,
    Give our hearts to thy obedience,
       Serve and love thee best of all.   *Cecil Frances Alexander*

Tuesday September 14   Matthew 18.21–35

Few of the demands Jesus makes of his followers are harder to meet than that of being continually ready to forgive. Peter thought he was almost ridiculously exaggerating when he suggested to Jesus that he might want him to forgive repeated injuries as often as seven times. What a surprise it was when Jesus said, 'No, Peter, not seven times but seventy times seven'!

Jesus did not mean that the limit of our forgiving should be a carefully counted four hundred and ninety times. He meant that our willingness to forgive should be unlimited.

If this should appear a lot to ask, the accompanying parable plainly indicates otherwise. We have been forgiven the greatest debt of all – it took the death of Jesus to cancel it – and we must therefore be forgiving towards others.

To be hard and unmerciful towards any of our fellows, in the face of what we owe to the forgiving love of God, is to act in very shameful fashion. Worse than that, it may be to deny forgiveness to ourselves. God does not force his forgiveness upon us and we shut the door against that forgiveness unless we are prepared to practise forgiveness ourselves. As George Herbert once put it, 'He who cannot forgive breaks the bridge over which he himself must pass.'

☐ *Help us, O Lord, to try really seriously to forgive as we have been forgiven.*

Wednesday September 15   Matthew 20.1–16

Perhaps no other parable that Jesus told has roused as much controversy as this one. However, most of this is seen to be irrelevant, when we remember that Jesus usually told his parables to convey one single truth. The details have no purpose beyond giving 'flesh and blood' to the bones of the story.

The point of this parable is the generosity of the love of God. The situation depicted is that of the hiring of casual labour by the day. Those who took up employment at the beginning of the day were promised a denarius (a penny AV), the normal day's wage. When the day's work was over they received that very amount – in other words they were paid in full. All other workers received a denarius, too; even those who started working at the last hour were given a full day's wage. The landowner was not unfair to the early starters – they all received the full day's wage, too – but he was more than fair to the late beginners.

The marvellous lesson is that no matter when a man comes to Jesus, be it early or late, he receives all that eternal life means. God cannot give more than everything his love has to bestow; he will not give less.

☐ *'Mine is an unchanging love,*
    Higher than the heights above,
    Deeper than the depths beneath,
    Free and faithful, strong as death.'

                                                    William Cowper

There are two parables in this section although they are set out as if the second were a continuation of the first.

● The first (verses 1–10) gives a reminder that the grace of God is so marvellous that there is a place in his kingdom for everyone who will accept it. No one is shut out except those who exclude themselves by refusing God's loving invitation.

● The second parable (verses 11–14) gives a reminder that accepting God's invitation involves responsibility as well as privilege. The king in the parable is not passing judgement on some poor guest because he could not afford to be better dressed. The guest simply decided not to take the trouble to dress appropriately.

The lesson of this second parable is that the man who decides to accept God's gracious invitation must bring with him a life which strives to match the bounty God's love has given him. As William Barclay puts it: 'The door is open, but the door is not open that the sinner may come and remain a sinner, but that the sinner may come and become a saint.'

☐   *O Love that wilt not let me go,*
      I rest my weary soul in thee :
   I give thee back the life I owe,
   That in thine ocean depths its flow
         May richer, fuller be.   *George Matheson*

In Jesus' day weddings could not be arranged for a precise hour nor even, if the bridegroom came from any distance, for a specific day. It was, however, part of the bridesmaids' duties to welcome the bridegroom whenever he should arrive, even if in the middle of the night, and escort him to the marriage. The bridegroom in Jesus' story did arrive in the middle of the night and half of the bridesmaids were caught so unprepared that they were shut out of the wedding celebrations.

Jesus wants every one of us to see to it that we are ready for that face to face encounter with God which lies ahead for us all. Not that he wants us to live in a state of unhealthy tension wondering every day if we should now prepare ourselves for judgement. Jesus wants us to have our spiritual affairs in such a state of constant readiness that we may live each day with serenity and also with gladness. He wants us, in other words, so to live our lives under his sovereignty that no matter when the final summons should come, we shall be found ready.

When Mary of Orange lay dying, her chaplain began to speak to her of her soul's salvation. 'My friend,' she said, 'I have not left this matter to this hour.' That is how Jesus wants it to be.

☐ *Help me, O Father, so to trust in Jesus that I may meet every day with the calm confidence that, whether I live or die, all will be well.*

Saturday September 18   Matthew 25.14–30

All of us hold our lives in trust from God. In this parable Jesus urges us to be good stewards of the life we hold and the opportunities it contains.

It would be plainly absurd to suggest that every person is endowed with the same abilities or given the same opportunities; and the story Jesus tells here recognises this. At the same time it makes it quite clear that we all have abilities and we all have opportunities; and Jesus wants us to do our best with what we have and are.

The fault of the servant with the one bag of gold, and the ground of his condemnation, was that he did not try. He wasted his opportunity simply because he refused to use it.

If we do our best for Jesus he will accept it gladly and bless it; and we shall gain his 'Well done!' If we fail even to try or if we are content to give him much less than our best, we condemn ourselves. What matters is not so much the talents and opportunities that life allots to us but the use we make of them.

A little mission girl was asked by a visitor what she did for the kingdom of God. 'Please, miss,' she replied, 'I scrubs.' She was doing her best for Jesus; and so may everyone.

☐ *Just as I am, young, strong and free,*
To be the best that I can be
For truth, and righteousness, and thee,
*   Lord of my life, I come.*   *Marianne Farningham*

For group discussion and personal thought

'It's hard to live a Christian life.' How do this week's readings show that to be true? Which of them do you think is the hardest to live up to? Why **must** we – and how **can** we – live by these teachings?

THOSE IN AUTHORITY

In a State where the Christian community is a minority, where the government is officially atheist or anti-Christian, would it be right to include national leaders in our prayers? This was the situation in the case of the early Church. Today's reading urges that such leaders **should** be prayed for. Two reasons are given:

● so that Christians might have a 'tranquil and quiet life' undisturbed by suspicions that Christians were enemies of the State;

● because Christianity is a faith which includes all people within the loving purpose of God.

It has been suggested that verses 5–6 may be part of an official Christian creed recited in worship at that time.

We seldom know what our prayers for other people achieve. We do believe that, if offered in genuine love, they may be means of bringing those for whom we pray within the orbit of God's love, enabling his love to become effective in their lives. So it is our privilege and duty to pray, not just for those dear to us, but perhaps especially for our enemies and for those with particularly heavy burdens to bear.

☐ *Pray now for the government of your country;*
the leaders in your community;
the leaders of your church.

DANIEL

Notes by Revd Richard Coggins, MA, BD

Richard Coggins, an Anglican, is a lecturer in Old Testament and Hebrew at King's College, London. He also assists in a parish in South London.

Few books of the Bible are the subject of more controversy than *Daniel*. On the one hand, there are fringe Christian groups who see in it veiled references to the political events of our own day, and find cryptic messages enabling them to denounce the iniquity of certain political systems. On the other hand, there is agreement among scholars that the book cannot have reached its present form until much later than its apparent date, and that it comes from second century Jerusalem and not from sixth century Babylon. It was 'published' at a time of crisis to encourage the Jews to be loyal to their faith in the face of persecution by the Hellenistic ruler Antiochus Epiphanes.

In the midst of the arguments about the origin and meaning of *Daniel*, much of the message of the book itself has often been neglected. So, during the next two weeks, we shall concentrate mainly on stories whose relevance does not depend upon a particular theory of their origin, and we shall ask what is their meaning for us today.

Suggestions for further reading

The Book of Daniel by R.J. Hammer, Cambridge Bible Commentaries on the New English Bible (Cambridge University Press);

Daniel: A Commentary by Norman W. Porteous, Old Testament Library (SCM Press).

Monday September 20   Daniel 1.1–21

The requirement of eating particular foods and abstaining from others is an important one in many of the world's religions. It is a major concern throughout the Bible, from the instructions given to Noah after the flood (Genesis 9.4) to the care shown by Paul for his converts in Corinth (1 Corinthians 8).

It is no surprise, therefore, to find that in times of crisis an important mark of self-identification for the Jewish community was strict adherence to the dietary laws. Here this is illustrated by a vivid story which also serves to introduce the main characters of the book – Daniel and his three young friends.

Many Christian churches no longer have specific food laws, but that does not make this chapter irrelevant. Let us note two points:

● A sensitive concern for adherents of other religions should bear in mind that Jews, Muslims and Hindus, for example, have particular dietary laws of which we should be aware.

● We need to ask whether we are exercising our stewardship of the world's resources as God would wish. Can the rich nations of the world legitimately go on consuming them at the present rate? Have vegetarians something to teach us, particularly in view of the large amounts of grain being fed to animals while millions of people are starving?

☐ *All that is in the world is the result of your bounty, O Lord; guide us in its proper use.*

Tuesday September 21   Daniel 2.1–24

The first chapter has introduced Daniel and his three friends; now this story in chapter 2 shows Daniel as a specially favoured servant of God. In times long past, Joseph, an exile in a foreign land, had been able to explain the meaning of the Pharaoh's dreams when they were told to him (Genesis 41); now Daniel, also an exile, is able to tell Nebuchadnezzar what he has dreamt as well as what it means!

Such a story might seem to smack of magic, or at least of a desire to poke fun at the pretensions of other religions. Perhaps these elements are present. But more basic is the prayer of Daniel (verses 20–23) which shows how he recognised the true source of all human wisdom and power.

It is essential for us in reading this story to distinguish between its transient and its lasting features. Our dreams may reveal much to psychologists, but we should be cautious of supposing that dreams will spell out the future, or provide a key to all that mystifies us in our daily lives. Yet, just as the Old Testament writer was able to look beyond the dream to the underlying reality of God's providence, so we also must look beyond the outward circumstances of our lives to their underlying reality and meaning in God's providence and love.

Wednesday September 22   Daniel 2.25–49

The dream of Nebuchadnezzar is now spelt out in detail, and its significance explained. It tells a story of lasting importance.

Throughout the world's history there have been those who have supposed that they controlled the lives of others. Later chapters of *Daniel* will underline the punishment which befalls those who overreach themselves in this way; for the moment the particular emphasis is on the transience of what may seem lasting and powerful. The mighty image of the vision was no stronger than its weakest parts (verses 33–34).

Of the lessons that could be learnt from this, one of the most important for the Church is the need to realise that much of what seems to be lasting and unchangeable in the power structures of the world is in fact no more than a passing fashion. Too often the Church has wedded itself to one political system or party, and has suffered when that system has undergone the fate of Nebuchadnezzar's image. We are a Church **in** the world, and as Christians we must be concerned with all its political, social and economic problems. Yet as a Church we must also learn not to tie ourselves too closely to any one particular political party or social grouping, for no such human institution can fully reflect the will of God for us.

☐ *Pray for Christians in positions of government, both local and national.*

Thursday September 23   Daniel 3.1–18

The story of the 'burning fiery furnace' seems to have an origin different from that of the other stories in *Daniel*, for here only the three young men and not Daniel himself play a part. But its essential purpose, of encouragement to maintain faith no matter how great the pressure, remains the same. As in the other stories, we find an element of mockery at other religions which are regarded as no more than idolatry, and a distrust of foreigners as potential betrayers (verses 8–12), whom we should hesitate to follow, although we can recognise how understandable such reactions are in times of crisis.

But in this first part of the story the climax is formed by the last three verses. The writer knew that God could not always be expected to intervene to rescue his servants from their torture, and so he emphasises that the service of God must be undertaken for its own sake, and not in the hope of escaping trials. Christian martyrs down the centuries have gained inspiration from the example of this story.

☐ *Pray for Christians living in countries where there is persecution, that they may have the strength to remain loyal to their faith.*

Friday September 24   **Daniel 3.19–30**

The dramatic story of the deliverance of the three young men will speak to each of us in different ways; but two particular approaches to its understanding seem natural.

● **We have the picture of God delivering his faithful servants** from even the most extreme danger. Jesus warned his followers that they must not necessarily expect such deliverance (Matthew 26.53–54), but the conviction of God's presence with us in the time of greatest trial and danger is still a precious one.

● **The description of a fourth being in the middle of the fire** (verse 25), so that the young men are now in the divine presence, gives a different dimension to the story. This suggests the hope of a future life, in which those who had remained faithful would be saved from all torments.

Thus these verses encourage the Christian both in his present struggle and in his future expectation. This encouragement led to the great hymn of praise sometimes known as the *Benedicite*, now found in the Apocrypha of our Bible, a prayer which even those who do not accept the Apocrypha as part of the Bible may nevertheless make their own. Here are two verses from it:

☐ *'O all ye works of the Lord, bless ye the Lord: praise him, and magnify him for ever.*
'O ye holy and humble men of heart, bless ye the Lord: praise him, and magnify him for ever.'
                    (The Song of the Three Holy Children 35, 65)

Saturday September 25   **Daniel 4.1–18**

The picture of Nebuchadnezzar in the book of *Daniel*, and particularly in this chapter, is in some ways an unexpected one. The ruler of the great empire which had ended Judah's independent existence, destroyed the holy city of Jerusalem and reduced its temple to ruins, might have been regarded as a godless tyrant. In fact we find words of praise put into his mouth (verse 3), and he shows great respect for Daniel (here given his Babylonian name Belteshazzar) because of his spiritual insight. When we read the rest of the story on Monday we shall notice how great was Daniel's own respect for the king.

But this story is no apology for Nebuchadnezzar. However great human achievements may seem, however sympathetically they may be understood, they must be seen as subject to divine control or disaster will follow. Verses 13 and 17 in particular set out the theme of God's rule being supreme over all human, earthly aspirations. The importance of this was never greater than in our own age when man's scientific and technological achievements are so impressive. Each time we hear of or benefit from some new 'breakthrough', we need to set it in the context of the overriding authority of God and to consider its proper use in furthering God's purposes.

☐ 'The Lord is King for ever and ever.' (Psalm 10.16)

For group discussion and personal thought

Read and study Daniel 3.1–18. We may not be required by the State to worship a golden image, but sometimes we may feel that some policies of our nation are contrary to God's will. Consider examples of these and how we should respond to them.

Sunday September 26   **Galatians 2.20 to 3.9***

THE PROOF OF FAITH

Many of the members of the Galatian churches were Gentiles. But some Jewish Christians were telling these new Gentile converts that true Christianity must include obedience to Jewish traditions. So what had begun for them as a joyous liberation from sin through their faith in Christ, was beginning to turn into a dreary effort to obey Jewish laws. Paul's 'good news' that life is not meant to be a grim legal imprisonment but a free personal relationship with God was in danger of being lost. No wonder he felt so exasperated! These verses put his exasperation into words. They contain the concept that when a person understands the meaning of Christ's self-giving, it is as if a new life begins for him – a Christ-centred life. What now motivates him is not an anxious following of rules, but the Spirit of Christ.

This ancient battle between 'salvation by grace' and 'salvation by works' is by no means dead. All too easily the joy and freedom of the Christian life turns into a grey, dull grind of 'trying to be good' – with all the guilt and sense of failure that accompany it. Christianity is not primarily an ethical or ritual system; it is the experience of friendship with God.

☐ *Father, may we know the joy and freedom of being your children.*

Monday September 27   Daniel 4.19–37

A characteristic feature of the book of *Daniel* is a symbolism which sets humankind over against the beasts as a closer representation of God's creation: the picture of the four empires in chapter 7 is a good example of this contrast. But men must learn that their differentiation from the beasts is part of God's pattern, not of their own achievement. That is the point of the description of Nebuchadnezzar's fate in verses 28–33. Because of his pride and the way in which he supposed that all his achievements were due to his 'own mighty power and for the honour of his majesty' (verse 30) he was reduced to animal status. Only when he acknowledged his limitations was his human dignity restored.

This vivid story enshrines a continuing truth about our status as human beings. It is not for nothing that pride has been described as the root sin, underlying all others.

Let us by all means rejoice in the wonder of humanity, provided that we recognise its proper place under the guiding hand of God. In particular the Church, as God's special instrument here on earth, needs to ensure that its achievements are measured by God's demands and not by worldly standards of success.

☐ *Pray for the leaders in our churches; that their aim may always be to discern and carry out God's will, not to further human ambition.*

Tuesday September 28   Daniel 5.1–31

The story of Belshazzar's feast sets out the writer's belief in the power of God over against blasphemous human pretensions, and it has much to teach us.

Unlike Nebuchadnezzar, Belshazzar is presented in a totally unsympathetic way. He symbolised the arrogant pagan ruler, confident in his own power, treating the dearest aspirations of his subject peoples with contempt. The blasphemous misuse of the temple vessels (verses 2–3) would have caused particular horror to those who first heard the story.

The book of *Daniel* reached its present form when the Jews were suffering persecution from another arrogant pagan ruler; and they were divided as to whether they should fight by every available means, or leave all in the hands of God. The author of *Daniel* took the latter view. He was confident that soon the writing would be on the wall for the impious tyrant and that God would soon deliver his people, who were to await that deliverance in passive obedience. Similar dilemmas have confronted the subjects of unjust régimes from that day to this.

☐ *In our prayers let us constantly remember those who have to decide whether to stand and fight or kneel and pray.*

Wednesday September 29   Daniel 6.1–28

It is sometimes said that the main concern of the stories in Daniel 1–6 is to spell out the right attitude toward unjust rulers; but this is only part of the story. Here Darius is pictured as actively supporting his favoured servant Daniel. The underlying theme of these stories is really the call to trust – trust in God's willingness to save.

In the Old Testament lions are used as a symbol for enemies (see, for example, Psalm 57.4). Consequently, a story which told of a faithful servant of God being rescued from ravaging lions would be especially significant. Daniel, like the psalmist, felt himself to be surrounded by enemies who could be pictured as lions. Here, with vivid irony, we read how the lion-like enemies were themselves consumed by lions (verse 24).

The theme of trust in God is also expressed in the book of *Daniel* by means of God sending protecting angels to guard his servants. In Daniel 10.13 one of these angels is called Michael. Today is Michaelmas Day, and it is appropriate both to renew our trust in God and to thank him for the protecting care which he has exercised over our lives in so many different ways.

☐ *Have you a decision to make? How can you best show your trust in God's power to help you to decide rightly?*

Thursday September 30

The first six chapters of Daniel tell stories from which any sensitive reader can gain a valuable message; the remainder of the book is in the more veiled form known as *apocalyptic*. During the remainder of this week we shall look at just three passages from this section.

▶ Read **Daniel 7.1–18.**

The visionary character of this part is established at once with the appearance of four mysterious beasts which symbolise the various empires under whose control Israel passed. In their turn they were succeeded by one 'like a man' or 'son of man' (RSV). Verse 13 has been of enormous importance for Christians, for almost certainly it provides the background for the application of the title 'Son of man' to Jesus in the Gospels. For the reader of *Daniel*, however, its most immediate significance lies in the assertion that God's people, Israel – 'the saints of the Most High' (verse 18) – could be considered as truly human where the great empires were likened to beasts.

It is an encouraging message, but also a dangerous one. Right through the history of Israel and of the Church it has been necessary to warn against the idea that membership of a particular group is by itself sufficient to ensure God's favour. We can thank God for our membership of the Church; but we must never presume that that membership by itself puts us right with God.

☐ *Use the last sentence above as the basis of your prayers.*

Friday October 1   Daniel 9.3–19

The series of visions which make up the second half of the book of *Daniel* is here interrupted by an extended prayer, somewhat unexpected in its present context, but of great importance for our understanding of the outlook of the author.

We saw yesterday that the idea of a particular nation or group as specially favoured by God is a dangerous one. Here our author shows himself well aware of that danger, and, using a type of prayer found several times in the Old Testament (eg Solomon's prayer in 1 Kings 8), he acknowledges how often Israel has failed to fulfil her responsibilities. After the confession of sin comes the supplication to God to remember his former mercies and to deliver his people once again as he had done in the past (verses 15–19).

How much today's Church needs such a prayer! Too often we are either complacently assured that as God's people all must be well with us, or we are so engrossed in our own plans that we fail to realise how much we fall short of God's demands upon us.

☐ *Let us make our own the words of verse 9: 'Compassion and forgiveness belong to the Lord our God, **though we have rebelled against him.'***

Saturday October 2   Daniel 12.1–10

Throughout much of the Old Testament we find the confident expectation that Israel, the people of God, would be restored, no matter how great the disasters she might have to undergo. By the second century BC, when the book of *Daniel* reached its final form, that belief was held as firmly as ever, but there was an additional complication. Who were the true people of God? It was a time when those who adhered strictly to their religion were being persecuted, and so Israel was divided; some had betrayed their sacred heritage and accepted pagan ways. In these verses the future hope is expressed in more individual terms: the faithful might look forward to a future life of bliss, while the traitors would receive their due reward.

There are passages in the Gospels where the idea of resurrection was greeted with incredulity, as something very strange to the disciples of Jesus (eg Mark 9.9-10). This is partly explained by the fact that this is probably the only Old Testament passage pointing forward to such a hope. But the Christian hope is grounded rather in the fact that, as God raised Jesus, so he will give new life to those who are loyal to Jesus. The Christian life is a life of confident expectation, just as the book of *Daniel* ends on a note of confident expectation.

☐ *The day of resurrection!*
   Earth, tell it out abroad!   *John of Damascus*

For group discussion and personal thought

The book of *Daniel* appeared at a time when the Jews were suffering fierce persecution. Consider why the writer was confident that God could be trusted to see them through their tribulations. Can we, for the same reasons, depend on God when we are faced with the temptation to compromise or co-operate with evil?

THE OFFERING OF OUR LIFE

It is an interesting exercise to discuss with friends what they would do if they knew they had only a few weeks to live. Various answers might be given: for example, sail round the world or visit as many old friends as possible to say goodbye. What would **you** do?

Peter was writing to people whom he believed would soon experience the 'end of the world'. And he advised them as to what they should do with their brief, remaining time:

● Live a calm, self-controlled life of prayer.

● Go on loving other people in depth.

● Use their gifts for other people's benefit and to the glory of God.

In other words, they were to carry on living as a Christian usually does!

It does not matter if the end of the world – or our own death, which is the end of the world for us – comes sooner or later. We do not live in the past or in the future. We live in the **'now'**; and quiet confidence in God, sustained by prayer, love for others and living our life to the full for God and for others, is the way to peace and joy.

☐   *His adorable will*
       Let us gladly fulfil,
       And our talents improve,
   By the patience of hope and the labour of love.

                              Charles Wesley

ROMANS 9–16

Notes by Revd Howard Booth

Having read the first eight chapters of *Romans* in May, we now return to this most important letter of Paul to read chapters 9–16.

In chapters 9–11, Paul writes about the problem of unbelieving Israel. Although this had led to the Gentiles receiving the offer of salvation, Paul still held to the conviction that ultimately the Jews would also be gathered into the Church of Christ.

Then, in chapters 12–16, Paul turns to the practical outworking of the Christian faith in daily life. We are saved to serve, and to live lives of integrity, pleasing to God.

Suggestions for further reading – see page 89.

Monday October 4   **Romans 9.1–18**

Paul wrestles with the problem of the relationship between Jews and Gentiles and the part played by the Jewish law in mankind's spiritual enlightenment.

Do not try to avoid the difficulties raised by these verses. It appears that Paul is saying that God chooses whom he wills to be blessed and similarly whom he wills to be cursed. But this is an exaggeration in order to make a supremely important point – that we are entirely dependent upon God's love and mercy.

I have learned a good deal about life by reflecting upon what has happened to me through the actions of people whom I thought were stubborn and lacking in love. The Jews were a highly privileged people but God could use even their rejection of Christ to good purpose. Through it Gentiles could see that the offer of a true Christian life did not depend on breeding; it was 'all of grace', and they were as much loved by God as their Jewish neighbours who had laid far too much stress upon their being 'chosen'.

☐ *Begin your reflection and prayer by thanking God that you are loved by him. This is where fruitful discipleship often begins – with a thankful heart. Then try to feel the pain Paul felt because of the actions of his own people. This could be the means of your creative witnessing to those you love who care little about Jesus.*

In the world of psychology there are those who believe that a man is the result of his conditioning. He is what his circumstances have made him; he cannot escape his fate. This view appears to surface here in theological language. But let your thinking get beneath the words. God has not made tin soldiers; he has made real people who can respond to love and be loving. Some people do seem to get a better start in life than others, but no one is completely unable to respond to God's love.

It is easy for a church to become a kind of religious club which is exclusive rather than inclusive. Years ago I heard a person say to a close friend as she came out of church: 'It isn't the same since all those new people started to come!'

There is something comforting at first in believing that you belong to a superior class but in the end it is devastating. Those who practise racial exclusiveness are finding this out, often with dreadful consequences.

☐ *Thank God for that part of your Christian faith which is real and vital and which is your very own. This is what you can build on. And remember that it all happened because God took the initiative in letting you know that you are loved.*

In pastoral work I have come to see the way in which some people's fierce independence can lead them to loneliness and even to breakdown. The people who will never let you do anything for them are the most difficult of people to have good relationships with. They may even want to do all manner of things for you but when you offer yourself to them in any way you are politely but firmly rejected.

Paul now shows that what the Jews believed to be a virtue was actually turning out to be a vice. They were a chosen people, but they thought they earned God's favour by their obedience to the law and by their good works. They refused what God had to offer them – his free grace.

In pastoral work there is little one can do with aggressive independence until it breaks down. It often does because the burden of maintaining a continually independent stance is too much to bear. People need each other – we are all 'bound up in the bundle of life' and thus we are interdependent. And further, we all need God.

□ *Think about your own attitude towards God and other people.*
Are you willing to accept help from others as well as to give it?
Reflect on verse 3 and remember that the only one who can put
you right is God himself.

Thursday October 7   Romans 10.5–21

Over the years I can recall a number of people whose personal
faith has been rekindled by the infectious enthusiasm of their
children. Indeed I myself have been challenged more than once
by the witness of my own children. It is so easy to get caught up
in formal religion, even to become absorbed in Church politics,
and yet, at the same time, to lose close contact with God and any
real sense of spiritual awareness.

Paul was aware that this had happened to many who claimed
to practise a detailed observance of the Jewish law and so he invited his readers to act positively by first believing and then
bearing witness to what had happened as the result of such faith
and trust.

When inward renewal takes place and the 'spiritual glow' is
restored then those who need to hear the good news will surely
do so. Paul wanted his fellow-Christians in Rome to know that
when at last he came to Rome he would proclaim the truths of
the gospel with all the power at his command. But what a
difference a lively, active, believing Christian community would
make!

□ *What are the factors which enable effective gospel communication*
in these days? Good preachers? Yes, there must always be those
who will preach with authority and conviction. But if there is to
be response there must also be the support of a virile and active
local Christian community. Are there ways in which you could
enable your Christian community to become more effective?

Friday October 8   Romans 11.1–12

The fact that the Jews had let God down meant that the Gentiles
could now hear and respond to the gospel. But this was not the
end. The aim was that out of this happening the Jews should
come back to their senses and return to the fold. Thus the
Christian community would cross racial barriers and so demonstrate reconciliation.

The 'remnant' principle (verse 5) has worked out again and

again in history and is being seen to be effective in our own day. At the time these notes are being written the Chinese government is allowing Christian minorities more privileges. Protestant churches are being allowed to train clergy again. As the veil is lifted so the 'remnant' is coming to life. It has always been there but, by the very nature of events, it has been hidden. Now, something of what has been going on has been revealed. And one of the good things we are hearing is that not all the believers are elderly. Some are young and eager to evangelise. Families have kept the flame burning by telling their children.

☐ *Reflect upon your own experience of spiritual isolation and perhaps even opposition. Such experiences can make or break a person. Tell God that you are going to trust him to deliver you if such times should ever come to you again.*

Saturday October 9   Romans 11.13–24

Christians must always recall 'the rock from whence they were hewn'. There could not have been a new covenant unless there had first been an old covenant. Christianity arose out of Judaism and for this we should always be grateful.

Paul's agricultural example (verse 17) was slightly wrong. The fruit-grower grafts the cultivated plant on to the stronger wild stock and not the other way round. It is possible, however, that Paul knew this quite well and was suggesting here that God does what human beings cannot do. 'Nature' may here be overtaken by **grace.**

Paul hopes that the Jews will come to envy the new status now possessed by the Gentiles and will want it for themselves. He knew how easy it was for both Jew and Gentile to become self-satisfied and complacent and to think that they had 'arrived'. Every age and every generation, including our own, has to discover a personal faith for themselves.

☐ *How easy it is to get caught up in ecclesiastical arguments about Church government, liturgical reform and the 'fine print' of Christian discipleship, while failing to be liberated and loving people! What holds us to Christ? Is it the 'earthen vessel' or the energising power of the gospel? Think hard – and then pray!*

● Have you remembered to make your **gift** for the **international work of the IBRA** (see page 175 for details).

For group discussion and personal thought:

Consider Paul's attitude to Jews and Gentiles as found in this week's readings. As Christians we believe that God's final revelation is in Jesus Christ but today, in many countries, there is a growing friendliness between Christians and those of other faiths. How far can a greater friendliness and mutual understanding be reconciled with traditional missionary zeal?

Sunday October 10   Romans 5.1–11*

THE LIFE OF FAITH

When you have quarrelled with someone, you may feel sorry but quite unable to heal the rift because you think your friend will never be able to forgive you. But if he stretches out the hand of friendship in spite of all you have done, then the way is immediately open for you to respond – and find that the old friendship is firmly restored. That is something like what has happened, says Paul, between men and God. In Christ he has stretched out his hand of friendship to us. If we respond to his act (the New Testament term for this is **faith**) then all is right between God and us again (the New Testament term for this is **justified**).

☐ *Think carefully about these phrases from today's reading:*
  'The sphere of God's grace' *(verse 2). Now our relationship with God is one of confidence, not fear.*

  'God's love has flooded our inmost heart' *(verse 5). That contains the clue to the changed relationship – an overwhelming certainty that we are loved by God.*

  'God's own proof of his love towards us' *(verse 8) – namely, the death and resurrection of Christ.*

  'Reconciled to him' *(verse 10). It is not God who is reconciled to us. The change takes place in us, not him.*

  'Saved by his life' *(verse 10). The main thing about Jesus Christ is not that he died but that he lives – in us every day.*

Monday October 11   Romans 11.25–36

William Temple once said: 'The world can only be saved by worship.' When I first read it years ago I did not understand what he meant. If the world was to be saved from its own foolishness it seemed to me that it would be by hard work – by people taking the Christian faith seriously and putting it into practice! But further reflection helped me to realise that William Temple knew that the basic problem was people's motivation. Only when we are aware that we belong to God and depend totally upon him, will we act in harmony with God's will. Saint Augustine said this in another way a long time ago: 'Love God and do as you like.'

In today's reading Paul is affirming the same truth but the way he puts it makes it difficult to understand. Once again he seems to be saying that God predestines some to find life in Christ and others not to. It is his way of saying that everything that happens goes back to God. But he also makes it clear on so many other occasions that God's will for you and me and for everyone is the direct outcome of his love. God loves Jews **and** Gentiles and the only response that is adequate is our awareness of this followed by our sincere adoration.

☐ *Take verse 36 and dwell on its implications. When you have let your mind wander around its massive truths join in the triumphant chorus of the last phrase.*

Tuesday October 12 **Romans 12.1–8**

In the earlier chapters of *Romans* Paul has wrestled with the relationships between God and both Jews and Gentiles, and the place of the Jewish law. We now turn to what John Wesley would call 'the plain, practical implications'.

In my own Bible I have written by the side of today's reading: 'These verses are about Christians developing their full potential.' Then I have added the following four sub-headings:

● **Inward transformation.**
● **Proper view of self.**
● **Use of gifts.**
● **Personal development arises out of sharing.**

Try to identify the seed thoughts in the reading which gave rise to these sub-headings. Then notice how they relate to one another. Our inner transformation encourages a proper valuation of ourselves. Modesty is called for but not self-denigration. We have gifts and they are to be used; your gifts will both complement and be complemented by the gifts of others.

□ *Ask yourself whether you do properly value your own worth as a person and whether you are using your gifts aright in co-operation with others. Then dwell upon your own inner transformation. This is an ongoing process and makes the fuller development of your potential possible.*

Wednesday October 13   Romans 12.9–21

Verses like these will speak to different people in different ways according to what is happening to each individual at the time of reading. Sometimes one particular phrase will leap out from the rest because it helps to clarify a current mood or challenges a recent experience.

One way to read these verses is to use them as a 'check list':

● **Go through each phrase** and put a tick or a question mark against each statement.

● **Then go through them a second time,** thanking God for what he has achieved in your life and reflecting upon those areas in which you feel that you need to grow as a person.

□ *It may seem to be an extravagant statement, but these verses could revolutionise your life! In every one there is a rich source of spiritual dynamic. Pray these thoughts into the very centre of your being and get every one of them down as deep as you can.*

Thursday October 14   Romans 13.1–7

Paul might almost be accused of suggesting humiliating acquiescence to the State at all times and under all circumstances. A few years after he wrote these words Christians were suffering terrible hardships and even death because they would not do what the legal authority told them to do – bow the knee to the emperor. History is full of the stories of men and women who defied the established order for conscience' sake. Paul himself had some sharp exchanges with magistrates and others in positions of authority.

If and when such testing times come to us then we must be prepared to stand up and be counted – but that is when we believe that what the authority is doing runs counter to God's will. At all other times we accept that those set over us in government have the right to expect our loyalty – even when we do not like some of the things they are doing.

□ *Examine your own role in the community in which you live.*
To pay up cheerfully and to obey both the spirit of the law as well
as the letter can be a very real way of witnessing for Christ. When
you have taken an honest look at your attitudes, make the
further test of seeing if you can offer them to God in prayer.

Friday October 15   Romans 13.8–14

As the crowds move towards Wembley Stadium, London, for an
international football match they often see men carrying
banners with words such as these written on them: 'The day of
the Lord is at hand. Prepare to meet thy God.' The people in the
crowds smile and walk on. Such sentences lack any kind of
meaningful reality for them. Even regular churchgoers take little
notice. The urgency has gone out of announcements of the
Lord's return.

If Wembley had existed in Paul's day he might well have been
one of the banner-carriers! He believed that 'the day of the Lord'
was not far away. This gave point to his message and added
urgency. If his readers were to be found asleep when the event
took place this would be a tragedy of the first order!

Our response to the gospel should not depend upon any time
factor. It is right to respond with love **now** and at **all times**.
Indeed, all our actions should arise out of love which is the only
adequate motivation.

□ *Dwell on the 'debt of love' concept. Realise afresh how good it is*
to be loved and what a difference this makes to your own ability
to be loving. A man who had pushed his wife fifty miles through
the African bush as she lay on pillows in a wheelbarrow to get to a
mission hospital, was surprised to be asked why he did it. It was
quite simple. He loved her.

Saturday October 16   Romans 14.1–12

Occasionally I have been at the receiving end of intolerance and
disapproval. Someone has thought my churchmanship faulty
or my theology 'unsound' or my social judgement on a certain
issue lacking fire! Quite often I have hit back sharply at my
critics with a public statement such as a letter to the newspaper,
or perhaps with a private telephone call. On reflection I can now
see that sometimes I have been guilty myself of the same kind of
faults I have condemned in others.

Food laws were common in Judaism – and still are. Those who break them are considered to be disloyal to their faith. In the early Christian churches there were those who felt bound by old taboos. Paul here asks for understanding of each other's position. He does not ask his readers to abandon their own convictions; he does not even ask them to accept what the other person is doing. He simply asks that they accept each other as responsible human beings.

If we heeded Paul's word today it could make a profound difference to inter-church discussions and to the varied debates we have had in recent years on controversial social issues.

☐ *Pray for those who have responsibility for guiding their churches in ecumenical relations and in formulating ethical judgements. Some attitudes seem to arise more out of personal inclinations than a careful assessment of the facts in the light of biblical teaching.*

For group discussion and personal thought

Christians with the same basic beliefs do seem to arrive at widely different conclusions on an extensive range of issues (for example: use of alcohol, pacifism, sexual behaviour, politics). Read Romans 14.1–12 and consider what should guide us in the way we react to those who hold different convictions from ours.

Sunday October 17   **Revelation 7.9–17***

CITIZENS OF HEAVEN

These verses are often read at funerals as a statement of the Christian hope of life after death. They form part of that mysterious and exciting book which is sometimes called the *Apocalypse*, a word which means 'unveiling'. In a time of intense persecution of Christians (probably about 95 AD in the reign of the Emperor Domitian), the author wrote primarily for seven churches in Asia to encourage them to stand firm whatever they might have to suffer for their faith in Christ.

The book consists of a series of 'visions'. Instead of attempting to interpret these visions in terms of forthcoming events, as so many do, the whole book should be read as we read poetry. John may indeed have had some future holocaust in mind, connected with the barbaric persecution meted out by some of the Roman emperors. We live beyond those days. But the basic message of the book – and of today's verses in particular – has value for all times. It is that God is the absolute ruler, that all history is under his control, and that if we are faithful, his victory over evil will be our victory too, now and after death.

☐ *I ask them whence their victory came;*
   They, with united breath,
Ascribe their conquest to the Lamb,
   Their triumph to his death.

Isaac Watts

Prayer to use during the Week of Prayer for World Peace (October 17–24)

God, our Father, we pray for the peace of the world. Help us to consider with courage and humility the things that cause enmity – our greed, prejudices, sheer ignorance of people who are not of our nation, race or tribe, and failure to recognise them as our brothers and sisters. We pray that knowledge, trust and love may grow between the nations and that the love of Christ may destroy the enmity and make us one family.

Monday October 18   Romans 14.13–23

In the days when Roman Catholics abstained from meat on Fridays, if we were entertaining Roman Catholic friends we would always offer them fish to eat. It would have been the height of discourtesy to serve them with roast beef!

In so doing we were faithful to Paul's reasoning. It is sometimes suggested that here is the classic New Testament argument for total abstinence from alcohol but, worthy a social attitude as this may be, it is not likely that it was in Paul's mind. It can hardly be that each individual conviction of every member of a Christian community must be accepted by all in order to save each other from stumbling. In most congregations there are pacifists, non-pacifists, vegetarians, meat-eaters, total abstainers and moderate drinkers. If, for the sake of each other we all tried to act according to each others' decisions the end result would be chaos!

The vital point being made, however, is that of our mutual

responsibility for each other before God. This is the guiding light for all our decisions and consequent actions.

☐ *This emphasis on the 'stumbling block' idea reminds us of the teaching of Jesus (for example see Mark 9.42). Do you allow your deep concern for others to motivate your personal customs and social habits? Think of particular instances.*

Tuesday October 19   Romans 15.1–6

People who work in the caring professions – medicine, social work, and so on – are sometimes taught that they must not get involved in their patient's or client's needs. They must maintain a professional detachment which, it is said, is the only way to survive.

Today's reading would seem to challenge this view. If we are to help the weak to carry their burdens we must feel the weight of those burdens ourselves. A young doctor I know broke down when he told a woman that her husband had just died. The next moment he was holding the woman in his arms and letting the depth of his feeling seep through to her. This did far more for her than an attitude of cold, professional detachment. Within that situation they supported each other and both were helped.

In Jesus we have our supreme example. He really entered into people's deep, personal needs. He 'sat where they sat' and he 'wept with those who wept'. The result was that people knew that he really cared. Of course this often meant that he was not able to please himself, but out of this self-discipline other people were blessed and strengthened.

☐ *Think of someone known to you who is in need. Have you really felt the extent of their distress? Have you allowed it to get through to the centre of your being? Out of a willingness to turn away from self and so become available to other people much 'fruit' can come.*

Wednesday October 20   Romans 15.7–13

My exchange ministry trip to the deep south of the USA was a wonderful experience, but it was also saddening – almost heart-breaking. As guest pastor to a white church sited in a predominantly black area I saw only a few black faces in the congregation and these belonged to the professional class. In the main there were black churches for black people and white churches for white people. Apart from a few honourable exceptions they did not accept each other.

Similarly, in Britain many black Christians have set up their own black churches. They could not find churches in which their own cultural expressions of the same faith were made welcome. They could come as guests but not as partners.

It was a similar kind of situation that Paul wrestled with and, as he draws near to the end of the letter to the Romans, he returns to the matter which has always been on his mind – the relationship between Jew and Gentile. He appeals to the Old Testament to show that God's intention, right from the start, was acceptance of the Gentiles. Now both communities need to accept each other.

☐ *To be accepted is a wonderfully healing experience. Think of some person known to you who you feel longs to be accepted. What can you do about it? Take the blessing in verse 13 and meditate on the central words – joy – peace – faith – hope – power. These are ours because we have been accepted by God, and their true meaning will be reinforced as we accept other people. And those people may begin to enjoy the same experiences through our acceptance of them.*

Thursday October 21   Romans 15.14–21

A young man I know has been unable to get a regular job since he graduated two years ago. His father said to me: 'He has lost faith in himself.' That he should do so is easy to understand: but somehow he has to be helped to go on believing in himself, in his own worth, and in the contribution he can make to society.

Paul believed in himself in a proper way and invites us to follow his example. He had not founded the Roman church and some might say that he had no right to counsel them. But Rome was to be a base from which he would reach out to new and unevangelised areas. His right to communicate with them was endorsed by the seal God had put upon his work. That seal was the conversion of so many Gentiles.

Paul describes himself as a minister of Christ who is in priestly service. Without doubt he has been the appointed means of extending Christ's saving work among the Gentiles. The evidence is clearly seen, and there is no point in false modesty. God has chosen and appointed him and he is right to know and appreciate his place in God's eternal plan.

☐ *Read 1 Peter 2.9 as a further commentary on today's reading. We also are priests. God has chosen us to share in his work. Let us not shrink from the task : we each have a part to play.*

Friday October 22   Romans 15.22–33

Whenever and wherever there is aching need in the world the followers of Jesus can usually be found extending a helping hand. Christian aid is given without any strings attached and is an expression of Christian love.

Paul was an agent of Christian aid as well as an evangelist. The money he had collected for the Jerusalem poor was an expression of Christian *koinonia* (fellowship); it was a reminder that Christians belong to each other, that simple caring is an essential part of the gospel message.

Care and **proclamation** go hand in hand – the one supports the other. After the aid had been distributed Paul hoped to continue on his apostolic journeyings. He sensed that his visit to Jerusalem might be dangerous and he needed their prayers.

Yes, Paul did visit Rome – but it was in chains! Perhaps **because** he did come as a prisoner this turned out to be 'for the furtherance of the gospel' (Philippians 1.12, AV). Many years later a man called Dietrich Bonhoeffer made a similar journey: he too was persecuted, imprisoned and killed. But through his testimony many have found faith – and are still finding it.

☐ *There are many different ways of commending Christ. Some readers of these notes will be surrounded by challenging circumstances at this moment. Can this searching experience be the very means whereby you 'offer Christ'?*

Saturday October 23   Romans 16.1–27

The many names and personal greetings which make up more than half of this final chapter suggest several important things:

● **The 'good news' had been spread through personal relationships.** Public preaching there had been but this had been backed up by loving and caring friendship.

● **Women played an important part in the early development of the Christian Church.** Their part in the creation of Christian communities was out of all proportion to their place in the society of that day.

● **The names mentioned belonged to Jews and Gentiles.** The 'middle wall of partition' had been broken down.

Yet they must still exercise great care because the powers of darkness were always hovering around. Their main defence would be praise, gratitude, thanksgiving. Paul's final doxology is the one sufficient answer to jealousy, animosity and divisions – **'To God be glory!'** Praising enables loving and loving ensures thankfulness and consequently more praise!

☐ *Think of three people : first one who has given you much through his or her friendship ; then a woman who has played a significant part in your life ; finally recall a 'reconciler' through whom you have been blessed.*

Can you follow their examples in ways which are open to you? Of course you can – and for this privilege, glory to Jesus!

For group discussion and personal thought

Read Romans 16, noting the variety of people to whom Paul sent greetings. This suggests that in many instances the gospel had been spread by personal commendation and that groups for fellowship and worship were held in people's homes. Consider these as ways of evangelism in our own time.

Sunday October 24   **Genesis 1.1–3, 24–31a***

THE CREATION

The Christian faith is a **historical** religion. It has a beginning and an end, although both beginning and end are beyond time. In between is the history – the story of the Jewish people and the continuing story of Christ and the Christian Church. The beginning we find depicted in the early chapters of *Genesis*, the end in the apocalyptic language of *Revelation*.

We are not concerned in Genesis 1 with a scientific account of how the universe came into existence; we **are** concerned with what **meaning** we may find in the created universe. To this fundamental question the answer of *Genesis* is clear: there is a purpose; there is **God**. More than that, of all God's creatures, human beings have unique status; they possess something the rest of creation lacks – something that enables them to be partners with God in the creative process, to have communion with God and to be the children of God. It is this unique status of human beings, stamped with God's image, which is the basis of our faith and hope.

JOSHUA

Notes by Revd Leslie A. Newman, BA, PhD

Leslie Newman is a Methodist minister now living in Brighton. During his ministry he has served at Scarborough, Newcastle-on-Tyne and the Dome Mission, Brighton, and he has travelled extensively abroad as a lecturer and preacher.

A pattern is clearly seen in the events recorded in the book of *Joshua*. After the introduction of Joshua himself, we are given a dramatic account of the conquest of the Promised Land. This is followed by a scheme for agricultural settlement which, in turn, leads to a plan for the religious life of the people. So first we have the warriors, then the workers, and finally the worshippers.

● **The warriors.** Violence did not seem wrong to the consciences of people in those primitive days. The only way they knew of getting rid of false gods and evil practices was by extermination. In the course of time ideas developed, and later it was perceived that we do not fight against flesh and blood but against evil.

● **The workers.** In chapter 13 the book turns from war to work. The territory was divided among the tribes who were to cultivate it. This was something new, for this strip of land had hitherto been a highway rather than a homeland.

● **The worshippers.** With chapter 22 we find the spotlight turned on the people's worship. Joshua was most anxious that they should choose the God who had chosen them. He reviewed their history and, in the light of it, urged them to make a covenant with the God of their fathers.

Suggestions for further reading

Joshua by G. M. Tucker, Cambridge Bible Commentaries on the New English Bible (Cambridge University Press);

Joshua and the Flow of Biblical History by Francis A. Schaeffer (Hodder & Stoughton).

Monday October 25   Joshua 1.1–9

As Joshua is called to be the leader of the Israelites on the death of Moses, consider the following:

● **Strength.** We admire the physical strength of the athlete, the intellectual strength of an Einstein, and the moral strength of a John Wesley. However, strength for its own sake needs to be looked at carefully. A father who said to his son, 'Be anything; but be strong,' was giving dangerous advice, for it all depends on what we do with our strength. So many catastrophes have issued not from the weakness of the weak but the strength of the strong.

● **Purpose.** Joshua was told to use his strength in keeping the law. Both he and his people were to be under its authority, which implies obedience, and this demands character, especially in the strong man. Notice that Joshua was not to belittle his strength but to use it responsibly. To do this would require the knowledge that he was not alone (verse 9).

● **Challenge.** Joshua was to banish timidity. If only men would use their gift of strength in a courageous, rightful way, what tragedies the world would be spared! If only nations, that have economic assets and political experience would realise the sacredness of strength, how speedily the world would become prosperous and peaceful!

☐ *Lord, may we be of good courage and responsibly strong as we face the challenges of life.*

Tuesday October 26   Joshua 2.1–16

Some regard Rahab as a heroine. This is surprising, for consider some unlovely elements in her character:

● She was **a liar.** The Bible teaches, and history demonstrates, that whatever may be the short term advantage of 'a lie of convenience', to betray the truth is to betray oneself.

● She was **a harlot.** Some commentators describe her as 'the keeper of a house of entertainment' who ran a hostelry for travellers. Possibly she represents a common type of heathen morality.

Alongside her treachery and her trade consider two excellent qualities:

● She was **a student of contemporary history!** Having pondered the significance of events, she believed that some great happening was about to intervene. So she sought to build a 'shelter' around herself and her family. How do we read current events? Living in a transitional period, full of expectation and uncertainty, how do we interpret it? Rahab may have been a sinner, but she was also a seer.

• She became **an important figure in history,** for she was the mother of Boaz who was the great-grandfather of King David, from whom Jesus was descended (see Matthew 1.1–16 and Luke 3.23–32). Although Jesus would not have approved of Rahab's trade, it is interesting to note that some of his important sayings were in connection with a woman caught committing adultery (John 8.1–11).

☐ *O God, may we, like Jesus, appreciate the good in everyone.*

Wednesday October 27   Joshua 3.1–17

These verses should not be read merely as history; for, surely, they also contain an acted parable. Ponder the following points:
• **It was a new beginning.** On the brink of a new life the Israelites knew that tomorrow's world would be different from today's (verse 5). Is not the situation today somewhat similar? We, too, are on the brink of the unknown. However, unlike the Israelites, we rely on self-effort and humanistic plans. A human leader there must be, but it is God who will 'magnify' him (verse 7).
• **They were a new nation under God.** Notice that Joshua did not offer his own ideas but told them of God's purpose (verse 9). Nor did he seek to be original or clever. His concern was to declare the intention of God.
• **God would lead them.** Joshua reminded them that they were pledged to God. Unlike a modern military leader, who would have discussed armaments and tactics, Joshua put the signature of God on the venture. Both ancient and modern unbelievers may wag their heads at Joshua's insistence on God first, but the failure of many humanistic efforts suggests that his emphasis was right.
• **It was a people's crusade.** Verse 12 expresses a rich thought. It suggests that Joshua declined to be a dictator and involved all the tribes in a form of representative government.

☐ *Only thou our leader be,*
   And we still will follow thee.   *John Cennick*

Thursday October 28   Joshua 4.4–14, 19–22

Israel kept her history alive. Again and again she raised stones of remembrance so that others might ask what they meant, what history was in them. Thus they were more than a memorial –

they were stones of witness. These 'sermons in stone' opened a door to a message from history.

● **Every person has his history.** He is building his life with the stones of experience and there are many 'Jordans' for each to cross. Of course, we may leave these experiences scattered about, like meaningless stones on the bed of a river. Alternatively, we may build them into a pattern which is meaningful to others as we declare: 'Such and such happened to me.' Nor should we wait for posterity to do this for us. Let us bear our own witness while we can.

● **Was it an accident that no way of retreat was provided?** Does this not suggest that life is a one-way street and we do not go back? As we pass over our various 'Jordans', especially the last one, they close behind us, leaving us no alternative but to go forward and face the future.

□ *Here I raise my Ebenezer;*
    Hither by thy help I'm come;
  And I hope by thy good pleasure,
      Safely to arrive at home. *Robert Robinson*

Friday October 29   Joshua 6.1–11

Modern military experts might think that to assault a fortress by investing it with a religious ceremony was impractical. Was it? Consider two hidden points:

● **Its effect on the Israelite army.** Think of the discipline involved in the daily march around the city. To be kept in check when the prize is before you, to possess arms and not to use them, to want to shout and yet remain silent: such discipline produces strength, just as indiscipline dissipates it.

Is not this a lesson we all have to learn – to have power and not to use it, to be filled with excitement and not express it? In this activist age we often do much and achieve little. Is not mob violence a sign of indiscipline?

● **Its effect on the enemy.** Wouldn't the daily march undermine the enemy's confidence and the religious character of the procession play upon their superstition? What secret weapon had an army which could keep so steady? When would the 'bomb' go off? A disciplined army, seemingly doing nothing, could have terrified an enemy by its intimidating silence.

□ *With shield of faith and mystic sword,*
    Go forth the knights of God. *Vera Walker*

Verses 18–19 reveal yet another aspect of discipline: 'Touch not, take not, handle not,' is the theme. After years of deprivation, suddenly the Israelites found themselves surrounded by things they were not to touch. When conquerors enter a city and yet behave themselves like honest men, are they not greater in their abstinence than they were in their assault? In such an attitude the quality of character is revealed.

This is an acute difficulty for some people. When surrounded by things they want, it takes a disciplined conscience not to appropriate them. Consider a starving man with only the law between himself and food, or a person who for years has been begging 'leave to toil' and a job could be his if only he would cheat. At such points the quality of a person is tested.

When we see people yield to great temptations, which would not tempt us, we should reflect lest hypocrisy conceal our real character.

The disciplined life discovers that abstinence is a positive virtue.

☐ *'Let anyone who thinks that he stands take heed lest he fall.'*
(1 Corinthians 10.12, RSV)

For group discussion and personal thought

Prominent in the story of the Israelites' crossing of the Jordan is the idea of 'stones of remembrance' (Joshua 4.4–7). Consider some modern 'stones of remembrance' (statues, war memorials, etc). What is the chief value of these? How could we profit more from them?

Sunday October 31   **Genesis 3.1–15***
THE FALL

There are two basic concepts of human nature in the Bible. One is that humans are stamped with God's image – made for communion with him. The other is that this image of God has become smudged by sin: the intended happy relation with God has been broken. Last Sunday we looked briefly at the first basic concept. Today's story is an attempt to state the second. We should not look for profound significance in every detail of the story but see its general meaning; namely that evil, corruption and sin are real elements in our human experience.

● **The serpent.** In ancient thought this is frequently a symbol of evil.

● **The tree in the middle of the garden.** The fruit of this tree was forbidden. What was the 'forbidden fruit' which would give the eater knowledge of good and evil? It was not moral knowledge but a knowledge of mysterious forces whereby the universe could be controlled – in other words the authority that belongs to God alone. What the man and the woman were tempted to do was to disregard their responsibility to God and to be gods themselves! Human beings, created to be God's junior partners, are always wanting to ignore God and 'run their own show'. But the universe will not work that way.

☐ *It has been said that sin is an alienation from God of which our sins are symptoms.*

Monday November 1   Joshua 9.3–23

The trick of the Gibeonites has much to say to our modern situation. It illustrates the pitiable ruses which men take upon themselves when driven by fear. How often people draw a mask over their faces, obliterating their true identity, in order to save their own skin! How often have businesses and nations misrepresented themselves in order to join alliances in which they do not really believe!

● **The truth men ignore.** The evidence of the Gibeonites' genuineness seemed complete – the travel stains, the mouldy bread, the old clothes and useless wine-skins. So why make it a religious problem? Why pray about it? The Israelites at first left out God (verse 14) and depended upon their own wisdom to make their decision – and they were deceived.

The challenge here for us is that even the smallest and seemingly clearest situations must be brought to God.

● **The truth that prevails.** The tricksters were tricked, for although they gained their lives, they became slaves (verse 23). The life of a lie is always suicidal. It stands only to fall. Inevitable exposure awaits it. Those who practise pretence should remember that nothing except truth finally stands.

☐ *This above all : to thine own self be true,*
And it must follow, as the night the day,
Thou canst not then be false to any man.   *William Shakespeare*

Consider the mystery of the missing day (verses 12–13). It has been shown scientifically that a whole day was found to be missing at the time of Joshua. Maybe! But are we limited to science and astronomy? After writing, 'We are upon an engagement very difficult through which we cannot get without a miracle,' Oliver Cromwell immediately set out to become part of the miracle. So it was with Joshua. He raced against time and it seemed to stand still.

● If we want something so much that we are willing to pay the price we are likely to get it. Joshua desired victory so strongly that he would risk everything. What success do we desire? Are we willing to race against time, making one day do the work of two?

● Within us are unsuspected energies. When asked to climb a tall drain-pipe a mother said, 'I can't do it.' But when her child was trapped in a fire-filled room she achieved it easily. The emergency released the energy. 'The sun stood still and the moon halted' for Joshua (verse 13). What profound poetic truth!

● Some might say that we cannot put into one day more than one day will hold. But two days **will** go into one if we want something enough.

☐   *Give heart and soul and mind and strength*
         To serve the King of kings.   *William P. Merrill*

The claim of Caleb to be 85 years young is very inspiring. Today he would have been 'pensioned off' many years earlier. Why does one person age while another keeps the strength of his youth? Is wear-and-tear a factor, or is it something to do with the spirit in which life is faced? Caleb's spirit certainly kept him young to his last day.

Notice that Caleb was not boasting of his youthfulness. His character is revealed in the words, 'Give me today this hill-country' (verse 12). He was the kind of man who would go where the risk was greatest and the hardship hardest.

How badly we need men and women of this spirit today – those who, even when old in years, are able and willing to serve! This might throw into chaos our retirement system, which does not allow that some may be as young at 85 as others are at 40!

The secret of this old man was a religious one (verse 8). God had given him the materials out of which to make a great life. Now he was to receive his reward.

☐   *Who would true valour see,*
     Let him come hither;
  One here will constant be,
     Come wind, come weather:
  There's no discouragement
  Shall make him once relent
  His first avowed intent
     To be a pilgrim.   *John Bunyan*

Thursday November 4   Joshua 23.1–16

This farewell speech is very significant. In it Joshua reminded the people that, although they might be safe from external enemies, they were less secure against the subtler foes within themselves.

Notice how precise was the old man's appeal. They were to review their history because it would show a pattern which was from God. The backward look should awaken their courage to keep the law of Moses. How true it is that often when we look at isolated incidents they seem to lack meaning but when we survey life as a whole the storm and sunshine form a meaningful picture!

Joshua also looked at the moral side. The Israelites may have dazzled other nations by their achievements but they could only please God by their goodness. His ways are ways of truth, integrity and holiness. His blessing rests on those who follow these ways. We stand by character and we fall by its absence. The theme of the 'wages' paid by goodness and 'pseudo-wages' paid by evil being inevitably wrapped up in the nature of things is developed by the later prophets. Life itself confirms it.

☐   *Make you his service your delight,*
     He'll make your wants his care.
                            Nahum Tate and Nicholas Brady

Friday November 5   Joshua 24.1–13

In this final speech Joshua reviewed the past and offered a philosophy of history. Indeed, the Israelites were the first among the many people on the world stage to sense that there is a divine intention unfolding itself through the experiences of men and women. They always believed in tomorrow because they were marching to a 'promised land' and Joshua's summary of past happenings was designed to show to later generations that their national history was no accident. By putting these 'handfuls of purpose' together Joshua both highlighted the purpose of God and exposed the fallacy – so popular today – that every man has a right to do as he pleases.

How important it is that we should think collectively! No one lives to himself; therefore none has the right to pollute the common air. Unpolluted air – and water – belong to all; so does the moral, spiritual and educational atmosphere. To teach that the world is a brotherhood and then to act as if each had a right to do as he pleases means that brotherhood is cancelled out by practice.

Like Israel, we need to see from where we have come and to where we are going and to realise that we are a band of pilgrims *en route* to a greater future.

☐   *Help us to help each other, Lord.*   *Charles Wesley*

Saturday November 6   **Joshua 24.14–28**

● **The choice.** Joshua exhorted the people to make a choice. There always comes a point when real religion becomes personal and voluntary. Does not the chief value of spiritual religion consist in the response made by mind and heart?

● **The example.** In Joshua's declaration, 'I and my family, we will worship the Lord' (verse 15), we have the secret of true leadership. Few will follow an exhortation if it is not linked to personal example. People are not won by our theology but by our reality. If the preacher is doubting or the believer is wavering it is little wonder that no lasting impression is made. It is words and resolution harnessed to action that make the greatest appeal. Joshua's life and character showed beyond doubt that he was completely on the side of God.

● **The response.** When the people had responded verbally they were reminded that this could have been from impulse rather than conviction. However, after assuring Joshua that they had not used mere words, they were invited to consolidate their convictions into a covenant. This would make the matter so personal that they would be their own witnesses and a stone of remembrance would tell others what they had done (see October 28).

☐ *God be in my head, and in my understanding;*
God be in mine eyes, and in my looking;
God be in my mouth, and in my speaking;
God be in my heart, and in my thinking;
God be at mine end, and at my departing.   *Book of Hours*

For group discussion and personal thought
In Joshua's farewell speech he urged the people of Israel to be
loyal to God. Read what followed in Joshua 24.21–27. How were
they to show their loyalty? How do we show our loyalty to God?
What more could we do?

Sunday November 7   **Genesis 12.1–9***

ABRAHAM

The Christian faith is rooted in history. Its origins go back far
beyond the birth of Christ, back indeed to the beginning of a
little nation which was to grow, through its experiences of joy
and sorrow, to a spiritual maturity which would make it possible at last for God to reveal himself fully. Today we read of that
beginning. It is the story of a man who, some 1800 or 1900 years
before Christ, was called by God to uproot himself and set out
for an unknown country.

Abram (later Abraham) travelled south from Harran and at
place after place he seemed to receive a conviction that God was
leading him. 'Through you I will bless all the nations' (verse 3,
GNB) must have seemed to him a mysterious promise. Little
did he realise that nearly two thousand years later he would be
put forward as a great example of faith.

It must have taken courage for Abraham to uproot himself and
his family and set forth 'without knowing where he was to go'
(Hebrews 11.8). Out of this act of faith sprang Judaism, Judaism's
growing knowledge of God and, ultimately, Judaism's gift of
Jesus Christ – and the possibility of reconciliation with God for
all humanity.

☐ *Lord, when you call me, may there be no delay in my response.*

● DON'T FORGET to order your copy of **Notes on Bible
Readings** for **1983**!

219

2 CORINTHIANS

Notes by Revd Ian B. Tanner, BSc

Ian Tanner is a minister of the Uniting Church in Australia. He was formerly minister of Scots Church, Adelaide, South Australia, and is now Director of Lay Education for the Synod of South Australia of the Uniting Church.

In the first century AD correspondence was penned on loose sheets of papyrus. No symbols of continuity were used; and there were no chapter or verse divisions – these were introduced many centuries later. Thus the papyrus sheets could easily become misplaced and be put in the wrong order. Most scholars believe that *2 Corinthians* consists of three distinct letters, or parts of letters. The order of the whole Corinthian correspondence is probably as follows:

● **2 Corinthians 6.14 to 7.1,** a fragment of Paul's earliest letter to the Corinthian church.

● **1 Corinthians,** written to deal with problems there. It is believed that Paul followed this up with a personal visit which was a failure.

● **2 Corinthians 10–13,** the severe letter that Paul had to send because the situation became worse.

● **2 Corinthians 1–9** (excluding 6.14 to 7.1), a letter of reconciliation which was sent after Timothy had returned from Corinth with the news that all was now well.

In no other letter of Paul do we come so close to the bared soul of the great apostle. Here we see Paul's anguish and intense love for this young and troubled congregation.

Suggestion for further reading

The Letters to the Corinthians by William Barclay, Daily Study Bible (Saint Andrew Press).

Monday November 8   **2 Corinthians 1.1–11**

When Jesus sent out his disciples two by two, he told them: 'Exchange no greetings on the road.' (Luke 10.4) The expla-

nation of this apparent lack of friendliness is that the disciples'
task was urgent, and they must not be side-tracked into pleasant
but empty chit-chat. Paul's letter illustrates the same sense of
purpose and urgency. The apostle wastes no time on empty
pleasantries. Even the customary formal greetings are adapted to
witness to God's grace.

A bishop in Australia was asked why he continued to wear a
pectoral cross as his badge of office. Wouldn't a badge saying,
'Smile, God loves you,' be more appropriate today? He replied
that many people are too involved in suffering of one sort or
another to smile much. The cross is a far more meaningful
symbol to those who experience suffering because it reminds
them that God shares our suffering in Christ and triumphs over
it. This is Paul's theme in verses 3–11. Our experience both of
suffering and of Christ's consolation equips us to share the comfort of Christ with others in their suffering. Notice particularly
verses 8–11. Paul is no theorist! He knew at firsthand what
suffering meant.

☐ *Meditate on verse 4, and make it the basis of your prayers.*

Tuesday November 9　　　　2 Corinthians 1.12 to 2.4

Verses 15–24 are an example of Paul's ability to take ordinary,
even mundane, events of life and turn them into superlative
acts of witness to the person of Jesus. Paul had earlier stated his
intention to visit Corinth on his journey to and from Macedonia,
but had not in fact done so. Some of the Corinthians accused him
of duplicity. They said he was like a person who says 'Yes' and
'No' in the same breath. Even as Paul offers his defence he for-
gets his own predicament and soars to a marvellous testimony to
Jesus. Jesus, said Paul, is never a blend of 'Yes' and 'No'. Jesus
is God's 'Yes' to all God's promises!

What does Paul mean by 'more than ordinary love' (verse 4)?
Sometimes we serve our friends very badly. We love them and
like to encourage and maybe flatter them. But it takes a special
kind of love to run the risk of correcting or admonishing them as
Paul does here. It takes 'more than ordinary love' to serve a
friend like that.

☐ *Do you love your friends or family enough to risk their disapproval by caring for them with the 'correction, which belongs
to a Christian upbringing' (Ephesians 6.4)?*

Wednesday November 10   2 Corinthians 2.5-17

In verses 5–11 there are some important guide-lines for the practice of Christian forgiveness. We do not know the details of the conflict that had occurred. We deduce that a member of the Corinthian church had caused unjust harm to Paul. But now the member must be forgiven and restored to membership by the Corinthian congregation. Paul was too great a man to rejoice in the humiliation of an enemy. He knew that Satan applauds and encourages the gloating of a victor in a human quarrel. Paul longed for this man's rehabilitation – 'more than ordinary love' again, indeed a reflection of God's love. Are you motivated by this love of God?

☐   *For the love of God is broader*
     Than the measures of man's mind,
   And the heart of the eternal
     Is most wonderfully kind.   *Frederick W. Faber*

Paul's mind moves on to other successes, notably in Macedonia. He instinctively uses the illustration of the triumphal procession of a Roman general, accompanied by the priests swinging their censers of incense. A Christian can never be a pessimist. The certain triumph of Christ must be the glass through which we see our own and the world's future.

Thursday November 11   2 Corinthians 3.1-18

I visit an old veteran of the First World War. No matter where our conversation commences it always ends up in the trenches of France, 1914–18! Some people – Paul among them – have the ability to turn every conversation and every allusion to the subject of their own interest.

Paul had probably been accused by his enemies of parading his credentials in order to assert his authority as a minister of Christ. He protested that he had no need of written credentials. The Corinthian church itself was a living credential to the effectiveness of his ministry. However, as soon as he contemplates the difference between the written word of a letter of introduction and the witness of a living person, Paul immediately thinks of the difference between the written law of the old covenant and the living Spirit of the new. He then goes on to compare the veiled and fading glory of God's old law with the clear, unconcealed splendour of the new gospel.

Have we, like Paul, cultivated the skill of seeing God's purposes in every part of life, and speaking about it to others?

☐ *So let me feel thy presence day by day*
In wind and sod,
That every bush I meet upon the way
Shall glow with God.

Adams Brown

Friday November 12   2 Corinthians 4.1–15

Anthony Sampson, writing of the people whose exercise of power guides Great Britain, says: 'Their most valuable asset is confidence – confidence both from themselves and from others.'

Paul exudes this quality of confidence. But Paul's confidence is not self-confidence, not the arrogance of assumed superiority over others. His confidence is based on God, and on knowing God's power to be within him. He thinks of this power as the power of the risen Christ. It is like a light shining within him, or as a treasure hidden within his life. You cannot put down a person who knows that to be true in his or her experience!

Paul's confidence is not unique. It is a characteristic of the life of every true believer. Even the psalmist was able to say:

☐ *The Lord is my light and my salvation;*
whom shall I fear?
The Lord is the stronghold of my life;
of whom shall I be afraid?
Though a host encamp against me,
my heart shall not fear;
though war arise against me,
yet I will be confident.

(Psalm 27.1,3, RSV)

Saturday November 13   2 Corinthians 4.16 to 5.10

William Temple was a big man physically as well as in faith. One hot day with a group of friends he climbed up the steep slopes to a look-out tower. He sat down perspiring and out of breath and gasped to his amused friends, 'I am so glad I don't have to believe in the resurrection of the flesh!'

Paul shared the same good news. His confidence in life beyond death did not depend upon belief in the resurrection of the flesh. He knew that our 'earthly frame' was mortal and expendable, and that we shall have a new body in the resurrection life. What that new body would be like he did not know; but he knew that it would be a new experience of putting on Christ – and of going 'to live with the Lord' (verse 8).

It is important to remember that when Paul wrote these words he was not an old man contemplating the end of his life. He was in the prime of his life. His reflections on life and death were prompted by the anticipation of violence and the attacks of assassins. What a comfort these words are to those Christians today who live in the midst of persecution and danger!

☐ *A man, at the conclusion of the funeral service of his friend, once said to me, 'I'd give my right arm to believe what you believe.' What would you have said in reply?*

For group discussion and personal thought

Those who respond to God through Jesus Christ are people within whom God has caused his light to shine (see 2 Corinthians 4.6). Consider what this personal experience means in terms of (a) illumination, (b) sheer joy, and (c) the reflecting of Christ's radiance to others.

Remembrance Sunday, November 14   Exodus 3.1–15*
MOSES

Abraham was the great pioneer of faith. Moses, who lived 600 years after him, was the champion of liberty. Moses doubted his ability for the task of liberating his people on two grounds: his own humble situation, and his uncertainty as to whether his people would accept that God had called him. 'Which god?' they might ask. 'What is his name?'

A god's name, indicative of his character, needed to be known in ancient cultures before it was considered possible to enter into relationship with him. The reply God gave to Moses was, 'I AM.' In this name there was the hint of a guiding, liberating spirit who is in all events. 'I AM' is not a distant God but an ever-present, moving God, alive here and now – and in the future, too. So, armed with the power of this ever-present God, Moses went to his people's rescue.

This redemption, liberation of men and women from physical bondage, was to prepare for the deepest kind of liberation of all, the liberation Christ brings from that which separates us from the love of God and reconciles us at last to him.

□ *Today we remember those who died fighting in the cause of freedom. Let us pray for the spiritual liberation which sets men free from the fears and jealousies that separate members of the human family from one another and which lie at the root of enmities and war.*

Monday November 15   2 Corinthians 5.11–21

Someone said that 'reconciliation' was Christianity in one word. Reconciliation means the restoration of broken relationships. The Bible's story of the human adventure is that mankind was made for fellowship with God and with one another. By disobedience and self-seeking the human race ended up estranged from God. On the cross Jesus took that sense of enmity away, and made possible the restoration of all the broken relationships.

God's work through Christ is reconciliation, 'and he has enlisted us in this service of reconciliation' (verse 18). Whenever we help patch up a quarrel, unite a family in strife, help settle a migrant, refuse to be prejudiced, create peace around us, bring others to faith in God, we are doing his work.

□ *The prayer of St Francis of Assisi is a beautiful expression of reconciliation. Let it be our prayer today:*

> *Lord, make us instruments of thy peace;*
> *where there is hatred, let us sow love;*
> *where there is injury, pardon;*
> *where there is discord, union;*
> *where there is doubt, faith;*
> *where there is despair, hope;*
> *where there is darkness, light;*
> *where there is sadness, joy;*
> *for thy mercy and thy truth's sake.*

Tuesday November 16   2 Corinthians 6.14 to 7.1

This part of *2 Corinthians* is held by most scholars to be a fragment of an earlier letter (see introduction on page 220), and is therefore not related to what precedes it or follows it in the letter we are reading now. This fragment may be part of the letter referred to by Paul in *1 Corinthians* 5.9. There Paul was concerned that influences and practices of the old pagan way of life were so easily carried over into the new life of the Christian fellowship.

In an atomic reactor there are substances called separators which keep apart the reactive elements to prevent them from generating explosively high energy. Often in a congregation active Christians are kept apart, and their enthusiasm nullified, by nominal Christians who act as separators. It is always difficult to set standards in the life of a Christian congregation or fellowship, and yet some criteria to establish the integrity of the local church are necessary for membership and discipline. Not to do so is to be careless about our stewardship of the gospel.

If someone asked you what were the standards required of members of your congregation, could you tell them?

☐ *Pray for an increase in the quality of your Christian life and the life of your congregation so that others may be challenged to make decisions about the standard of their own discipleship.*

Wednesday November 17   2 Corinthians 7.2–16

Some people think that Christianity is a marvellous ideal but impossible to put into practice. The reading for November 15 about reconciliation (5.11–21) is one of the great theological expositions of the New Testament. But for Paul it was no theory. In today's reading he demonstrates the practice of reconciliation. He shows the process of reconciliation in his own dealings with the Corinthian congregation.

Notice how Paul takes the initiative even though he candidly professes he is the innocent party. Nor does he attempt to 'put down' the Corinthians and make them feel humiliated for their misdeeds. He tells them he is proud of them and then encourages them with his appreciation. He had risked his relationship with the Corinthians by sending them the 'severe letter' but the risk was justified because they had accepted the rebuke 'in God's way', and now they see things from a different point of view. In all this there is a delightful illustration of reconciliation.

It is not much use preaching about reconciliation to others unless we practise it ourselves in our own lives. James said, 'Be doers of the word, and not hearers only.' (James 1.22, RSV)

☐ *Is there anybody to whom you need to be reconciled? Have you sought God's way of effecting it?*

Thursday November 18   2 Corinthians 8.1–15

The stewardship of money is a great responsibility. Some

biblical scholars claim that Jesus spoke more about money and material possessions than any other subject. This passage in *2 Corinthians* is of more than general interest because Paul sets out very clearly his own understanding of the principles of Christian stewardship.

The need arose because of the poverty within the Jerusalem church. Whether their condition was made worse by famine or persecution we do not know.

Notice how Paul seeks to persuade the Corinthians of their financial responsibilities to the wider Church – the example of another congregation; their own adequate resources; their own reputation. But above all there was the example of Jesus.

A visitor to a leprosarium in India tells of watching a nursing sister cleaning the festering sores of a leper. He said, 'I wouldn't do that work for a million dollars.' 'Neither would I,' the nun answered, 'but I do it for him,' as she nodded in the direction of a crucifix on the wall.

☐ *Love so amazing, so divine,*
   Demands my soul, my life, my all.   *Isaac Watts*

Friday November 19   **2 Corinthians 8.16–24**

When people give money for the Lord's work it is essential, both for their own confidence and for the witness of the Church, that no questions can be raised about the proper accounting and use of such funds.

Paul's problem was that this collection of funds for the Jerusalem church would have to be gathered in cash or kind and physically transported to Jerusalem. There was no banking system to transfer the gift by letter of credit or likewise. Neither were there effective audit practices for such a situation. Paul's guarantee of the integrity of the gift funds was to appoint a group of three men, all of honourable character – and probably of burly physique considering the physical dangers of carrying large sums of money a considerable distance!

Once, a plan was suggested to the enemies of Abraham Lincoln to discredit him by falsely accusing him of embezzlement of government funds. 'It wouldn't work,' one of them said sadly. 'No one would ever believe Lincoln would do that.'

☐ *Is that your reputation? Is that the reputation of your church and its officials?*

Probably one of the best known (although often misquoted) texts in the Bible is 'The love of money is the root of all evil.' (1 Timothy 6.10, AV) It is important to remember that this text does not indict **money** as the root of all evil, but the **love** of money. Today's reading suggests another truth – the love of **giving** is the root of all **good.**

Paul has used persuasive arguments to encourage the Corinthians to give generously to this cause which was so close to his heart. He does not think it unchristian to use the competitive element to spur on the Corinthians or to warn them of the shame of failure. Nor does he think it immoral to canvass the idea of reward. But the climax of Paul's appeal to the Corinthians is to highlight the public witness of such a gift. The Jerusalem church will overflow with thanksgiving to God as well as to their generous Christian brethren.

☐   *The gift which he on one bestows,*
     We all delight to prove ;
   The grace through every vessel flows,
     In purest streams of love.

                                  Charles Wesley

For group discussion and personal thought

From 2 Corinthians 8–9 make a list of the arguments Paul used to persuade the Corinthians to contribute generously to his Jerusalem fund. How far are they appropriate for encouraging Christians in their giving today?

Sunday November 21

THE REMNANT OF ISRAEL

The prophet Elijah lived at a time when Israel was at a critical point of decision. The worship of Jehovah had come into conflict with the fertility-cult of Baal. Each fought for Israel's allegiance. In the contest on Mount Carmel, Elijah tried to win the people for Jehovah. After seeming to succeed, he fled from the vengeance of the queen. It seemed as if all was lost, as if Jehovah was vanquished, as if Elijah's life-work had ended in failure, as if he alone remained faithful.

▶ Now read **1 Kings 19.9–18.***

Thus Elijah learned that it is not through powers and wonders that God works his way with men, but through the persuasion of their inner consciousness. This was to be the way God's servants were to seek people's allegiance to God. The results of this way of persuasion might seem small, with few people responding, but, as Elijah learned, God is on the throne and is never defeated.

☐ *A word of encouragement for all who preach today:*

'*It pleased God by the foolishness of preaching to save them that believe. For the Jews require a sign, and the Greeks seek after wisdom: but we preach Christ crucified . . . the power of God, and the wisdom of God.*' (*1 Corinthians 1.21–24, AV*)

Monday November 22   2 Corinthians 10.1–18

This chapter begins a new section of *2 Corinthians* (see introduction on page 220). All the evidence points to the fact that chapters 10–13 were written before chapters 1–9, and probably constitute Paul's 'severe letter' which he refers to in 2 Corinthians 7.8.

So now we must look at the content of this 'severe letter'. The introduction has presumably been lost, and we face the difficulty of neither knowing the content of the preceding pages or even the precise nature or cause of the problems about which Paul is writing.

It is important to notice how Paul responds to the challenge to his authority. Obviously he has enemies and detractors in the Corinthian congregation. Why does he not 'bless those who curse him; pray for those who treat him despitefully' (from Luke 6.28), instead of reacting with such aggression and toughness? Because it was not Paul who was defamed, but Christ.

It is one thing to suffer insults offered against oneself. It is a different matter when others are suffering unjustly, and especially the Lord 'in whom we boast'. We are not meant to turn the other cheek when God's truth and love are being ridiculed!

☐ *Recall some occasions when Jesus stood up against those who victimised the innocent.*

Tuesday November 23   2 Corinthians 11.1–15

An elder was not impressed after a visiting preacher had tongue-lashed the congregation. 'I suppose we deserve it,' he said, 'but it's not the gospel when there is judgement and no mercy.' In today's reading Paul confronts the Corinthian congregation with both judgement and mercy. He addresses them directly and forthrightly about their sins and yet shining through it all is his love and concern for them. 'Is it that I do not love you? God knows I do.' (verse 11)

The Corinthian church had apparently been beguiled by other 'evangelists' whose message and character were contrary to Paul's. From the content of today's reading we presume they were persuasive speakers, they charged for their services, and they claimed apostolic status.

It is sometimes difficult for a pastor to warn his flock against dangerous influences – 'Satan himself masquerades as an angel of light' (verse 14). So often it sounds like jealousy or pique to warn against one who proclaims 'another Jesus' (verse 4), and yet we are told to 'test the spirits to see whether they are from God, for among those who have gone out into the world there are many prophets falsely inspired' (1 John 4.1).

☐ *What tests would you apply today to determine the authenticity of a preacher of Jesus?*

Wednesday November 24   2 Corinthians 11.16–33

A friend of mine who is a very capable pastor of a large congregation told me how he learned an important lesson early in his ministry. He was not a perfectionist but he always strove to be thoroughly prepared and gave the impression of supreme competence. One day he lost his temper at a congregational meeting and forthrightly apologised to the congregation. Afterwards one of his elders said to him, 'I'm so glad to know you are human. I was beginning to think you were perfect and I nearly stopped listening to you.'

Paul's outburst here is full of emotion and he knows he is going beyond his own rules of Christian modesty. He himself wrote, 'Love is never boastful.' (1 Corinthians 13.4) But how pleased we are to know that he is human! Otherwise we would never have known the full rigour and suffering of his discipleship.

When a white minister was killed and others physically attacked for taking part in Martin Luther King's protest marches in Alabama, a sympathetic newspaper editorial said that perhaps it was time for the Church to reinterpret the meaning of 'the laying on of hands'. We prefer the laying on of hands in a quiet service of commissioning or ordination or healing. But we ought not to forget that many Christians in our own day endure another sort of 'laying on of hands' which, as in the case of Paul, is physical violence because of their steadfast witness to the gospel.

☐ *Pray for the martyr Christians of our own time.*

Thursday November 25   2 Corinthians 12.1–10

Paul continues his list of credentials. The 'Christian man' of whom he writes (verse 2) is undoubtedly Paul himself. The credential of having visionary or ecstatic experiences would have been of help to some of the Corinthian congregation. It implied a prophetic spirit greatly valued in the first-century Church.

Someone said of a notable Churchman that he was so heavenly-minded that he was of no earthly use! The trouble with those who have heavenly visions is that often they are tempted to lose touch with the harsh realities of life. Paul acknowledges the danger and interprets his own malady ('a sharp physical pain') as a counterbalance to the ever-present sin of pride. We are not told the nature of his illness.

Almost accidentally we are made aware that Paul not only had to suffer the most incredible outward persecution and hardships, but also that he had to endure painful recurring physical illness. However, by this he knew that what he accomplished was not because of his own strength, but only through 'the power of Christ' which overcame his weakness. If we pride ourselves on being strong and healthy and capable, we may never know the power of God. But when we know we are weak, then we can also know where to find strength to live.

☐ *Meditate on Paul's words in verse 10 : 'When I am weak, then I am strong.'*

Friday November 26   2 Corinthians 12.11–21

There is value in constructive criticism from those who love us. But it is difficult for a leader to continue if all he receives is criticism and fault-finding. When did you last encourage your own leaders?

In today's reading Paul seems to be responding to another charge that, while he may not have accepted money for preaching, he had gained a financial advantage through the devices of some friends, notably Titus and an unnamed helper. Paul refutes this charge as being without any basis and adds a further 'mark of a true apostle' by his willingness to 'gladly spend what I have for you – and spend myself to the limit' (verse 15). What more can anybody say or do?

Paul did, of course, go on spending himself in the care of his congregations and, according to tradition, did finally spend himself to the limit of his own death. What greater credential can there be than love like this? The people we meet are not likely to be persuaded by our zeal for Christ unless at the same time they know we care deeply for them with Christ's kind of love.

☐   *But O my friend!*
    My friend indeed,
    Who at my need
    His life did spend.

                                                              Samuel Crossman

Saturday November 27   2 Corinthians 13.1–14

'My whole prayer is that all may be put right with you' (verse 9) – shining through all of Paul's words of rebuke, anguish and assertion of his apostolic authority is his deep concern for the Corinthian congregation. If our understanding of the division of *2 Corinthians* is correct and these latter chapters precede chapters 1–9, then we know that this severe letter did in fact win over the Corinthian congregation to repentance and restoration.

As we reflect on Paul's 'severe letter' we may see how he fulfils his own definition of love in his previous letter to the Corinthians: 'Love keeps no score of wrongs; does not gloat over other men's sins, but delights in the truth.' (1 Corinthians 13.5–6)

Paul concludes positively and constructively. Whatever has been written, it leaves his readers in no doubt of his affection; his 'more than ordinary love' for them.

The closing words are still ringing round the world as a constantly repeated and loved benediction: 'The grace of the Lord Jesus Christ, and the love of God, and fellowship in the Holy Spirit, be with you all.'

☐   *Is the order of Paul's closing benediction important? Make this*
    benediction a closing prayer of intercession for all God's people
    everywhere.

For group discussion and personal thought

In 2 Corinthians 10–12 what does Paul suggest are the marks of a true apostle? Can you put together a profile of a true Christian leader today?

Advent Sunday, November 28   Isaiah 52.1–10*

THE ADVENT HOPE

In the eyes of pagans, the history of the Jewish people must have seemed one long succession of calamities. In fact, it was a period of training. Through every event that had befallen them, some word of God was being spoken – a word of discipline or encouragement or hope. Through men like Abraham, Moses and Elijah and the prophets, there came an understanding of the oneness, goodness and love of God which was leading them more and more deeply into the conviction that he had a purpose for Israel. This conviction found expression in the preaching of a sixth-century prophet usually known as Second Isaiah (the writer of *Isaiah 40–55*).

The prophets believed that God would raise up a deliverer to re-establish Jewish national independence and prosperity. They were wrong in the details; but they were right in their basic certainty. The deliverer **did** come, but he brought something greater than any national liberation – he brought spiritual freedom for all mankind.

☐ *O God, help us to prepare ourselves for the coming of Jesus who is ever ready to enter our lives; and set us free from all that separates us from you.*

A REMINDER

Have you remembered to order your copy of **NOTES on Bible Readings** for 1983? If not, do so straightaway. The year's scheme is on page 256.

ISAIAH 40–55

Notes by Revd Christopher Ellis, MA, MPhil

Christopher Ellis is a Baptist minister serving as a member of an ecumenical team in Swindon, England. He previously ministered in Brighton, Sussex, and Cardiff, South Wales.

In the year 586 BC Jerusalem was destroyed by the armies of Nebuchadnezzar. A large number of the people of Judah including all the leading citizens were marched into exile in Babylon, in an attempt to break resistance in Palestine and probably to provide cheap, skilled labour in the metropolitan centre of the empire.

About forty years later the Babylonian empire itself was threatened by the rising fortunes of the Persian soldier-king, Cyrus. His methods of running an empire were different and it seemed likely that, when Babylon fell, the exiled Jews would have an opportunity to return home. But much had happened to their faith and their hopes in a not uncomfortable exile and they had to be made ready for the opportunity when it came.

An anonymous prophet, a disciple of Isaiah of Jerusalem, addressed the dispirited and apathetic exiles and prepared them for the return home. We usually call him 'Second Isaiah' and his prophecies are found in chapters 40–55 of the book of *Isaiah*. We shall look at a selection of these prophecies under three weekly themes.

Suggestions for further reading

Isaiah 40–55 by Christopher R. North, Torch Bible Commentaries (SCM Press);

Isaiah 40–66 by A. S. Herbert, Cambridge Bible Commentaries on the New English Bible (Cambridge University Press);

THE RETURN HOME

Monday November 29   **Isaiah 44.21–28**

People have very definite ideas about what they call 'real life' or 'the real world'. For the Old Testament prophets the 'real world' was not simply the place of political, economic and social activities, but the arena of God's saving actions. Sometimes events were seen as judgement for faithlessness and disobedience, like the destruction of Jerusalem and the exile in Babylon. The prophet of Isaiah 40–55 saw the impending victory of Cyrus over the Babylonians as the activity of God, the surpassing of judgement by mercy, the opportunity for Israel to start again as the covenant people of God in the Promised Land. It was like a prisoner being told that his fine had been paid and he was free.

'I have fashioned you,' 'I have swept away your sins', 'I have ransomed you' (verses 21–22) – this is all in the past tense. What Israel had to do was to seize the freely offered opportunity of new life and accept the hopes and the risks of the promises of God. Things have not changed: we still receive from God more than we can ever give. But his gifts mean action as well as gratitude, creative hope as well as peace.

☐ *Thank God for life and all it contains – and for the new life, forgiveness and hope which he offers through Jesus Christ.*

Tuesday November 30

In the ancient world people believed in many gods. There might be one special god for a particular nation or locality, but it was not until the time of Amos and later that belief in the existence of just **one God** came to the fore, even in Israel and Judah. With the destruction of Jerusalem and the end of all normal life in Judah, it was natural that some should say that the Babylonian gods were more powerful than Jehovah. This was underlined when the exiles, far from home, were overwhelmed by the size and sophistication of urban life in Babylon and the magnificence of the temples and palaces – all dedicated to the foreign gods.

The prophet affirmed that there was only one true God – the Creator, the God who set them free from Egypt and gave them all they had. Many of the prophets had forecast disaster so that the exile too could be seen as the work of God and not the victory of foreign powers. Second Isaiah ridiculed the idolatry of Babylon: 'You must worship your Creator, not something which is your own creation!'

▶ Now read **Isaiah 44.6–8, 12–20.**

There is still the temptation to worship what we have made. The prizes of our society become our gods. Yet they are not worthy of our worship. Adoration is not only God's due, it becomes our salvation!

☐ *Quietly think about the greatness of God and then offer him a prayer of praise.*

Wednesday December 1

The prophet turned his attention to the great power of the Babylonian civilisation which surrounded the exiled Jews. He announced the impending destruction of the Babylonian empire. On the surface of current affairs it could be seen as the result of the military advances of Cyrus but, underneath, the prophet exposed the corruption which had come under the judgement of God.

▶ Read **Isaiah 47.1–11.**

This could easily be a portrait of the world in which **we** live: a lack of concern for the poor and the powerless (verse 6), a proud but naïve belief that nothing can change (verse 7), and a smug and illusory complacence. In his words to the smug Pharisees, Jesus implied that people need to realise that they are sick before a doctor can help them (see Mark 2.17).

Pride is like an hallucinatory drug which makes a man believe he can fly – as a result of which he jumps out of a window to his death. Christian hope, on the other hand, is born of a realistic assessment of where we are and of the greatness of God's mercy.

☐ *Why restless, why cast down, my soul?*
    Hope, still, and thou shalt sing
    The praise of him who is thy God,
    Thy health's eternal spring.

                                    Nahum Tate and Nicholas Brady

Thursday December 2

The difference between a **good** painter and a **great** one is that the great painter shows us something new. Both might paint the same face or landscape, but one shows us what we expect to see while the other reveals things which we have not seen before. So it is with poets and prophets.

▶ Read **Isaiah 45.1–13.**

Anointing with oil was a symbol of God's commissioning and it was done over the heads of kings, priests and prophets. Eventually it became a technical term for a man supremely sent by God who would usher in the golden age for the Jews (*Messiah* = 'anointed one'). This is the only place in the Old Testament where, even in a figurative sense, anointing is applied to a non-Jew (see verse 1). Cyrus was sent as an agent of God's plans – God was working through him.

To those who first heard these words they would have been as profoundly shocking as the story of the good Samaritan was to the Jewish listeners of Jesus (Luke 10.30–37). The prophet showed them something new – God working through everyday events and the most unlikely people. It is always tempting to corner the market and claim that God will only work through people like us, the official party members of the Church. But it is not so.

☐   *God is working his purpose out as year succeeds to year.*

Arthur C. Ainger

   Can we see signs of this in the world today?

Friday December 3

There is more than one way of running an empire. Whereas the Babylonians strengthened their control by crushing initiative and national identity in the subject areas and by centralising human resources (like the Jewish exiles) in Babylon, Cyrus had a different way. He relied upon national strength and allowed considerable freedom amongst the conquered countries; national culture and religion were allowed to have free expression. So, with Cyrus poised to crush Babylon, the prophet saw that the exiles could soon have an opportunity to return home.

In preparing these dispirited and apathetic people for the return he drew on their history and their faith. Their national identity had been forged in the exodus from Egypt – now they were going to embark on a **new** exodus and return through the desert to the Promised Land. God the Creator would do this.

▶ Read **Isaiah 51.1–5, 9–16.**

Somebody has called the Church 'the people of God on the move'. But we are not aimless tourists flitting from one curiosity to the next. Rather, we are pilgrims summoned forward by the promises of God and empowered by hope.

☐   *They cared not, but with force unspent,*
   Unmoved by pain, they onward went,
   Unstayed by pleasures, still they bent
     Their zealous course to God.   *Thomas T. Lynch*

Here is poetry to uplift the most downcast spirits. Forty years of exile had taken their toll. Some Jews had lost their faith, overwhelmed by the magnificence and sheer size of the Babylonian civilisation; their faith had crumbled with the ruined walls of Jerusalem. Others had survived by becoming Babylonians themselves, no longer the people of God looking expectantly for their God to act. Others had turned inwards, worshipping a God of the past but failing to expect from him any new future. To all these the prophet proclaimed the God who could do the impossible.

The experience of the exile had been overwhelming and the prophet likened it to the great flood in the story of Noah (verse 9). But God is merciful and forgiveness now made possible the renewing of the covenant relationship which Israel had spoilt. Never again would God be angry. Five hundred years later the cross and the empty tomb became the symbols of that promise. Man's relationship with God is for ever seen as costly forgiveness and life-giving hope.

☐ *Pray for those overwhelmed by despair. Ask God to make you an instrument of his peace, love and hope.*

For group discussion and personal thought

The declining membership in some western churches has been likened to the experience of the Babylonian exile. If this is so, what does the prophet of Isaiah 40–55 have to say to these churches today? Look particularly at Isaiah 44.21–28.

2nd Sunday in Advent, December 5   Isaiah 55.1–11*
(Bible Sunday)

THE WORD OF GOD IN THE OLD TESTAMENT

We are living in a time when people everywhere demand more and more material goods. Yet there remains with men and women a terrible hunger, a growing sense of having missed the point of living. The words, 'Man cannot live on bread alone but lives by every word that comes from the mouth of the Lord' (Deuteronomy 8.3) are as true now as they ever were.

The emphasis of today's reading is upon the **word of God,** which can be heard when people will really **listen** (verse 3). The differences between our greed for things and God's offer of spiritual riches are referred to in verses 8–9. One reason for the spiritual starvation of our times is the widespread neglect of the regular reading of the Bible and the daily discovery of the words from God that can be found in it, words which can open for us a whole new dimension of living.

How important it is for people to discover God's word again – and especially his supreme word which he offers to us in Christ! Jesus spoke of himself as the 'bread of life', the source of 'living water', the giver of true life.

◻   *Thou art the Bread of life,*
        O Lord, to me,
    Thy holy word the truth
        That saveth me.   *Alexander Groves*

OUR GOD

Monday December 6

A few years ago a religious newspaper held a poll to find out the favourite hymns of its readers. It was interesting to see that the top choices were hymns such as: 'And can it be that I should gain an interest in the Saviour's blood?', 'Blessed assurance, Jesus is mine', and 'The Lord's my shepherd, I'll not want'. They are happy hymns but the happiness is based upon what we have received from God. It is always a temptation to think of God as the provider of eternal goodies rather than to worship him for his own sake.

If our faith is based merely upon an experience of divine blessing then rough times may tempt us to give up God. The Jews had lost their land, their temple and, in some cases, their faith. The prophet's strategy was to raise their eyes from their own joys or troubles to the wonder of God their Creator.

▶ Read **Isaiah 40.12–25.**

The exiles' ideas of God had been too small, dwarfed by the magnificent surroundings of Babylon. Let us ponder the unknown size of the universe and then allow our minds to be lost in wonder of the God who has made the immeasurable.

◻   *Let all things their Creator bless,*
    And worship him in humbleness,
        O praise him, hallelujah!   *St Francis*

Yesterday we read about the greatness of God. Today's reading tells us that God is not so great that he is inaccessible but that he entered into a caring relationship with Israel. It was not deserved (verse 8), it was an act of love. However rootless and fragile the Jews might have felt in a foreign land, they were told that they **belonged**. They were reminded of their destiny as the covenant people of God.

Their special relationship had not protected them from the buffets of international turmoil, for the people of God are exposed to the cruelties of human power and the frustrations of human failure like anyone else. But God said, 'Have no fear; for I am with you.' (verse 5)

The prophet's predecessor, Isaiah of Jerusalem, had spoken of *Immanuel* – 'God-with-us' (Isaiah 7.14). Some five hundred years later a crucified carpenter showed us that God is not remote from our troubles but comes and shares them – for that is what love is about.

☐ *Jesus said: 'I am with you always, to the end of time.' (Matthew 28.20) Think prayerfully about where you have been and where you will go this week and resolve to live in the light of this marvellous promise.*

In Britain there are a number of church buildings which seat at least a thousand people but where the Sunday congregations are pitifully small. If a visitor were to suggest changes in the pattern of church life, the amalgamation of close congregations or new forms of worship, he would be politely told that God requires faithfulness not experiment! The buildings were erected in a time of revivalist expansion at the beginning of the century and the people quietly wait for another revival to fill the decaying monument.

The prophet told his hearers that faithfulness was not about slavishly copying the past but expecting God to act in new ways in the future and being ready to co-operate with him. William Carey said, 'Expect great things from God; attempt great things for God.' In today's reading the prophet told the exiles to stop brooding about all the good times of the past when God brought them out of Egypt and gave them the Promised Land. They must live in the present and for the future.

Notice that the new escape from Babylon is described in terms of the first exodus from Egypt. The new comes out of the old. The new Israel, the Church of Christ, was to emerge from the old Israel. God creates our new life out of the raw materials of the old.

☐ *Lord, set me free from the shackles of the past and help me to have the faith of anticipation.*

Thursday December 9

For someone to fall off a mountain, he has to climb up there in the first place. Fatigue is not a symptom of laziness but of energy already expended. But lethargy can sometimes be a counterfeit tiredness and is often an accompaniment of depression. The exiles were depressed and their depression had sapped their strength. If they were to be ready to return to the Promised Land then they needed hope and encouragement. To give them that hope the prophet directed their thoughts away from their troubles and doubts and reminded them of the greatness of God.

▶ Read **Isaiah 40.26–31.**

What marvellous promises! The God we worship and serve is the giver of life and so we must turn to him to find the source of life and strength he offers. Depression can make us concentrate on our problems until they block everything else out of our sight. The prophet called, 'Lift up your eyes.' (verse 26) Conversely, over-confidence in one's own ability can thwart God's giving of strength to his struggling pilgrims and we are told in verses 30–31:

'Young men may grow weary and faint,
    but those who look to the Lord will win new strength.'

☐ *Teach us, good Lord to serve thee as thou deservest;*
to give, and not to count the cost;
to fight, and not to heed the wounds;
to toil, and not to seek for rest;
to labour, and not to seek for any reward,
save that of knowing we do thy will.   *Ignatius Loyola*

Friday December 10

Deliverance was near. The armies of Cyrus were advancing and the defeat of Babylon was certain. The prophet painted a picture of chaos as Babylonians fled from their homes before the Persian onslaught. Like countless refugees before and since, they would take all that could be carried from their homes. Amongst the things strapped on to the backs of their beasts would be the idols they worshipped. The prophet ridiculed gods which needed to be carried to safety. Surely a god should carry his people!

▶ Read **Isaiah 46.1–13.**

Martin Luther said that if God did not exist then man would have to invent him. The fact that we are creatures makes us look outside and beyond ourselves for something or someone to worship. The tragedy is that the substitute gods we manufacture – whether they be dreams of affluence or even a good cause – are not worthy of us. Like the Babylonians, many people are bigger and stronger than their gods. Only the Creator is big enough to be our God – only he is able to carry us.

☐   *O God of life, whose power benign*
     Doth o'er the world in mercy shine,
     Accept our praise, for we are thine.   *Arthur T. Russell*

Saturday December 11   Isaiah 49.1–13

In today's reading we are shown more of the relationship, between Israel and God, that was called the covenant. Verses 1–6 are one of the four *Servant Songs* in Isaiah 40–55. Who the servant was supposed to be is still strongly debated but it seems clear that in this song the prophet was speaking in the name of Israel. Although their sense of vocation had lapsed, it was now strong again. The exile was coming to a close and there was work to be done.

Verses 7–13 are very poetic and verse 13 reminds us of the psalms. But this is no timeless literature. It is embedded in a history full of activity and change. God was at work and tables were being turned, prisoners were being released and new hopes were being offered.

When Jesus read the manifesto of his ministry in the Capernaum synagogue (see Luke 4.16–19) he used a later passage of *Isaiah* (61.1–2) possibly based on these verses. The coming of God's kingdom means liberty and healing, light shining in darkness and life overcoming death. Our world today needs this kingdom more than ever. Let us ensure that we side with the oppressed peoples everywhere and not with the forces of cruelty and injustice.

☐   *Pray for prisoners of conscience that they might have courage, hope and love.*

For group discussion and personal thought
Study Isaiah 40.12–31. What difference do these words make to
your understanding of God's greatness, and in what ways does
this affect your life?

3rd Sunday in Advent, December 12   Isaiah 40.1–11*
THE FORERUNNER

While still in exile, the people of Israel in the sixth century BC
were given hope that their long ordeal under the Babylonian
tyrant was ending. The poet-prophet put this hope into words
for them. They were words of **comfort, authority, assurance**
and **tenderness.**

God comes to end oppression; but he also comes as a shepherd
to enfold his people. The prophet's words had an immediate
reference to the political situation of his time. But they also had
a deeper reference recognised some centuries later by John the
Baptist. When John set out to prepare his people for the coming
of Christ he said, 'I am a voice crying aloud in the wilderness,
"Make the Lord's highway straight." ' (John 1.23)

☐ *The message of Isaiah and John is relevant for us in this
twentieth century, amid the tensions and bewilderment of our
time. Sometimes it may seem to us that this sceptical and harsh
modern world has gone out of control; that hope has dwindled;
that, indeed, 'all mankind is grass'. But the Christian's message
is still the same: 'The word of our God is here,' and 'He will
tend his flock like a shepherd'.*

ISRAEL MY SERVANT

Monday December 13   Isaiah 42.12–24

Nothing is as destructive as meaningless suffering. Before the
depressed Jews could be rehabilitated into the servant people of
God they needed to come to terms with the crushing experience
of the Babylonian exile and its meaning. The prophet told them
that they had been blind to the activity of God. Their suffering
was seen as a consequence of denying their task as the covenant
people. They needed to rediscover themselves and this had to
begin with a realistic view of past failures.

But before the condemnation of failure the prophet pointed to the salvation of God. Our hopes rest not on our feeble attempts at changing ourselves and our world, but on the salvation of God, who enlists us in his mission. Knowing that the foundation of Christian hope is not the Church, or ourselves, but God himself, enables us to examine our problems and mistakes more realistically. He used mightily people like David who had plenty of personal faults. Jesus called twelve disciples, but one betrayed him, the others ran away and the leader of the early Church, Peter, denied even knowing him.

Our adoration should naturally lead to confession. Better still, it will be followed by forgiveness and re-enlistment.

☐ *Father, may your love release me to see myself as I really am – and to seek your forgiveness and help.*

Tuesday December 14

The prophet spoke again in the name of the almighty Creator. The turmoil which was threatening Babylon was the Lord's doing and the Jewish exiles had to be ready to move out.

▶ Read **Isaiah 48.12–22.**

'If only . . .' (verse 18) are words of regret, but God was giving them another chance to live up to their calling and it was important to show them the cause of their first failure. These words are in line with the message of many of the prophets, including Amos, Micah, Hosea and Isaiah of Jerusalem. Israel's problems stemmed from disobedience, for the troubles that she had endured were judgement. She had not kept the laws of God – laws which were intended to build a just, compassionate and reverent society that reflected the very nature of God.

Love brings responsibilities and the grace of God is not a blank cheque to pamper God's favourites but the means by which he recreates lives and shares his hopes. Dietrich Bonhoeffer wrote that if we just take from God, without allowing our lives to be altered, then we cheapen his grace.

☐ *'Cheap grace is the preaching of forgiveness without requiring repentance . . . grace without discipleship.' (Dietrich Bonhoeffer)*

Wednesday December 15   Isaiah 50.1–11

The covenant between God and his people was often likened to a marriage and in today's reading the prophet may have been using the picture of a law court. God was in the dock, accused of rejecting Israel for no cause. How often do people blame God when things go wrong? The prophet argued that the break was made by Israel's faithlessness.

Verses 4–9 contain another of the *Servant Songs* and here it appears that the servant was the prophet himself. Despite the greatness that we now recognise in his writings it appears that he had a rough ride and that his message of **hope**, which in turn meant **action**, was at first unpopular (verses 6–9).

Look again at verses 10–11. It is often easy to judge ourselves and others with the benefit of hindsight. For example, the disciples of Jesus seemed to have been stupidly slow to understand his teaching. We sometimes say, 'If I had known how it would turn out I wouldn't have done such and such.' But living is about making decisions 'in the dark' and **faith is about trusting in the dark.** Of course the alternative to living by faith is to rely on oneself – to light the torch of false certainties. Faith is difficult and agonising – but it is the true way to life.

☐   *Lead, kindly light, amid the encircling gloom,*
        Lead thou me on;
    The night is dark, and I am far from home;
        Lead thou me on;
    Keep thou my feet; I do not ask to see
    The distant scene; one step enough for me.   *John H. Newman*

Thursday December 16   Isaiah 42.1–9

Why did God choose one nation from amongst all the others and lavish upon it all he did? Was this an example of sheer favouritism? No, for the calling of Israel was the calling to a task. Privilege should always involve responsibility.

In the *Servant Song* in verses 1–4 Israel is the servant and her vocation is described as the calling to be like her God. This was the purpose of the laws which were given at Sinai. 'Be compassionate as your Father is compassionate,' said Jesus (Luke 6.36), and this was to be the task of Israel. In order to reveal himself to men, and to reveal to men their true destiny, God wanted a people who would reflect his goodness and love – a compassionate society (verse 3) based on justice.

Israel was to be a beacon shining in the darkness so that when other nations saw Israel they would also see a reflection of Israel's God. But Israel failed yet again and the Servant who became 'the light of the world' called **his** followers to share in the shining. When someone said that 'a saint is a person through whom the light shines' he was not talking about saints in stained glass windows!

☐ *Lord, help* **me** *to be a bringer of light, a sharer of your love.*

Friday December 17   **Isaiah 52.13 to 53.12**

It is right that this wonderful passage should be linked with Jesus but we must be careful about the nature of the link. For centuries people have seen it as a foretelling of the crucifixion – as in Handel's *Messiah* – as though the prophet were looking through a telescope into the future. But, in fact, the prophet was meditating about his own experience and the experience of Israel, and how suffering often accompanies being faithful to God's call even though it must eventually lead to vindication. Naturally, the early Church applied this theme to Jesus and it is likely that he himself found in these words inspiration for the way of the cross and for the meaning of his ministry (see Mark 10.42–45).

● The prophet glimpses the mystery of a faithful servant of God whose suffering brings blessing to others. The way of the cross is given meaning.

● He recognises that the way of suffering cuts right across the way of the world. 'We despised him.' Nobody likes a loser; yet Jesus ultimately revealed the magnificence of God's love as a loser – on the cross. Today's world is full of losers – homeless, hungry, those who are denied jobs and dignity – not because they have lost in a fair fight but because the way of the world favours the strong and keeps the weak in their place!

☐ *Lord, grant me the love and the strength to take up my cross and side with the oppressed and the dispossessed.*

Saturday December 18   **Isaiah 54.11–17**

There is such a thing as 'poetic licence' and the prophet uses it to the full here. His picture of the new Jerusalem is so exaggerated that no one would claim that he misled the people with a deceitful 'commercial' for the purposes of God. What he was concerned about was to inspire the Jews so that they would be ready to return home. 'Think big,' he said to them.

Then he used a dream to give them a goal to aim for. It was not the sort of dream we have when we are asleep but the kind of dream which calls people to strive and look forward to the future. Such dreams are important – but we must remember that their fulfilment is the work of God as well as man. It is a matter of co-operation and no amount of frenzied human activity is sufficient.

In Morris West's novel *Summer of the Red Wolf* one of the characters asks the story-teller why his own dreams only bring trouble while the others' bring peace of mind. The story-teller answers, 'Perhaps because you want to make them all come true.'

> ☐ *Though what I dream and what I do*
> *In my poor days are always two,*
> *Help me, oppressed by things undone,*
> *O thou, whose deeds and dreams were one.*   *John Hunter*

For group discussion and personal thought

Consider the Servant Song in Isaiah 52.13 to 53.12, and see how it can be applied to the suffering and death of Jesus. In what ways can **our** suffering bring blessing to others?

4th Sunday in Advent, December 19   Isaiah 11.1–9*

OUR HOPE IS FULFILLED

The prophet sees a stump of a tree which, for him, represents the house of Jesse, from which King David had come. He sees a green shoot growing out of it. Thus he begins this poem which describes an ideal future king.

In fact, Israel never did have such a king. But the ideal remained and became the basis of the messianic hope. Such a leader would be a man possessed with the spirit of true wisdom, compassion for the oppressed, justice and integrity. Under such a leader, the world would enter upon a state of unparalleled peace, and all men would know God.

No earthly ruler has ever fulfilled this prophecy. But this week millions of us are rejoicing that it **has** been fulfilled. The King has come. The Son of David is in our midst. Let us open the doors of our hearts and invite him in to rule our lives and re-kindle our hope that one day all mankind will acknowledge his Lordship.

☐ *Use Romans 15.12–13 as the basis of your meditation.*

THE SAVIOUR COMES!

Notes by Revd Paul Beasley-Murray, MA, PhD

Paul Beasley-Murray is minister of Altrincham Baptist Church, Cheshire. A member of the Baptist Union Council of Great Britain, he formerly taught in the National University of Zaire, and has also researched into the subject of Church Growth.

With the approach of the Christmas season, we are reminded that the Christian faith stands or falls with the person of Jesus. Christianity does not offer a philosophy which dispenses ideas but a gospel – a gospel which proclaims what God has done for the world in Christ. The gospel is **good news**; and the coming of Jesus is the beginning of this good news.

During the remaining days of December our readings will tell the story of his coming. First, we shall remind ourselves of the facts; and then, we shall reflect upon the significance of Christ's coming.

Monday December 20   Luke 1.26–45
MARY SETS AN EXAMPLE

Mary was 'betrothed to a man named Joseph'. Betrothal then was far more serious than engagement today. It was as binding as marriage and could only be dissolved by divorce.

In this reading Mary sets a threefold example to us:

● **An example of God's grace.** 'Greetings, most favoured one!' said the angel. Why did God privilege her to be the mother of Jesus? In the final analysis there was no real reason – it was all of grace. This is true more generally of God's dealings towards us. We are saved by grace – it is not of our deserving!

● **An example of faith.** 'I am the Lord's servant; as you have spoken, so be it.' Mary was willing to trust God, whatever the consequences. She might well have expected Joseph to break the engagement, and yet she accepted God's will. Are we willing to trust God, come what may?

● **An example of the paradox of blessing.** 'God's blessing is on you above all women,' said Elizabeth. And yet that blessing was to prove painful – for one day Mary was to see her Son on a cross. What is true of Mary is true often of us: in Christ, God has wonderfully blessed us, and yet we are called to go the way of the cross.

☐ *In rejecting the Roman Catholic veneration of Mary, are Protestants in danger of according her no honour?*

Tuesday December 21   Luke 1.46–56

MARY'S DREAM OF REVOLUTION

Every mother dreams of great things for her son. Mary was no exception. But little did she know that while 'all generations' would count her 'blessed', they would also call her 'Our Lady of Sorrows'. Mary believed that God was going to start the revolution – and that her Son was to be the leader. But far from Jesus putting the mighty down from their thrones, they put him down. Seen as a social revolutionary, Jesus was a failure. However, we know that Jesus came to deal with a more fundamental problem than that of the redistribution of wealth. He came to liberate people not from the Romans, but from sin and death.

Yet we must take care not to over-spiritualise the *Magnificat*. Jesus may not have been a social reformer, but that does not mean that Christianity has nothing to do with the world of politics and economics. The *Magnificat* can be taken literally and be seen as prophetic of the revolution Jesus did start – the revolution of love. In the light of the cross all men have an inestimable worth – they are men for whom Christ died. Precisely because of this, Christians are now committed to economic change and social action.

☐ *How can I join the revolution? What, for instance, can I do this Christmas-time to satisfy the hungry with good things – so that they too may rejoice in God our Saviour?*

Wednesday December 22   Luke 1.57–58, 67–80

GOD KEEPS HIS PROMISES

The *Benedictus* (verses 68–79) is a song of praise and prophecy.
● **Praise.** Zechariah praised God for fulfilling his promise. There must have been many times when God did not seem to be keeping his promise. But he had a plan and he worked it out in

the coming of Jesus. God also has a plan for the present. Bismarck said: 'The statesman must try to reach for the hem when he hears the garment of God rustling through events.' God has a plan for the future – 'to bring all creation together, with Christ as head' (Ephesians 1.10, GNB).

● **Prophecy.** Zechariah spoke of his son as 'the forerunner' who would announce the coming of the Messiah. He would 'lead his people to salvation', by telling them of the one who had come to save. Zechariah turned from his son to the Christ himself – 'the morning sun from heaven will rise upon us'. Without Christ we are lost in the darkness, but with him life gains direction and by him we are led to God. No wonder Zechariah praised God.

☐ *Ours is a dark world – there is much suffering and unhappiness. Pray for those who are in darkness, that the light of Jesus may shine on them.*

Thursday December 23   Matthew 1.18–25

INSIGNIFICANT – YET IMPORTANT

Joseph is one of the unsung heroes of the Bible.

● **He co-operated with God in fulfilling his purposes.** By taking Mary as his wife Joseph, the 'son of David', enabled Jesus to be his legitimate son in the line of David, and in this way he enabled the Scriptures to be fulfilled.

● **He obeyed God and went against the stream.** The natural course of action in the circumstances would have been for Joseph to have broken his engagement. Indeed for 'a man of principle' there was no real alternative. Yet, for God's sake, Joseph was willing to go against the stream and take Mary to be his wife.

● **He proved a true father to Jesus.** A man has not fulfilled his fatherly duties merely by causing his wife to become pregnant. A true father accepts responsibility for a child by giving him a home, surrounding him with love, teaching and training him to become a complete person. Joseph must have been a true father to Jesus – otherwise it is unlikely that Jesus would have called God, 'Abba, Father' (Mark 14.36).

☐ *Joseph was a comparatively insignificant figure and yet he had an essential part to play in God's plan. We may not all get the limelight, and yet we are all needed. God has a purpose for each one of us.*

WHAT A CHRISTMAS!

It was only eighty miles from Nazareth to Bethlehem, but in those days the journey had to be made on foot or on a donkey. Furthermore, Mary was nine months pregnant. To cap it all, when they arrived in Bethlehem they could not find anywhere to stay – a stable had to suffice. To Mary that 'first Christmas' must have seemed a nightmare.

Many Christmas cards depict an outhouse as the birthplace of Jesus. However, Justin Martyr, one of the early Church fathers, who lived in the second century AD and who came from the district of Bethlehem, tells us that Jesus was born 'in a certain cave near the village'. This is quite possible, in so far as the houses in Bethlehem were built on the slopes of a limestone ridge, with the result that it was common for them to have a cavelike stable hollowed out in the rock below the house itself. Indeed to this day a cave is shown in Bethlehem as the birthplace of Jesus and above it the great Church of the Nativity has been built.

☐ *The innkeeper had no room for a couple in distress. How much room have we? Jesus said: 'When I was a stranger you gave me no home . . . I tell you this: anything you did not do for one of these, however humble, you did not do for me.'*

(Matthew 25.43, 45)

LET ALL COME TO THE SAVIOUR!

Luke's Gospel is the Gospel for the underprivileged, so it is no coincidence that the author includes the story of the shepherds. Shepherds ranked amongst the lowest of the low. They were despised by the orthodox of Jesus' day because they were unable to keep the details of the ceremonial law. For instance, they could not observe the meticulous hand-washings demanded by the law – their flocks made too constant a demand on them. But God 'is no respecter of persons'; he loves all men – shepherds as well as wise men were told of their Saviour's birth.

The shepherds' response is a lesson to us all:

● **They sought.** The shepherds exhibited as much a scientific approach to the angels' chorus as the wise men to the star – for by going to Bethlehem they put the 'vision' to the test.

● **They found.** Their search was rewarded with success – 'God

. . . rewards those who search for him.' (Hebrews 11.6)

● **They praised God.** Like the angels, they saw that this was no ordinary child.

☐   *See how the shepherds,*
    Summoned to his cradle,
  Leaving their flocks, draw nigh to gaze;
    We too will thither
    Bend our joyful footsteps:
      O come, let us adore him, Christ the Lord.

                                                       Anon

For group discussion and personal thought

In Christ, God's love was 'embodied'. How can we (a) as individuals, (b) as churches, embody God's love in today's world? What parallels can we draw between our efforts and what God did for us in Christ?

Sunday December 26   **Matthew 2.1–12★**

THE WISE MEN

For the past seven Sundays our readings have traced the growth of the Jews' understanding of the redemptive purposes of God. While their hopes were largely directed towards their own nation and time, there was underlying it all an increasing search for one who should liberate the whole world from its sin and alienation. In the story of the wise men, that ever-widening hope is crystallised into fulfilment; the world's Saviour is discovered in a child. The wise men were Gentiles and sincere seekers after truth. In this Jewish child they found what they sought. What **did** they find?

● A **King** whose rule of love was sufficient for all people.

● A **Healer** whose compassion could make men and women whole.

● A **Saviour** who was able to reach across the gulf and bring mankind back to the Father.

Still there are those who will not have him. Perhaps even in ourselves – we who acknowledge him – there is selfishness and fear that would reject him. Today's story is not all joy; not everyone rejoiced at Jesus' coming.

Our year of Sunday readings ends with an invitation and a challenge. Jesus invites us to accept his gentle rule. He challenges

us to pull down any barrier that still keeps us apart from him –
and from God.

☐ *No ear may hear his coming;*
  But in this world of sin,
Where meek souls will receive him, still
    The dear Christ enters in. *Phillips Brooks*

Monday December 27 **Philippians 2.5–11**

JESUS OUR EXAMPLE

Almost certainly Paul is here quoting an early Christian hymn
which celebrates the humiliation and exaltation of Jesus.

● **Humiliation.** Jesus, the Lord of glory, humbled himself in
becoming man. He assumed 'the nature of a slave' and became
subject to earthly limitations, passions and desires. He took 'the
form of a servant' (RSV) and in so doing fulfilled the Servant
prophecies of *Isaiah* (eg Isaiah 53), which we read earlier this
month. Jesus humbled himself yet further in his dying – 'in
obedience (he) accepted even death – death on a cross'. In the
eyes of a Jew no man could sink further than a cross. But Jesus
endured the curse of separation from God in order to remove the
barrier of sin which stood between God and man.

● **Exaltation.** The equality with God at which Christ refused
to snatch is now his – for in bestowing the new name of 'Lord'
God has enthroned Jesus as Lord of all. The hymn envisages
everyone acknowledging his Lordship. This is not just some
future hope, it is a process which has already begun!

☐ *Paul's hymn celebrates the Lordship of Jesus. But he included it*
  in his letter as an illustration of the attitude of humility and love
  which Christians are called to have toward one another. Reflect
  on the example of Jesus.

Tuesday December 28 **Galatians 4.1–7**

GOD'S TIME IS ALWAYS RIGHT

'When the right time finally came' (verse 4, GNB) God sent his
Son. Consider some of the factors which pointed to the time
being right.

● **The Roman empire had reached its peak.** Rome had
conquered the known world and in doing so had built many
roads. These roads facilitated the spread of the gospel. Jesus may

have been born in a Roman backwater, but thanks to the Roman communication system, the babe of Bethlehem became a household word within a matter of decades.

● **Greek had become the 'lingua franca' of the empire.** The Roman empire was composed of many nations and many tongues. For the purposes of trade a common language was needed. In the first century this common language was Greek, and it facilitated the spread of the gospel throughout the empire.

● **Men hungered for God.** Nobody really believed in gods who frolicked on Mount Olympus. Men were looking for a religion that was real and satisfying. This was the time of the growth of the mystery religions, but these also failed to satisfy. Many Jews too were dissatisfied; they longed for the true freedom which God's Messiah would bring.

☐ *God's timing is always perfect. We see this in the incarnation. Is it not also true in our own experience?*

Wednesday December 29   Hebrews 1.1–9

THE WONDER OF THE INCARNATION

No New Testament writer has a higher understanding of the person of Christ than the author of the letter to the Hebrews. This is clearly expressed in the first chapter.

● **Christ is the Word of God,** the agent of creation (verses 2–3; see also John 1.1–3 and Colossians 1.16). When *Hebrews* was written, Jesus was a man still in living memory, and yet he could be described in these terms! Note the present tense in verse 3: he 'sustains the universe by his word of power'. This suggests a continuing relationship with the world!

● **Christ is the Son of God** (verses 2–6). Here the ascension is depicted as the moment of his accession to power. Whereas in Philippians 2.9–11 the name he received was that of 'Lord', here it is 'Son of God'.

● **He is God** (verses 8–9). By quoting Psalm 45.6–7, *Hebrews* makes a direct equation of the Son with God. It is not that the author is unaware of the humanity of Jesus – indeed he emphasises this aspect more than any other New Testament writer. But for him Jesus was both God **and** man.

☐ *Jesus – the Word, risen, God himself become man.*
  Reflect on the enormity of the step from eternity into time and space.

RECOGNISING CHRIST

> *Comfort, comfort my people . . .*
> *speak tenderly to Jerusalem*
> *and tell her this,*
> *that she has fulfilled her term of bondage.*   (Isaiah 40.1–2)

In the birth of Jesus, Simeon saw the ultimate fulfilment of these words of the prophet. Along with many other devout Jews, Simeon had been looking for the 'restoration' – literally, the 'consolation' – of Israel associated with the coming of the Messiah. Then, in the baby Jesus, he saw God's anointed. This divinely-given insight caused Simeon to break forth into praise and prophecy:

● **Praise** (verses 29–32). Simeon's joy was so full that he was ready to die – for a Saviour had come, who would bring 'light' to the Gentiles as well as 'glory' to Israel.

● **Prophecy** (verses 34–35). The Saviour would receive a mixed reception: but those who rejected him would in the end 'fall', whereas those who accepted him would 'rise' and enter into God's salvation. Alas, the one who was to bring comfort to Israel would bring little comfort to Mary – suffering lay ahead for him and, therefore, for her also.

Anna too shared in the insight given to Simeon. Although no prophecy is recorded, her thanksgiving implies that she too recognised Jesus as the Messiah, who would bring 'liberation' to the people of God.

☐ *It was 'at church' – in the temple – that Simeon and Anna recognised Christ. Pray that in your church this week there may be somebody who discovers Christ for the first time.*

'GOD WITH SKIN ON!'

One summer night a mother tucked her small daughter into bed, while outside the lightning flashed and thunder shook the house. But the little girl did not remain settled long. After a few minutes she ran downstairs and threw herself into her mother's arms: 'Mummy, I'm scared.' The mother comforted her and then sent her upstairs with the words: 'Remember, darling, God loves you and he'll take care of you and keep you safe.' But five minutes later the girl was back downstairs; 'I know God loves me. But, Mummy, I want someone with skin on to love me.'

This is a parable of the incarnation. Someone 'with skin on' has come to love us. In Jesus, God took an undiluted dose of humanity – in Jesus, God has proclaimed his love for all to see.

This, too, is the basic message of the opening words of John's Gospel, although it is couched in popular philosophical language: 'The Word became flesh.' In Jesus, God has spoken a word of love. Augustine said that in his pre-Christian days he had read and studied the great pagan philosophers and their writings: he had read many speculations concerning the divine *Logos* (Word), but he had never read of the Word becoming flesh. In Jesus, the unthinkable becomes real – God 'with skin on' has come to love us!

☐ *The Church, as the body of Christ, is called to embody God's love. What practical act of love can I do today? What resolve can I make for 1983 so that through me God's love can be more clearly shown to others?*

SCHEME OF READINGS FOR 1983

January 1–16	**Luke's Gospel** (selections)
January 17–30	**Hosea**
January 31–April 10	**John's Gospel**
April 11–May 1	**Genesis 12–35**
May 2–22	**1 Corinthians**
May 23–June 12	**One in the Spirit** (Ephesians)
June 13–July 3	**Exodus**
July 4–17	**James**
July 18–31	**Isaiah 56–66**
August 1–14	**Philippians**
August 15–September 4	**1 Samuel 1–16**
September 5–25	**1,2 Timothy and Titus**
September 26–October 9	**Harvest**
October 10–30	**Ezra and Nehemiah**
October 31–November 13	**Peace and Justice**
November 14–27	**Ecclesiastes and Song of Songs**
November 28–December 18	**Revelation**
December 19–31	**The Promise of God** (Christmas readings)